For Instructors Only

We are currently creating and implementing a *Student Portal* for this textbook that is expected to go live effective Spring 2020 semester. Designed for students to complete the Global Pretest Diagnostic and Chapter Pre- and Posttests online, the *Student Portal* will help instructor's track the individual scores of each of their students in one convenient location.

Meanwhile, while we prepare the *Student Portal*, Onziéme Edition will work with instructors to help facilitate the testing process for their students. To this end, we will provide a one-semester, written legal authorization to approve the use of Canvas quiz modules for instructors should they wish to put the Pre- and Posttests online in Canvas.

To request a temporary, one-semester written legal authorization from our company to use Canvas for the Pre- and Posttests, instructors must

1. Have already adopted this textbook for the Fall 2019 semester;
2. Email us at flippingenglish@onziemedition.com requesting this temporary written authorization.

Instructors who wish to use Canvas following the Fall 2019 semester must again email us prior to the start of each semester they expect to use Canvas. We cannot guarantee continued authorization.

Instructors are not legally authorized to put Pre- or Posttests on Canvas without our pre-approval.

Onzième Edition
PUBLISHING COMPANY

FLIPPING ENGLISH

Creating a Pathway to Success

David Moton, Gloria Naso,
&
Michael McNellis

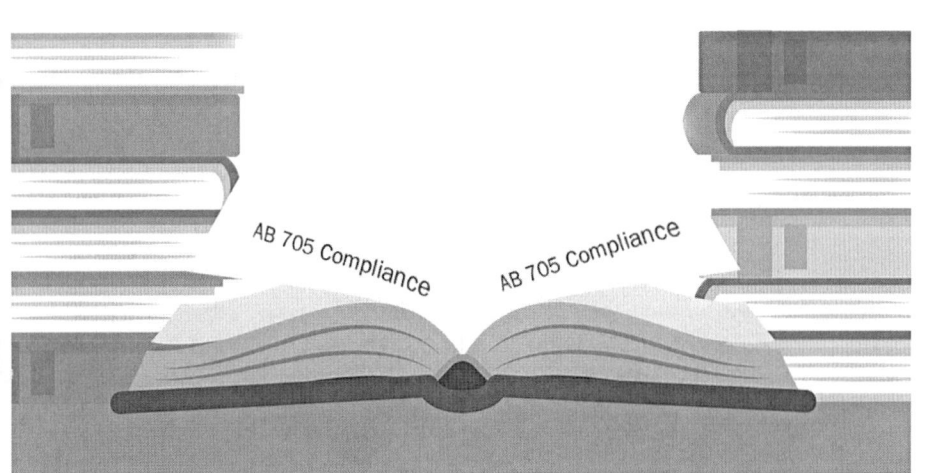

Onzième Edition
PUBLISHING COMPANY

Copyright © 2019 by David Moton, Gloria Naso, and Michael McNellis

Published by Onzième Edition
http://www.onzieme11edition.com
Book50f09

ISBN 978-1-7322439-3-4

Onzième Edition is a registered trademark of Onzième Edition Publishing Company.

Inquiries: www.onzieme11edition.com

Printing number: 9 8 7 6 5 4 3 2 1

Printed in the United States of America

For our students

CONTENTS

CHAPTER 1.
How to Think, Read, and Write Critically
19

CHAPTER 2.
How to Master All Steps of the Writing Process
71

CHAPTER 3. How to Craft Expository, Analytical, and Argumentative Thesis Statements
95

CHAPTER 4.
How to Properly Organize an Essay
113

CHAPTER 5.
How to Breakdown the Components of Arguments
141

CHAPTER 6.
How to Use Rhetorical Techniques to Persuade an Audience   171

CHAPTER 7.
How to Learn and Use College-Level Vocabulary   191

CHAPTER 8. How to Write Grammatical and
Properly Punctuated Sentences   221

CHAPTER 9.
How to Use the Basics of MLA Format
261

CHAPTER 10.
How to Identify and Avoid Plagiarism

301

PREFACE

Introduction and a Pedagogical Discussion

In the fall of 2019, California Assembly Bill No. 705 (also called AB 705) took effect. The odds are if you are reading this preface, then you know the details and potential impact of the law. Simply put, the law makes every community college in California all but eliminate remediation in math and English with a view, at least in theory, to move all students through the transfer level class within one academic year. Unfortunately, it may have the opposite effect if we cannot help bring less-prepared students up to speed. Now, your authors cannot "solve for X" to save their lives, but we do know something about English. To this end, we focus on the impact the law has on English classes, realizing compliance requires a new approach to traditional remediation modalities. Even if you teach at a university or high school, you undoubtedly have mounting pressure on your end to move students as rapidly as possible through more fast-paced "pathways to success." For California community colleges, however, campuses *must* be compliant with AB 705, and that means changes in approaches to teaching. For many colleges, change means adding a co-requisite class that runs alongside the regular transfer-level class. For others, change means retooling writing centers, hiring target tutors, enhancing services, rethinking lab work, or developing other new methods and services. Regardless of the pedagogical and service strategies, the bottom line is this: freshman composition just got a whole lot trickier to teach.

We will be now faced with a classroom full of students who have wider skill gaps between one another than ever before, and this book aims to minimize these gaps as quickly, efficiently, and effectively as possible to help students succeed. Whereas some students need only a small amount of MLA instruction and a refresher on punctuation and grammar rules to pass transfer-level English, others need a whole lot more—for example, learning something as basic as subject-verb agreement. How do we teach students with such a disparate set of skill levels who are in the same class? That is the very question this book answers.

Flipping English centers on the need for "flipping" the classroom to get students to self-diagnose their own weaknesses as readers and writers and to use that diagnosis to hone their skills—without taking up valuable classroom time. The students take responsibility for their own learning. As instructors, we take the role of mentors and guides and help them by providing a battery of diagnostic pre- and post-tests at the beginning and end of concise chapters that focus on specific skills. Emphasizing individualized instruction below transfer-level skills, *Flipping English* was written with versatility in mind, making it a low-cost supplemental text for traditional transfer-level classes, co-requisite courses, or even lab or tutoring environments.

Let me say that as one of *Flipping English's* authors, I know this individualized instructional approach works. It did for me. As a first-year freshman at California State University, Bakersfield (a long, long time ago), my placement scores were almost good enough to get into the English transfer-level course…but not quite. I was lucky in that I could enroll in a one-credit co-requisite class that helped me hone my English skills. In fact, as many community colleges are currently revising their curricula to adopt a more individualized approach to instruction and from my direct experience those many moons ago, I can say this model works. After all—here I am working with two great colleagues writing an English textbook.

How did the flipped model work for me? Using the same individualized strategies as those that are pedagogically in fashion now, the flipped model accelerated my learning. The co-requisite class I took at CSUB provided the supportive framework and approach to help the students in the class identify their own writing foibles, pitfalls, and strengths through a battery of diagnostic tests. It allowed us to read chapters and complete practice exercises at our own pace. We could only pass the class when we took a posttest that showed we had mastered the skills needed to succeed in the transfer class in which we were concurrently enrolled. And it worked. I recognized my weaknesses, understood my strengths, and worked on my deficiencies. The instructor guided me and an English tutor assigned to the class helped students. That tutor (Gloria Naso) happens to now be a co-author of this book.

I immediately recalled this class from the late 1980s once AB 705 became law. Our English Department quickly recognized the inevitability of change. Over discussions of creating a resource that could help what may be a sea of near-drowning students struggling to pass transfer-level English, I thought of that life-saving class, and suddenly the methodology of this book was formed. It allows students to self-diagnose, learn, and pass posttests on their own with some gentle guidance from professors and tutors.

Note for Instructors

The premise of *Flipping English* is simple. Students start by taking the Global Pretest Diagnostic—see Appendix A. Structured to link each set of basic English skills with a corresponding and specific chapter, the global pretest provides scores in a clear, systematic, and effective way to help students develop a learning prescription, creating time-saving, focused instructional opportunities. Guided by the learning prescription, the student reads and completes only the chapters that relate to the student's needs. Each chapter contains the critical learning content followed by exercises and workshop tasks to be completed at the student's own pace (or a pace set by you as the instructor). At the end of each chapter, a posttest is provided to measure the skill level achieved by the student. The results highlight which aspects of basic English skills were mastered and which were not. Instructors employing their pedagogical skills, content knowledge, and resources can use this book to guide students along the pathway to success.

The layout of the book is simple and straightforward and designed for students to be able to navigate it themselves:

Global Pretest Diagnostic. This is a multiple-choice test that the students will take. It can be simply taken via Scantron and graded by you. Once you have the numbers that are right and wrong, you can compare it to the key to generate a learning prescription for the students, a tool that will guide them to the chapters on which they need to focus.

Content Chapters. The chapters cover the basics of composition writing at the college level. Each chapter focuses on one specific skill set: critical thinking, reading, and writing; the writing process; essay organization; logical arguments;

thesis statements; rhetorical modes; collegiate vocabulary; grammar; MLA format; and avoiding plagiarism. These are written for pre-transfer students in order to get them ready for the transfer-level content. Each chapter contains the following:

- *Chapter Pretest*. Each chapter contains a pretest to let the students identify the areas on which they need to focus.
- *Content*. This is the bulk of the chapter. It is the reading material that will help the students learn the basics of the skills and concepts covered in the chapter.
- *Workshop*. This section contains a set of tasks designed to assist in the mastery of the chapter content. Some of them are global and focus on the entirety of the skills laid out in a chapter, whereas others are more focused and explore only one or two sections. The students can select these for themselves, or you can choose which ones to assign.
- *Chapter Posttest*. Each chapter has a posttest, the results of which help students identify the requisite skills that have not been mastered.

Designed with two goals in mind, *Flipping English* was written (1) to get students through the pathway of English in one year without traditional remedial classes (and therefore be AB 705 compliant) and (2) to help instructors provide differentiated ways of teaching without losing valuable class time. As we know, having to dedicate too much time to one group over another often leads to taking instructional time away from another. This book allows you to focus on the students' individual needs both equitably and efficiently without losing even more sleep than you already are. Whether you are teaching at a high school, a community college, or a university, and whether AB 705 directly impacts your curriculum, *Flipping English* will help you reach all of your students as individuals and leave no one behind on their pathway to success.

Note for Students

A new law was recently passed called California Assembly Bill 705 (or AB 705). This law says that every community college must do everything in its power to help students get through math and English classes and be transfer-ready within one school year. This means the elimination of the old-school way of teaching

English through a series of remedial classes that may take a couple of years before you reach the transfer-level English class.

It also means that many of you are going to be placed into your college class based on nothing but your cumulative high school GPA instead of a placement test or writing sample as has been done in California for decades. While this is going to get a lot of you into transfer-level classes for your first semester of college, the unfortunate truth is that many California community college students who find themselves in these classes will simply not be ready. According to 2010 findings by The National Center for Public Policy and Higher Education and Southern Regional Education Board (SREB), only about one quarter of incoming community college students are fully prepared for college-level courses. This means 75 percent of you who are first year community college students need pre-transfer-level work—and that is statistically significant.

Writing at the college level includes a wide and varied series of skills: grammar, syntax, vocabulary, critical thought, MLA format, reading skills, knowledge of essay structure, knowledge of thesis construction, and understanding rhetorical modes of writing. What used to take years for you to learn in a series of remedial classes will now be expected to be completed in one semester—and this textbook, *Flipping English*, is designed to help you meet that challenge.

This book is unlike other English textbooks you may have read in the past. Each chapter focuses on different skill sets and has content for you to read in order to come up to speed, and yet it does something more. It allows you to take some self-diagnostic tests to determine what your own strengths and weaknesses are, and it then takes you on a journey that you will lead yourself, a journey of mastering college writing. Your instructor will be there to help guide you, of course, but this is a type of self-guided learning that has come to be called a "flipped classroom."

The flipped classroom is one that isn't like traditional courses. Instead of a professor lecturing on stage and you taking notes (and, let's face it, trying not to fall asleep), you take control of your own learning. The instructor gives you the tools, information, exercises, and readings you need in order to succeed, and then he or she helps you master the material on your own. It's the type of teaching style that makes online learning work, and since AB 705 goes into effect Fall 2019, this individualized learning model will be seen in more and more community college classrooms.

If you are reading this student introduction, it means your instructor has embraced the flipped classroom model, which means that your instructor has faith that you are smart enough and dedicated enough to walk this path on your own.

How the book works: *Flipping English* works through a series of diagnostic tests. The Global Pretest Diagnostic that you will take before you read any of the chapters of the book will show you both where you are already strong and where you need to improve. The results of this Global Pretest Diagnostic will guide you to the chapters you need to focus on based on questions you have gotten wrong (through application of what we call a learning prescription).

From there, you'll discover that each chapter has a similar structure. There will be a chapter diagnostic you take to see how you do on the skills covered in that chapter (such as essay structure, grammar, rhetorical modes, vocabulary, or critical thought, just to name a few). You will read the chapter to get more information and then work with your instructor to see what exercises you should complete in order to practice these new skills and ultimately master them. To do so, you'll look at the set of Workshop exercises in each chapter and complete the ones you need. Once done, you will take a chapter diagnostic posttest to see how you have improved and will work with your instructor to make sure that you are ready to move on to the next section as outlined in your learning prescription.

We think you'll be pleasantly surprised at the results of your chapter postests after completing the requisite exercises and tasks. Whether you have picked this book up on your own, been assigned it in a traditional transfer-level English class, been assigned it as part of a co-requisite class, or even taken it on as part of tutoring or supplemental instruction activity, following its method and completing your learning prescription will get you ready for anything that college professors throw at you. Good luck on your journey down this pathway to success.

David Moton
Spring 2019

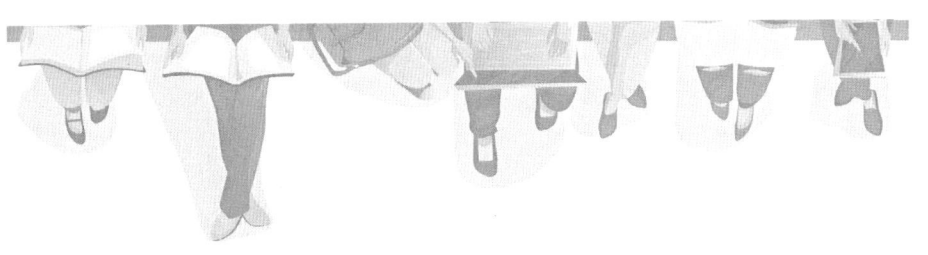

CHAPTER 1

How to Think, Read, and Write Critically

In this chapter, you will learn about the following:

Part One: Strategies for Critical Thinking
1. What is Critical Thinking?
2. Necessary First Steps for Critical Thinking
3. Emotional Self-Management
4. Skills for Critically Thinking about Other People's Ideas

Part Two: Strategies for Critical Reading
1. What is Critical Reading?
2. Reading Notebooks
3. Contextualizing, Reflecting, Annotating, Paraphrasing, and Summarizing
4. Double-Entry Note Taking
5. SQ3R
6. The Rhetorical Précis
7. The CRAAP Test
8. Finding Good Sources for Papers
9. Critically Evaluating Sources
10. Research Information Sets

Part Three: Workshop

PART ONE

Strategies for Critical Thinking

1. What is Critical Thinking?

Critical thinking simply consists of objective analysis and evaluation in order to form a judgment about something. While most people would probably say that they know how to be objective and form their judgments based on careful thought, that is not necessarily the case. There are many personal and emotional issues that interfere with critical thinking that we are not always aware of. Critical thinking involves "metacognition," which means thinking about how we think—developing an awareness and understanding about our own thought processes. This, in turn, can help us to better understand the thought processes of others.

2. Necessary First Steps for Critical Thinking

Will Storr, author of *The Unpersuadables: Adventures with the Enemies of Science*, made the following observation:

> By the time you have reached adulthood, your brain has decided how the world works—how a table looks and feels, how liquids and authority figures behave, how scary are rats. It has made countless of billions of little insights and decisions. It has made its mind up. From then on in, its treatment of any new information that runs counter to those views can sometimes be brutal. Your brain is surprisingly reluctant to change its mind. Rather than going through the difficulties involved in rearranging itself to reflect the truth, it often prefers to fool you. So it distorts. It projects. It lies.

Scientific research backs Storr up. This leads us to a discussion of the important first steps in critically thinking about any issue:

1. Know *what* you think.
2. Know *why* you think it.
3. Try to come up with evidence and arguments *against* your own beliefs.

Why are these the necessary first steps? Because you can't objectively evaluate anyone else's arguments if you don't recognize what could interfere with either accepting or rejecting their conclusions. If you already feel a certain way about something, you are going to be less likely to spot flaws in the arguments of people whose views are like yours, and you are going to be more likely to not give careful consideration to people whose views differ—you may simply reject them out of hand or come up with superficial reasons that won't stand up to careful analysis.

Being told to know what you think may seem like silly advice—doesn't everyone know what they already think? Political pollsters often ask people questions like "Are you in favor of gun control?" or "Are you in favor of women having complete access to abortions?" Anyone can accurately say "yes" or "no" to these questions, right? Not necessarily. People's attitudes are often a lot more complex. While there are people who are absolutely against these things no matter what the circumstances, other people who would automatically answer "no" to the abortion question might feel differently about a twelve-year-old girl who is pregnant because her father raped her. People who might automatically answer "no" to the gun control question might consider it reasonable to prohibit people with psychoses and a history of violence against other people to purchase military-style automatic weapons. People who might automatically answer "yes" to the two questions might balk at allowing women to choose abortion a week before a baby is due on a whim when there is no danger to their own health. They might think it is fine for people to own guns in any number of circumstances—just not all circumstances. Don't operate on automatic—examine your ideas and test them by imagining the various nuances of your own opinions.

Being told to know *why* you think something may also seem like silly advice— don't we tend to assume that we think what we do because we have carefully and objectively thought about it? In reality, we may think the way we do because of how we were raised; what political party our parents belonged to when we grew up; what religion we are (if we are religious); what our friends think; even what most people in our city, county, or state think. Our reasons for believing things may seem absolutely logical to us, but they may seem that way due to our emotions, not actual logic. In fact, research has proven that our brains are set up to make quick assumptions and to jump swiftly to conclusions. We are simply more satisfied and comfortable when we are "fast" rather than "slow"—but we need to slow down in order to make sure that we do not ignore relevant evidence.

Being told to try to come up with evidence and arguments *against* your own beliefs might seem counterintuitive—but the point about critical thinking is that you don't want to depend upon intuition—the apparent ability to understand something immediately, without the need for conscious reasoning. Some people are genuinely intuitive about some things, but too often we trust what seems like intuition or what we call "common sense" just because we are more comfortable doing so. Also, frankly, trying to come up with evidence and arguments against your own beliefs sounds unpleasant, time consuming, and may take work—but that is exactly why it is so important. To be blunt, you are not going to be able to carefully, critically evaluate other people's beliefs if you cannot first do the same with your own.

Understanding something scientists call "confirmation bias" is helpful. Confirmation bias is the very human tendency to selectively choose ideas and information that confirms our existing emotions and beliefs. Confirmation bias explains why people with totally opposite beliefs about a topic can look at the same evidence and believe that it proves that they are right and that the people who disagree with them are clearly wrong. People often favor, interpret, and remember information in a way that suits them, and they are not even conscious that they are doing so. They think they are being logical and intellectually honest—and that people who interpret information differently are either being stupid, intellectually dishonest, or both. This type of cognitive bias is most pronounced in relation to ingrained, ideological, and emotionally charged issues. (Think about what happens at a big Thanksgiving dinner with relatives you see only once a year and the subject of politics comes up.) Only by understanding how confirmation bias works can we learn to identify it in ourselves and in others. Always be cautious about information if it seems to immediately confirm your views. You probably need to dig deeper—and to actively look for information to challenge your views.

3. Emotional Self-Management

Stella Cottrell, former director of Lifelong Learning at the University of Leeds, who is an expert on study skills and critical thinking, advocates what she calls "emotional self-management." She suggests that people employ three written reflection exercises to understand ourselves and our thinking processes better. You can use a notebook, a tablet, or a computer. If you are using a notebook, be sure to give yourself enough room to be thorough. You could even put the prompts on different pages. The following is adapted from exercises in her book *Critical Thinking Skills: Effective Analysis, Argument and Reflection*:

TABLE 1.1. Reflection Exercise Worksheet on Self-Management

Reflection: Emotional Self-Management

For me, the emotions that are most difficult to manage when others disagree with me are

I will deal with these by

Reflection: Influences on My Thinking

For me, the influences on my own thinking that I need to be most aware of so they don't prejudice my thinking are

I will deal with these by

Reflection: Challenging Opinions

For me, the things I find most difficult about challenging the opinions of other people are

I will deal with these by

To Cottrell's three reflection exercises, we would like to add the following one:

TABLE 1.2. Added Reflection on Self-Management

Reflection: Challenging My Own Opinions

For me, the things I find most difficult to challenging my own opinions are

....

I will deal with these by

4. Skills for Critically Thinking about Other People's Ideas

Critical thinking takes work. It involves, at a minimum, the following steps. As a critical thinker, you should try to do all of the following:

1. Accurately identify other people's ideas, evidence, arguments, and conclusions.
2. Objectively and fairly evaluate alternative points of view.
3. Analyze how people reject, choose, combine, and order information to reach their conclusions.
4. Objectively and fairly evaluate all the evidence presented on each side of an issue, recognizing that there may be more than two sides.
5. Look deeply enough at an issue to identify and evaluate unspoken assumptions.
6. Recognize strategies used by each side on an issue to persuade people, including identifying logical fallacies and emotional appeals.
7. Seek substantial evidence and draw your conclusions based on logical reasoning and empirical evidence, not simply generalizations or what makes you feel most comfortable.

PART TWO
Strategies for Critical Reading

Critical thinking helps you to read critically. It enables you to recognize and retain information that might make you uncomfortable. In college, issues and questions are often a lot more complicated than what you are used to. We might be used to looking at issues in a right or wrong, black and white kind of way, but important issues are a lot more complex. In logic classes, students learn the structure of arguments and common patterns of bad arguments, some of which are called fallacies. While there are various types and names of fallacies, one that gets used a lot is the false dichotomy. This type of fallacious reasoning occurs when only two choices are presented even though more exist or a variety of possible choices exist between two extremes. People who deliberately employ this fallacy when advancing arguments will choose the alternative they believe in and contrast it only with an extreme one that they feel their audiences will reject. We may fall into the habit of thought that makes us feel like something is either right or wrong, when reality may be far more nuanced. When we read, we have to be careful not to project assumptions onto the material we are trying to analyze. To be critical readers, we should be critical thinkers.

This part of the chapter contains the following sections: What is Critical Reading?; Reading Notebooks; Contextualizing, Reflecting, Annotating, Paraphrasing, and Summarizing; Double-Entry Note Taking; SQ3R; The Rhetorical Précis; The CRAAP Test; Finding Good Sources for Papers; Critically Evaluating Sources; Research Information Sets.

1. What is Critical Reading?

"Reading critically" doesn't mean automatically criticizing what you read—it means being able to evaluate and analyze what you read. And, obviously, you must first be able to understand what you read—which can often feel very difficult when trying to read the texts assigned in your college classes. (By the way, "text" refers to any written material, not just what you think of when you hear the word "textbook.") In this section, we'll explore various time-tested strategies for critical reading. But they all come back to this point: critical reading at the college level requires that you read the assigned material multiple times. You aren't reading for fun. You aren't reading for the plot. You may get bored out of your mind. Learn to live with that. And you will find, as you get better and better, that you are likely to get less and less bored and more and more fascinated.

Time management is crucial. Schedule designated times for your reading. Even before reading the assigned text, read and re-read the instructions for the assignment that the reading is connected to. Simply reading instructions once basically guarantees that you will forget something important. Having a clear purpose when reading will help you to determine which of the reading strategies that we explore will be best suited for you and the specific task at hand.

It is also helpful to think of critical reading as involving two stages of reading: (1) reading to *understand* the author's views and (2) reading to *question* the author's views. Why is questioning important? Questioning is crucial to thorough comprehension because the activity of questioning, seeking answers to questions, and then asking further questions keeps reading focused and clear. The first stage is necessary for the second stage to be possible. Reading in these two stages enables you to develop your own ideas after making sure that you understand the author's ideas. We'll show you strategies for how to do this.

Critical reading is important not just to help you be a successful student, but also to help you be an engaged and analytical person throughout your life. It is connected to what is called "critical literacy." Basic literacy simply means the ability to read and write, which is obviously important. Critical literacy is the ability to actively read texts in a manner that encourages a deeper understanding of socially constructed concepts. It helps you to understand and question the values, attitudes, and beliefs of the people who produce not just written texts, but spoken words and even visual applications.

This chapter is intended to introduce you to tools that may be completely new to you or that you already use and how they can be used even more successfully.

2. Reading Notebooks

Keeping a reading notebook is useful because it gives you a place to jot down ideas that you can later refer to, it gives you a place to make notes that you can later incorporate into essays and research papers, and it helps you to keep track of what you have read and what you have gotten from your reading. Using a binder instead of a spiral notebook works best because you can divide your reading notebook into sections, move things around, and even discard and replace material when needed. You probably know that you are supposed to take notes when listening to lectures, but taking notes while you read is just as important because it supports better understanding of what you read. There are multiple ways to approach this kind of note taking, and we will cover a variety of them.

3. Contextualizing, Reflecting, Annotating, Paraphrasing, and Summarizing

The five most basic critical reading tools are contextualizing, reflecting, annotating, paraphrasing, and summarizing.

Contextualizing

Context refers to the circumstances that form the setting, background, and roots for something, such as a statement, idea, or argument. When we read, we need to understand context—what kind of context depends on what we are reading. Contexts can be historical, political, cultural, social, economic, scientific, and more. And these categories are not mutually exclusive—if you are evaluating an argument that someone is making in support of or in opposition to a piece of legislation, for example, all of the categories we've just named could be important to understanding the issue. In your reading notebook, you can write down what you can determine about the context of the issue that the writer is exploring.

Reflecting

Reflection refers to our capacity to exercise introspection and have a willingness to learn more about *why* we think and feel *what* we think and feel. When we read, we should be able to consciously and objectively **reflect** on challenges to our own beliefs, feelings, and values. This, however, can be very difficult because it can make us feel uncomfortable, even angry. Our own convictions are often so firmly fixed and established that we simply take for granted that our gut reactions are correct. We may say, "It's just common sense." Sense often has little or nothing to do with it—our emotions and habits of mind are in control. When we do this, we are not critically thinking—we are on automatic, simply protecting our own belief systems. To truly understand and evaluate what we read, we have to try to put that defensive part of our emotions on hold. It can be hard. We are all human—and humans are often fearful of any kind of change. (So are cats, dogs, birds, rodents, and anything else with a brain—but only humans can read and write.) To read critically, we need to understand how texts emotionally challenge us. If you feel annoyed, angry, threatened, or disturbed by something that you read, don't just think, "That's stupid!" and reject the ideas in the text on that basis. Identify the parts where you are feeling challenged, and analyze why you feel that way. At this point, it can be a good idea to write your reasons down—this doesn't have to be in an annotation—in fact, we advise against that because of the space factor. Label what you are doing in your reading notebook. Writing down your own reactions can help you to look at your own existing beliefs objectively—and that can help you to look at the text objectively.

Annotating

An **annotation** is a note, explanation, other comment, or a marking that you add to a text as you read. You can highlight or underline important parts, like thesis statements, paragraphs' topic statements, and key explanations. A thesis is the author's main point of a work. A topic sentence is the main point of a paragraph. Identifying these helps you grasp what the writer is trying to say. (Not all works have explicit thesis statements, though—sometimes the main points are implied.) Annotating includes circling, underlining, or highlighting what seem to be key words or words you don't understand to remind you to look them up and writing comments and questions in the margins. Even adding a question mark in the margin will remind you that you need to go back to parts of the text to unravel the meaning.

Paraphrasing

You **paraphrase** when you put the ideas presented in a text into your own words. A paraphrase is more detailed than a summary because the point is to convey the complete meaning of the passage being paraphrased. In fact, a paraphrase can sometimes be a little longer than the original passage because you are using your own words to fully express the ideas conveyed. Paraphrasing helps you to test yourself to see if you really do understand the passage. You are never going to paraphrase an entire chapter of a book or an entire article, but paraphrasing is very helpful when you are testing your own comprehension. Think of it as simplifying the passage without altering or losing any of its meaning. And do not add your own ideas—if you do, it is no longer a paraphrase. Stay true to the original.

Summarizing

As with paraphrasing, you **summarize** when you put the ideas from a text into your own words, but, unlike a paraphrase, the point is to convey only the main points. A paraphrase of a paragraph can be as long as or even longer than the paragraph. A summary is typically just one or two sentences. A summary of an entire article, for example, could consist of putting the thesis (main point) into your own words—which you would have to do anyway if there was no explicit thesis statement—and putting the topic sentences into your own words. A more useful summary could be longer—for example, along with the topic sentences, you could briefly explain key points of evidence or reasoning in support of the topic sentences. Just remember that both paraphrases and summaries, while they involve your own words, should not convey your own feelings or ideas.

4. Double-Entry Note Taking

With double-entry note taking, you divide pages into two columns. A common approach is "Record and React." In the first column, record the ideas you have taken from the source: (1) the main point—the thesis—of what you have read and (2) a summary of the main points about the evidence and arguments given in support of the author's thesis. In the second column, write down your reactions to the writer's evidence and arguments, questions about the writer's content and approach, and even questions about what you need to know about the subject that are not presented in the reading. You can also write about how the work relates to your assignment. Create a work-cited entry in MLA format as best you can and put that at the top of the entry.

TABLE 1.3. Work Cited Entry	
Notes on the Reading	**Notes on Your Reactions**
Thesis	What do I think about this issue?
Main Point 1	Why do I think what I do?
Main Point 2	How does the author's approach work or not work?
Main Point 3	What do I need to know about this topic to better
Main Point 4	evaluate the work?
Main Point 5	Can I use this work? How?
Main Point 6	(And so on.)
Main Point 7	
(And so on.)	

There are other approaches to "Record and React" double-column note taking. You can go into more detail in both columns.

TABLE 1.4. Work Cited Entry	
Notes on the Reading	**Notes on Your Reactions**
	What do I think about this issue?
	Why do I think what I do?
Outline	How does the author's approach work or
Summaries	not work?
Paraphrases	What do I need to know about this topic to
Quotations	better evaluate the work?
Facts	Can I use this work? How?
Examples	Are there connections with other readings?
Statistics	Are there connections with the course
Arguments	material?
	Can I think of any examples from experience?
	Can I generate any counter arguments?

5. SQ3R

SQ3R (sometimes referred to as SQRRR) is a critical and reading comprehension method named for its five steps: Survey, Question, Read, Recite, and Review. Francis P. Robinson first introduced this method in his book *Effective Study* (1946). SQ3R can be applied to a wide range of reading purposes because it is flexible and recognizes that a reader has to change reading speeds—taking this into account is a crucial reading strategy.

TABLE 1.5. SQ3R: Survey, Question, Read, Recite, and Review	
S Survey	This relates to skimming the text. At this stage, you are simply attempting to get a general idea of the material.

TABLE 1.5. *(continued)*	
Q Question	You should have a question or set of questions to direct you even before you begin to read. Having a purpose helps you to learn and retain information. Having questions changes reading from a passive to an active pursuit. Examples of questions include "What do I already know about this subject?" "What are my own opinions about this subject?" (Be willing to challenge them.) "How does this material relate to my research questions?"
R Read	The main activity of serious reading means carefully considering the meaning of what the author is trying to convey. You must evaluate and analyze what you read.
R Recall	If you do not make a conscious effort to recall what you have just read, you will forget a lot (maybe most) of it. As you read, see if you can recall what you have just read. You may be thinking, "Well, of course I can recall it—I just read it!" But often that really is not the case. Recalling from time to time allows you to focus upon the main points; this, in turn, aids concentration. One definition of "recall" is to "bring something back into one's mind, especially so as to recount it to others." So a good way to test whether you really can recall what you have read is to picture yourself trying to explain it to someone else. If you can't, then you didn't really understand it completely. Recalling makes you think about and assimilate what you have just read, keeping you an active, not a passive, reader. Remember—passive readers are moving their eyes over the words and maybe even understanding all those words—but they are not really understanding what all of those words amount to. A significant element in being active is to write down, in your own words, key points. Again, picture yourself trying to explain what the text means to someone else.

TABLE 1.5. *(continued)*	
R Review	The final step in SQ3R is to review the material that you have recalled in your notes. Did you understand the main points of the work? Did you understand the reasoning and evidence offered in support of any arguments? Did you identify all the main points? Are there any gaps? Don't take for granted that you have recalled everything accurately—review the text again to make certain and to clarify.

To put SQ3R into practice, follow these steps:

Step 1: Survey

Skim—that is, **survey**—the passage to identify the subject matter, the point of view, and the overall purpose of the passage.

Step 2: Question

Before you start the next phase of reading—the one that you will spend a lot of time on—come up with questions to answer, like "What is this passage about?" "What is its purpose?" "What implied questions are this passage trying to answer?"

Step 3: Read

Start reading the passage actively. The most important claims and conclusions are frequently found in the first and last sentences of a paragraph. Underline, highlight, or circle claims and key words. (Highlighting is useful because you can use different colors for different purposes.) Make notes in the margins. Is the author supporting an idea? Put a plus sign in the margin. Is the author rejecting an idea? Put a minus sign in the margin. Is something surprising to you? Put an exclamation mark in the margin. Is something confusing to you? Put a question mark in the margin. Pay attention to "contrast words," like *but, yet, however, nevertheless, although,* and *not.* These often signal a shift in the author's argument or indicate a counter-argument made by the author to potential arguments raised in the piece.

Step 4: Recall

This is the considered the most important part of successful active reading. After you read each paragraph, write notes to yourself explaining what it is about, using your own words. By doing this, you can either prove to yourself that you understand what you just read or realize that you need to go back and read it again.

Step 5: Review

Once you reach the end of the selection, explain to yourself what the point of the whole work is, also using your own words.

6. The Rhetorical Précis

Margaret K. Woodworth developed the rhetorical précis, a very specific type of summary, in 1988. It helps with reading comprehension and using source materials. A rhetorical précis is a useful tool for approaching assigned readings to make sure that you understand their main points, strategies, purpose, and intended audiences. A rhetorical précis has exactly four sentences, each of which has specific guidelines:

1. **Sentence one provides the name of the author, the genre, the title of the work, the date in parentheses following the title, a rhetorically accurate verb** (such as "asserts," "argues," "suggests," "posits," "questions," or "claims"), **and a "that" clause containing the major assertion (thesis) of the work.** Optional: an appositive (a phrase describing the author) following the author's name.
2. **Sentence two provides an explanation of how the author develops and supports the major assertion (thesis)**, usually in chronological order.
3. **Sentence three provides a statement of the author's apparent purpose, followed by an "in order to" phrase**. This may reflect the author's thesis, but should also include the author's apparent motive for writing the work.
4. **Sentence four provides a description of the intended audience and the relationship the author apparently wishes to establish with the audience.** (Establishing the tone of the piece can be helpful.) Also, it is easy to describe the intended audience of a scholarly journal article or a book by a scholar:

these are intended for an audience of fellow scholars in particular disciplines and for students interested in learning more about the subject.

Following is an example:

Rhetorical Précis of "Seeing White: Children of Color and the Disney Fairy Tale Princess"

In the scholarly journal article "Seeing White: Children of Color and the Disney Fairy Tale Princess" (Summer 2005), Dorothy L. Hurley argues that children's perceptions of their self-image are greatly influenced by the stories and characters they see portrayed in various forms of media and that children of color are rarely able to see themselves reflected in the stories they are exposed to, consequentially leading them to internalize ideas about white privilege. Hurley supports her argument with detailed analyses of the most popular Disney versions of the classic fairy tales, focusing on the surprisingly prevalent theme of white vs. black found in all the movies she discusses, which helps to cement her idea that young children of color are going to be exposed to media that will affect how they view themselves and their peers. Her purpose is to inform the reader of the racial biases found in the popular adaptations of fairy tales today in order to spark change in how we teach and raise the youth of today, keeping in mind how the media we expose them to will shape their views on race. Hurley is speaking to an audience of educators and parents who have the power to expose the children they are around to a wider range of fairy tales and stories so that the children can form more well-rounded ideas of their own self-image.

While a rhetorical précis should be written as a paragraph, as in the preceding example, it can help to understand how the student writer succeeded in writing a successful précis by looking at it sentence by sentence:

Sentence one provides the name of the author, the genre, the title of the work, the date in parentheses following the title, the rhetorically accurate verb "argues," and a "that" clause containing the major assertion of the work:

> In the scholarly journal article "Seeing White: Children of Color and the Disney Fairy Tale Princess" (Summer 2005), Dorothy L. Hurley argues that children's perceptions of their self-image are greatly influenced by the stories and characters they see portrayed in various forms of media and that children of color are rarely able to see themselves reflected in the stories they are exposed to, consequentially leading them to internalize ideas about white privilege.

Sentence two provides an explanation of how the author develops and supports her major assertion:

> Hurley supports her argument with detailed analyses of the most popular Disney versions of the classic fairy tales, focusing on the surprisingly prevalent theme of white vs. black found in all the movies she discusses, which helps to cement her idea that young children of color are going to be exposed to media that will affect how they view themselves and their peers.

Sentence three provides a statement of the author's apparent purpose, followed by an "in order to" phrase:

> Her purpose is to inform the reader of the racial biases found in the popular adaptations of fairy tales today in order to spark change in how we teach and raise the youth of today, keeping in mind how the media we expose them to will shape their views on race.

Sentence four provides a description of the student's assessment of the intended audience and the relationship the author apparently wishes to establish with that audience (what she would like people to do):

Hurley is speaking to an audience of educators and parents who have the power to expose the children they are around to a wider range of fairy tales and stories so that the children can form more well-rounded ideas of their own self-image.

Examples of Terms That Can Be Used in a Rhetorical Précis

TABLE 1.6. List of Commonly Used Terms in a Rhetorical Précis				
Genre	**Rhetorically accurate verb**	**Verb followed by evidence**	**In order to**	**The author's tone is**
article	argues [that]	comparing	convince	formal
book	asserts [that]	contrasting	inform	grave
review of ____	claims [that]	defining	persuade	earnest
chapter in ____	explains [that]	describing	point out	humorous
excerpt from ____	implies [that]	exploring	demonstrate	concerned
column	suggests [that]	explaining	show	informal
editorial	questions [that]	illustrating	suggest	serious
prologue to ____	proposes [that]	questioning	stress	ironic
speech	insists [that]	examining	influence	Strident

How to Think of the Four Sentences in a Rhetorical Précis

TABLE 1.7. Breakdown of the Four Sentences in a Précis	
How to think of the first sentence	**WHO are you talking about?** **WHAT is their background?** **WHAT did they write?** **WHEN was it published?** **WHAT is their point?**
How to think of the second sentence	**HOW do they support their thesis?** Do they offer research data? Expert primary sources? Secondary sources? Anecdotes or stories
How to think of the third sentence	**WHAT are they trying to do?** Are they trying to inform their audience? To get them to feel a certain way? To make them change their minds? **WHY is that their purpose? In order to accomplish what?**
How to think of the fourth sentence	**WHO is the author trying to address?** Consumers? Community members? Voters? Parents? Students? Scholars? **WHAT relationship are they trying to establish? Tone is important—are they . . .** Formal? Friendly? Informal? Sarcastic? Serious? Humorous?

7. The CRAAP Source Test

The CRAAP Test was created by Sarah Blakeslee of the Merriam Library at the University of California, Chico (2004). You can use the CRAAP Test to critically read and also evaluate how accurate and reliable a source is—in other words, to tell the difference between what is "crap" and what isn't. Here are the five sections:

TABLE 1.8. Critical Reading and Evaluation: The CRAAP Source Test	
C Currency	Currency can be more important in some fields than in other fields, but having current information is usually recommended. When was this work published? Does the author use recent information? Are the references current? Does currency matter for this topic? Why or why not?
R Relevance	Relevance is the quality or state of being closely connected or appropriate to a specific topic. A common problem for many college students is using sources that do not have a strong relationship to the topic their papers are supposed to explore. Which of your research questions does this source help to answer? What is the intended audience? Does this source provide new information or a new perspective? Is this source too technical or too general?
A Authority	Authority lets us know that someone with expertise in the topic is sharing knowledge. Authority, however, is contextual. Having a Ph.D. in electrical engineering does not make a person an expert in Holocaust studies, for example. What credentials does the author have? Are they relevant to the topic being explored? Does the author have any affiliations with a respected university or organization? What can you find out about the author online? Has the author published on this subject before? Is the publication reputable? Does it tend to have a cultural or political bias? Does it tend to endorse particular values?

TABLE 1.8. *(continued)*

A Accuracy	Determining the accuracy of a source aids you in finding information that is supported by evidence and free from errors. Does the author use reputable sources to support claims? Has an article been peer reviewed? (Peer review is when experts in a field review work in the same field before it is published in a scholarly journal.) Has a book been reviewed by experts? Does empirical evidence support the conclusions reached? Does this source align with other reputable sources that discuss this topic? Does the information seem complete, or are facts missing? Does the source contain any false information or errors?
P Purpose	Material may be written to educate readers, but it can also be designed to persuade, to support biases, to mislead, to sell something, and so on. Understanding the purpose helps us to see if there are any biases or underlying motives that may affect the way the information is presented. Is the information biased in one direction? Why is this information being shared? Does this source present multiple points of view on the topic? Is the language used objective, or is it meant to evoke an emotional response?

The following worksheet was adapted from the Merriam Library's original version. (See https://library.csuchico.edu/help/source-or-information-good.) Some professors may ask you to turn in worksheets like this one in with ratings added to each of the five sections, such as 0 points for the lowest rating and ten for the highest.

TABLE 1.9. CRAAP Test Worksheet

Work Cited

[Provide details of source here]

Type of Source

☐ Scholarly Article   ☐ Magazine Article   ☐ Newspaper Article   ☐ Book
☐ Selection from a Book
☐ Article from a Professional Organization's Website
☐ Article or Posting from a Non-Professional Website
☐ Other _____

Currency of the information

When was the information gathered?	
When was the work published?	
Does your assignment require only current information, or will older sources also work?	
If the information comes from a website, when was the site last updated?	

Relevance of the content and its importance to your assignment

Is the information detailed enough to be helpful to you?	
Is the information presented at an appropriate (not too elementary or simplistic) level?	
Can you picture how you could use this in your assignment?	

TABLE 1.9. *(continued)*

Authority (expertise) of the source

Who is the author? Publisher? Source? Sponsor?	
What are the author's credentials and organizational affiliations?	
If the work is presented by an organization and not a named author, is the organization a professional one? An established NGO? Or is it presented by a group with a biased agenda?	
What are the author's or organization's qualifications to publish on this topic?	
Is contact information provided, such as a publisher, mailing address, or email address?	
If the information comes from a website, does the domain name descriptor reveal anything about the source? (.com, .edu, .gov, .org, .net, .mil)	

Accuracy (reliability and truthfulness of the source)

Where does the information the author or organization presents come from?	
Is the information supported by empirical evidence, not just generalizations or opinions?	
Can you verify the information using other sources?	
Are there any spelling, punctuation, grammar, or typographical errors? People who are sloppy in these areas may be sloppy about information, too, even if they are not consciously trying to present biased or inaccurate information.	

TABLE 1.9. *(continued)*	
Purpose of the work (authors' or organization's intent and motives)	
Do the authors or organization make their intentions or purposes clear? Is the purpose to inform, teach, sell, entertain, or persuade?	
Does the point of view appear objective and impartial?	
Are there any political, ideological, cultural, religious, gender, identity, or personal biases?	

8. Finding Good Sources for Papers

College essays and research papers require that you take evidence to support your arguments from scholarly sources. Some scholars publish books, but the majority of scholarly research is published in scholarly journals, also called "academic journals" and "peer-reviewed journals" (articles are only accepted after being reviewed by a "jury" of peers—other experts—in the field). A scholarly journal is a particular type of periodical aimed at fellow experts and at other people—like students—doing research to learn more about a subject. Scholarly journals are sources of what we call *primary research*. Primary research presents information on experiments, investigations, tests, and so on carried out to gather data first hand, rather than taking it from other published sources (secondary and tertiary research). When magazines feature articles about scientific research, they publish secondary (second-hand) or tertiary (third-hand) information. The periodicals your professors want you to look for are journals, not magazines (which are aimed at the popular, not the scholarly, market). Magazines can have useful information, but scholarly journals are preferable. Some magazines are aimed at particular ideological groups and will be more biased than more neutral sources, both in terms of how articles are slanted and the issues they cover. Authors of articles may "cherry pick" what information they present, including information that may be accurate but out of context and ignoring accurate information that does not support their own biases.

Finding Scholarly Journal Articles Online at Your College Library
Start by going to the homepage of your college's library. Choose a database—
EBSCOhost is a good place to start.

Welcome to the Grace Van Dyke Bird Library

Find a Book

- Bakersfield College Library Catalog
  Locate print books and ebooks in the BC Library collection
- Bakersfield College eBook Collection
  Collection of over 170,000 ebooks from EBSCO
- Gale Virtual Reference Library
  Electronic reference books

Find Books & Articles

- EBSCO Discovery Service
  Search BC's book catalog, ebooks, and research databases simultaneously

Digital Archives

- JSTOR
  Digitized back issues of academic journals
- Gale 19th Century U.S. Newspapers
  Facsimile-image database of American newspapers of the 1800s
- Gale Slavery and Anti-Slavery
  History of slavery from the original books

Find an Article

- EBSCOhost
  Journal and magazine articles from various disciplines
- Gale Academic OneFile
  Journal and magazine articles from various disciplines
- Gale Biography in Context
  Reference, journal, and magazine articles regarding significant people, past and present
- Gale Literature Resource Center
  Overviews, literary criticism, and reviews on writers from all disciplines
- Gale Opposing Viewpoints
  Viewpoints, reference articles, and statistics covering today's hottest social issues
- CQ Researcher
  In-depth coverage of the most important issues of the day
- EBSCO Applied Science & Technology Source
  Journal and magazine articles in the applied sciences and computing disciplines
- Oxford Music Online
  Includes Grove Music Online and other Oxford music reference resources
- EBSCO Newspaper Source Plus
  Full-text coverage of many of today's major newspapers, newswires and news magazines
- EBSCO Full Text Finder
  Find which journals and magazines are available full-text in BC's databases.

Figure 1.1. Adapted Homepage of Grace Van Dyke Library at Bakersfield College (source: http://www.bakersfieldcollege.edu/library, 2019)

Once in EBSCOhost (or any other service your library may have), you'll see a list of databases. *Academic Search Complete* and *Psychology and Behavioral Sciences Collection* are both good for many of the topics assigned in college English classes.

EBSCO*host*

Choose Databases

To search within a single database, click the database name listed below. To select more than one database to search, check the boxes next to the databases and click *Continue*.

    Continue

☐ Select / deselect all

☐ **Academic Search Complete**

Academic Search Complete is the world's most valuable and comprehensive scholarly, multi-disciplinary full-text database, with more than 8,500 full-text periodicals, including more than 7,300 peer-reviewed journals. In addition to full text, this database offers indexing and abstracts for more than 12,500 journals and a total of more than 13,200 publications including monographs, reports, conference proceedings, etc. The database features PDF content going back as far as 1887, with the majority of full text titles in native (searchable) PDF format. Searchable cited references are provided for more than 1,400 journals.

Figure 1.2. An Example of a Database Listing Using EBSCOhost (2019)

Once in your database, enter search terms. You can add to the default number of three rows, but three isn't a bad number to start with.

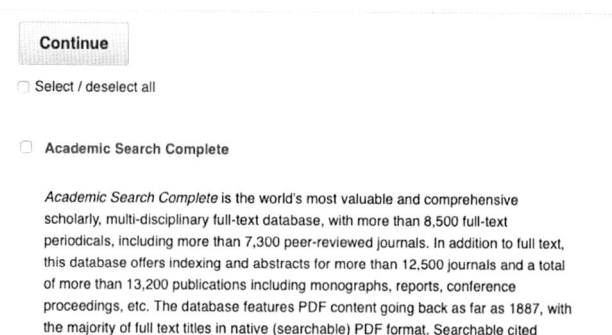

Figure 1.3. Modified Search field for Academic Search Complete database Using EBSCOhost (2019)

Just be sure to narrow your search to both "Full Text" and "Scholarly (Peer Reviewed) Journals" when you are looking for scholarly sources. You can also choose the publication date range.

Figure 1.4. EPSCOhost Refine Search Options Located Alongside the Results of Your Search Inquiry (2019)

If you decide not to limit your search to academic journals, make sure you know how to tell magazine and newspaper articles from journal articles. Scholarly journals will have an icon with a label that says "Academic Journal."

Academic
Journal

Figure 1.5.

Magazines will have an icon with a label that says "Periodical." (Even though journals, magazines, and newspapers are all periodicals, this is the terminology that the databases use.)

Periodical

Figure 1.6.

Newspapers will have an icon with a label that says "News."

News

Figure 1.7.

Book reviews will have an icon that says "Review."

Review

Figure 1.8.

Finding Scholarly Journal Articles Outside the College Library

You can also try Google Scholar. You can access Google Scholar through http://scholar.google.com. Using its search page, you can find numerous journals, theses, abstracts, and articles covering a wide range of disciplines. However, these are not all free of charge, unlike what you will find using your library's databases. Use advanced search options to get the best results. You won't have the same success if you use key words or plain language searches like you would on any other Internet search engine. Your results will be a list of citations in order of relevance. Be sure to check the dates because they are not ordered chronologically, and older articles may be outdated. Click a result to get publication information. If it's available, you can view the full text free of charge.

Figure 1.9. Search Field for Google Scholar Database

The Directory of Open Access Journals (DOAJ) provides a number of scholarly journal articles that you can access free of charge. The DOAJ includes scientific and academic journals covering a variety of fields and written in many languages. All of the articles on the DOAJ are completely open access, so you can read or print the full text of the articles free of charge. You can access DOAJ through https://doaj.org/.

Figure 1.10. Search Field for Directory of Open Access Journals (DOAJ)

You can also, of course, just do a regular Internet search—just remember to follow guidelines on evaluating what you find. The following section discusses how to do this.

9. Critically Evaluating Sources

The world is full of "information"—however, it is increasingly apparent that not all of it is valid, useful, or accurate. More and more often we see the spread of misinformation that can actually be dangerous. "Fake news" is being generated with a variety of motives on the parts of the people who create it. Take, for example, Jestin Color. The following information comes from an NPR story, "We Tracked Down a Fake-News Creator in the Suburbs":

> Coler's company, Disinfomedia, owns many faux news sites—he won't say how many. But he says his is one of the biggest fake-news businesses out there, which makes him a sort of godfather of the industry. At any given time, Coler says, he has between 20 and 25 writers. And it was one of them who wrote the story in the Denver Guardian that an FBI agent who leaked a presidential candidate's emails was killed. Coler says that over 10 days the site got 1.6 million views. He says stories like this work because they fit into existing conspiracy theories. "The people wanted to hear this," he says. "So all it took was to write that story. Everything about it was fictional: the town, the people, the sheriff, the FBI guy. And then . . . boy it spread like wildfire."

What motivated Coler? Was he deliberately trying to influence the election? Not at all. His motivation was simply to profit by creating fake news. When people go to the sites that host these stories, the stories spread.

> As these stories spread, Coler makes money from the ads on his websites. He wouldn't give exact figures, but he says stories about other fake-news proprietors making between $10,000 and $30,000 a month apply to him. Coler fits into a pattern of other faux news sites that make good money, especially by targeting certain political groups.

How is this profitable? The following comes from a story in the *Los Angeles Times*, "Without These Ads, There Wouldn't Be Money in Fake News" by Paresh Dave [Paresh really is his first name]:

> Fill out a short form and copy-paste some code to get ads on your website. Every 1,000 visitors earns you at least a dollar or two with traditional banner ads sold through Google—boxes typically pitching products that readers have browsed online. But the same readership generates three times the income through recommended content ads. Usually displayed in a familiar grid, they couple crazy headlines with scintillating pictures—a must-click combination dubbed chum.

> But the advertising technology companies that offer these easy-to-use services impose few regulations, inspiring sites that publish fake news to maximize revenue.

> They take advantage of a general rule in online publishing: the crazier the story, the greater the interest. Capitalizing off this year's presidential election, they post exaggerated political news articles — some with made-up quotes and details—that millions of consumers can't resist opening.

In many cases, of course, people generate fake news because they *do* want to have an impact on a country's future. Motivation, however, is ultimately less important than results. But the increasing prevalence and influence of fake news further illustrates why carefully looking for reputable sources is important—and not just for research papers. This statement is not indented to be overly dramatic—people's health and lives have been affected by people believing in information promoted as facts that have no basis in reality.

Falsehoods spread extremely rapidly on social media, outdistancing genuine information, researchers reported in 2018. Looking at Twitter, they found that false news was re-tweeted more often than true news was, and it was carried further. "Falsehood diffused significantly farther, faster, deeper, and more broadly than the truth in all categories of information, and the effects were more pronounced for false political news than for false news about terrorism, natural disasters, science, urban legends, or financial information," according to Sinan Aral of the Massachusetts Institute of Technology and his team. Their report was published in the journal *Science*. "It took the truth about six times as long as falsehood to reach 1,500 people."

Damage has been caused by the scientifically totally debunked claim that vaccines cause autism. In 1998, a British researcher named Andrew Wakefield released a paper claiming to have linked the measles, mumps, and rubella (MMR) vaccine to autism. No other scientist has ever been able to match his findings, and replicability—the reproducibility of experiments—is a vital part of the scientific process. Brian Deer, an investigative journalist, discovered that greed had motivated Wakefield to falsify data. He was working for a company developing a vaccine they wanted to market, and they wanted to discredit the existing vaccine. An ethics review board ruled that he had indeed falsified the data in his report, and the journal that published his article retracted it. He also lost his UK medical license.

Jenny McCarthy, a former Playboy Bunny and TV personality, began speaking out against vaccines in 2007, claiming they had caused her son's autism. She has written books (including one with a foreword by Wakefield) claiming that vaccines cause autism and that she has cured her son's disorder with alternative treatment. (Based on the descriptions of her son's symptoms, some experts believe the boy actually has Landau-Kleffner syndrome, not autism, which cannot be "cured.") McCarthy's celebrity status gave her a platform to urge parents not to vaccinate their children. The anti-vaccine movement that McCarthy and others started has caused devastating results for many families who did not know how to critically evaluate information. Studies from the independent, non-profit Institute of Medicine, the World Health Organization, and the Centers for Disease Control and Prevention have all found that there is no link between vaccines and autism spectrum disorder. The studies demonstrate that vaccines are overwhelmingly safe, with very rare cases of side effects. They protect children from dangerous and preventable diseases and help to reduce the prevalence of many diseases—some of which are now coming back due to the anti-vaccine movement.

Wakefield moved to the United States after he lost his license to practice medicine in the UK, but he continues to profit by his ability to fool credulous people. In 2016 the film *Vaxxed*, directed by Wakefield, was released. Capitalizing on many Americans' propensity to believe outlandish conspiracy theories, he claims that the U.S. Centers for Disease Control and Prevention, the nation's health protection agency and one of the major operating components of the Department of Health and Human Services, conducted a nefarious conspiracy to cover up the "true" reason for America's rising autism diagnosis rates—vaccines. Despite the fact that his claims have been continuously discredited and that he has been proven to lie and falsify other evidence in his defense of himself, Wakefield still has followers. His actions and the damage that he and celebrity followers have caused provide further examples of why people need to know how to evaluate information objectively and critically.

As stated earlier, there are three basic principles of critical thinking that apply to academics and to "real life": Know exactly *what* you believe, know *why* you believe it, and know what evidence exists to *challenge* what you believe. This last part is very important—most people look only for evidence to support their beliefs, so they tend to limit the "information" and opinions they seek out to those that satisfy them emotionally by reinforcing their belief systems.

What is a Scholarly Source?

Scholarly sources (also called academic, peer-reviewed, or refereed) are written by experts in a field and serve to keep others in that field up to date on the most recent research. These resources provide the most substantial and trustworthy information for research papers. Use of scholarly sources is an expected attribute of academic course work. How can you tell if a source is scholarly? The following pages will give you tips on how to distinguish reliable sources from unreliable or less useful ones, and the following criteria can help you differentiate scholarly sources from those that are not.

Authors
- Are authors' names included?
- Are authors' credentials provided? Are they relevant to the information provided?

Publishers
- Who is the publisher of the information?
- Is the publisher an academic institution, scholarly, or professional organization?
- Is publisher's purpose for publishing this source evident?

Audience
- Who is the intended audience of this source?
- Is the language geared toward those with knowledge of a specific discipline?

Content
- Why is the information being provided or the article written?
- Are sources cited?
- Are there references to other writings on this topic?
- Are research claims documented?
- Are conclusions based on evidence provided?

Timeliness (Currency)
- Is the date of publication evident?
- Is currency of the information crucial to your research?

Tips for Evaluating Specific Source Types

Each specific resource type will also have criteria that can be applied to that source.

Books
- Date of publication and currency
  - o Is the information current enough for your purposes? (You need to be careful—research can be supplanted by later research.)
  - o Is a historical perspective important?
- Publishers
  - o University presses likely to be scholarly.

         o Professional organizations and the U.S. Government Printing Office can also be indicators of scholarly content.

- Are there any book reviews?
  - o Check sources such as *Book Review Index* and *Contemporary Authors.*
  - o Search databases in the subject area or your topic to locate book reviews.

Articles

- Is biographical information for the author provided?
- Who is the publisher?
- How frequently is the periodical published?
- Are there advertisements in the periodical? If so, how many and what kinds of advertisements are present? For example, is the advertising clearly geared towards readers in a specific discipline, age group, or occupation?
- For more specific guidelines in identifying periodical types, see "Is It Scholarly? Distinguishing Periodical Types" later in this section.

Websites

- What is the domain of the page?
- Who is publishing or sponsoring the page? "Strip back" the URL to discover the source.
- Is contact information for the author and publisher provided?
- How recently was the page updated?
- Be particularly wary of bias and inaccuracies when viewing web pages. False information, sloppy research, and mistakes are prevalent.
- For more guidelines on evaluating web pages, see "Evaluating Websites" later in this section.

Tabloids

There is a type of commercially published "information" source not discussed above that will also not be included in the section on distinguishing periodical types. Tabloids, known in the trade as "sensational news," originally referred to papers having pages half the size of those of a standard newspaper and dominated by outlandish headlines, bizarre photographs, and sensational stories. Tabloids exist to make profits by shocking people and arousing other strong reactions. In highly regarded newspapers like the *New York Times* or *Wall Street Journal,* the facts in a news story are meticulously checked and confirmed with multiple sources. When errors occur, the newspapers publish corrections. Editors and writers understand and conform to journalistic standards. Tabloids ignore these standards.

Go to a supermarket checkout stand, and you'll see quite a few with headlines that may claim celebrities have just been seen drunk or drugged in public, are having affairs, are getting divorced, have committed murder or other crimes, and so on. They may also include stories like "Elvis Statue Found on Mars." Occasionally these stories—though not the ones about Elvis—may turn out to have some basis in fact. But that isn't because the tabloid sellers care about facts. Many credulous readers believe tabloid stories for two reasons: (1) they simply want to believe them, and (2) they believe they must be true or the celebrities would sue for libel. However, libel laws actually protect the lies of tabloids to a certain extent. Libel and defamation of character laws are heavily weighted in the tabloids' favor.

The standards of libel and slander for public figures is high, making cases difficult to win, and anyone who becomes famous is considered a "public figure," whether or not the person ever sought fame. A "public figure" has to prove "actual malice"—that the tabloid is not just negligent, but that the publisher knew that the story was false but nonetheless displayed a reckless disregard for the truth and for any harm that might be caused. And while there are standards in criminal law that must be met in order to find someone guilty of a crime, proving that someone is innocent of something reported in tabloids is different. And tabloids can be cagey in the way they word accusations or in the way they present them. How can anyone prove that an "anonymous" source did not say something about a public figure, true or not? After all, the tabloids' lawyers argue, they are just reporting "claims."

There are other reasons tabloids are willing and able to knowingly publish lies. In his book *I Watched a Wild Hog Eat My Baby: A Colorful History of Tabloids and Their Cultural Impact*, Bill Sloan, who has been the editor of the *Globe* and the *National Tattler*, a writer for the *National Enquirer*, and friends of editors, writers, and reporters at four other major tabloids, wrote that publishers recognized two reasons why most wouldn't sue "gutter-level" publications even in clear-cut cases of libel: (1) they may fear that the publicity surrounding the suit could be more damaging than the original lies, and (2) the cases can drag on for years. Many tabloid publishers often didn't have the money to pay damages anyway, and even when they did, the amounts were often reduced.

Distinguishing Between Periodical Types

TABLE 1.10. List of Periodical Types			
Criteria	Scholarly (Academic) Journals	Professional & Trade Periodicals	Popular & Special Interest Magazines
Purpose for Publication	Inform and report original research. Provide in-depth analysis of issues related to a specific discipline.	Current trends, news, and research in a specific field. Provide career information.	Entertain, inform, and persuade without in-depth analysis.
General Characteristics	Lengthy articles. Citations, bibliographies, charts, graphs, and tables.	Some research articles. Statistics and forecasts. Sources cited.	Articles usually fairly short. Sources generally not cited.
Frequency of Publication	Often quarterly.	Often monthly.	Monthly or weekly.
Author Information	Scholars and professors. Researchers in the field. Author credentials.	Scholars. Staff writers. Freelance journalists.	Freelance journalists. Editorial staff. Authors may not be identified.
Article Characteristics	Generally lengthy. Focus on a narrow subject or piece of research.	Varying lengths. Research articles. Field news.	Usually short. General information and little detail.
Words and Jargon Used	Terminology used by scholars in the discipline.	Language specific to those in a given profession.	Common language and sentence structure.

More Help with Evaluating Websites

Every source that you use in a paper must be evaluated, and you must submit evaluations of the sources in your research paper information sets. Resources that you find on the Internet range widely—many merely provide opinions or information in support of specific, partisan viewpoints. A first step in evaluating an online source is to look at the "About Us" page. Who sponsors the site? Don't assume a scholarly, nonpartisan-sounding statement of purpose is always accurate—you should look up the sponsoring organizations and, when provided, their sponsors, too. University-sponsored sites, organizations of professionals in different disciplines, and reputable nongovernment organizations (NGOs) and nonprofit organizations (NPOS) are often very useful.

Following are questions that you can ask about websites:

Authorship
- Does the site have an author?
- What are the author's qualifications or expertise in the area?
- Is the contact information for the author or the sponsor/publisher given?
- What is the relationship between the author and the sponsoring institution?

Accuracy
- Is the information accurate? (Does it correspond to other information on "vetted" websites?)
- Has the information been edited and fact-checked?
- Is the information verifiable?
- Does the site document the sources used?
- If the information is historical or biographical, are the dates of events accurate?
- How does the information compare with what you already know?

Currency
- Is the site up-to-date?
- When was the information first provided and last updated?
- Are the links expired or are they current?

Point of view

- Whose point of view/perspective is given?
- Is the author promoting an agenda?
- To what extent is the information trying to sway the opinion of the audience?
- Who sponsors the site? If a sponsoring organization is given, look at its "About Us" section, but don't stop there. Sponsors want to present themselves in the best light possible; no group that intends to suppress information and promote only biased perspectives is going to announce that. Also, if you can find pages about a sponsoring organization, can you find what its sponsors are—for example, political groups or corporations?
- Is there advertising on the page? If so, what kinds of products are being advertised?

What is the purpose of the website?

- Do a quick scan of the site. Can you determine its general purpose? Is it meant to do any of the following?
    1. Provide research and scholarly information?
    2. Provide educational or factual information?
    3. Entertain?
    4. Advertise, market or sell something?
    5. Advocate ideas? Persuade you?

Who is the intended audience?

"URL" is an acronym for Uniform Resource Locator. It has two main components: the protocol identifier, like "http," and the domain, or resource, name. For the URL http://example.com, the resource name is *example.com*. A resource name can indicate the site's intended audience. Knowing this provides clues as to the site's value. Domain names are organized right to left, with general descriptors to the right, and specific descriptors to the left. For example, cdc.gov is the domain name for the Centers for Disease Control and Prevention (commonly referred to as CDC). The full URL of its homepage is https://www.cdc.gov.

Most common domain name descriptors.

TABLE 1.11. Common Domains		
Domain	**Meaning**	**Example**
.edu	Created at a college or university.	www.indiana.edu
.gov	Created by an official U.S. federal agency or office.	www.federalreserve.gov
.org	Varies—in most cases the site was created by a nonprofit organization or an individual.	www.npr.org
.com	Varies—in most cases the site was created by a for-profit organization.	www.amazon.com
.net	Varies greatly—often indicates that the site was created by a person, group, and so on that uses an Internet service provider.	www.earthlink.net
.mil	Created by the U.S. military.	www.usmc.mil
.in.us	Created by state-supported institution of Indiana - the .us domain requires a state code as a second level domain.	www.monroe.lib.in.us

As stated earlier, always look at a site's "About" or "About Us" page. As an example, on the following pages, you will see part of the Pew Research Centers "About" page. It is very thorough.

About Pew Research Center

Pew Research Center is a nonpartisan fact tank that informs the public about the issues, attitudes and trends shaping the world. We conduct public opinion polling, demographic research, content analysis and other data-driven social science research. We do not take policy positions.

Quick links

Contact us

Follow us

Media resources

Our mission

We generate a foundation of facts that enriches the public dialogue and supports sound decision-making. We are nonprofit, nonpartisan and nonadvocacy. We value independence, objectivity, accuracy, rigor, humility, transparency and innovation. Read more

Our research

We study U.S. politics and policy; journalism and media; internet, science and technology; religion and public life; Hispanic trends; global attitudes and trends; and U.S. social and demographic trends. Read more

Our methods

We're committed to meeting the highest methodological standards — and to exploring the newest frontiers of research. Read more

Our people

We are led by Michael Dimock and have a staff of more than 160 people. Our experts combine the observational and storytelling skills of journalists with the analytical rigor of social scientists. Pew Research Center is stewarded by a nine-member volunteer board.

Our funding

We are a subsidiary of The Pew Charitable Trusts, our primary funder. We partner strategically with philanthropists and institutional funders who share our commitment to impartial research and data that drive discussion. Read more about our funding. Learn more about supporting Pew Research Center and making a contribution on the Center's behalf.

In February 2019, the Pew Charitable Trusts and the Pew Research Center created Living Facts, a place that brings facts about Americans to life – who we are, how we live and what we do.

Our history

We originated in a research project created in 1990 called the Times Mirror Center for the People & the Press. In 2004, The Pew Charitable Trusts established the Pew Research Center as a subsidiary to house its information initiatives. Read more

Figure 1.11. Information on the "About" Webpage of the Pew Research Center

To the right of the preceding section, you will find the following, with links to even more information, such as exactly who is on its governing board—you simply have to click the link. Once there, you can click links to find even more detailed information about these people and their affiliations.

ABOUT PEW RESEARCH CENTER

About Pew Research Center

Our Mission and Code of Ethics

Our Research

Our Leadership & Staff

Our Governing Board

Our Funding

Support Pew Research Center

Our History

Careers

Find an Expert

Terms of Use

Privacy Policy

Figure 1.12. Other Links Located on the Far Right Column on the About Webpage of the Pew Research Center

Our Governing Board

Michael Delli Carpini, professor of communication, Annenberg School for Communication, University of Pennsylvania

Jana Bennett, founder and MD, JebRoc Media

Susan Glasser, contributing writer, The New Yorker

Robert M. Groves, provost, Georgetown University

Henry W. McGee, senior lecturer of business administration, Harvard Business School

James McMillan, senior vice president, general counsel and corporate secretary, The Pew Charitable Trusts

Arati Prabhakar, Technologist

Maria Thomas, Startup Advisor and Investor

Duncan Watts, principal researcher, Microsoft Research

Michael Dimock, president, Pew Research Center (non-voting)

Figure 1.13. Results after Clicking the Our Governing Board Link Located on the Far Right Column on the About Webpage of the Pew Research Center

10. Research Information Sets

Decades ago, students would create note card sets using index cards for projects like research papers. Today, this can be done with computers. This is a way to help read critically and to organize your information in such a way that after you have done your research, you can more easily put your paper together. Here are suggestions for creating your own information sets.

Each set should have the following components:

A work cited entry in MLA format.

An annotation, for example, a rhetorical précis or other type of short summary.

An evaluation, which should be from an objective source, not simply your own opinion (See "Critically Evaluating Sources").

Notes from the source, including in-text citations. Adding in-text citations now will save you a lot of time and trouble later. The information in the notes should be from your source, not your own opinion of the information. You can keep a notebook or other file where you record those impressions. You don't want to find yourself confused about where the information in your notes come from—your source or your opinions.

Sample #1

Following is a sample student research information set for a book. The student uses "qtd. in" in some of her citations. This is correct because the source was quoting someone else, which she notes before the quotations. Only use "qtd. in." when a source is quoting someone else—not when you are quoting the source. This student wrote a rhetorical précis for her annotation. This sample shows just five of her notes; naturally, you are not restricted to five notes per source.

Research Information Set #1

Work Cited

Taylor, Philip M. *Munitions of the Mind: War Propaganda from the Ancient World to the Nuclear Age*. Manchester UP, 2003.

Annotation

Philip M. Taylor, in his book *Munitions of the Mind: War Propaganda from the Ancient World to the Nuclear Age* (2005), argues that misguided wars are more easily launched and maintained when a single propaganda source gains a monopoly over the information and images that shape people's thoughts. Taylor provides a history of war propaganda from its earliest known instances, examines the psychological methods used to make a country's people fight war and the methods used to try to get people on the other side to abstain from fighting, and analyzes the role war propaganda plays today. His purpose is to help readers gain an understanding of both the negative and the positive aspects of war propaganda in order to recognize when they are being manipulated to support the military and political goals of forces in their own countries and to analyze the effects of propaganda on other populations in the world. The book appears to be aimed at people interested in a serious analysis of cultural history, military history, politics, and media and communications.

Evaluation

Excerpts of reviews of this book were found in our library's *Book Review Digest*. The scholarly journal *History* called it a "classic work." The reviewer said, "the book has an extraordinary range and offers an original and cohesive analysis," making it "an ideal text for . . . media and communications studies, cultural history, military history and politics." According to *SourceWatch*, a wiki encyclopedia "of people, issues, and groups shaping the public agenda" ("About"), Dr. Taylor is a professor based at Leeds University (UK), and his research interests are "Government-media relations, public and cultural diplomacy, propaganda, psychological operations/warfare, information operations/warfare, military-media relations, international film, radio and television (international communications), all in an historical or contemporaneous context."

Note #1

According to Philip M. Taylor, a professor of International Communications in the Institute of Communications Studies at the University of Leeds and a noted expert on propaganda, Goebbels was Hitler's "evil genius" of propaganda, and he spent six years, starting in 1933, preparing the German population to accept the idea that Germany should wage war against other European countries in order to achieve what Hitler and his followers considered Germany's "rightful" place in the world. Hitler's Ministry for Propaganda and Public Enlightenment had twelve separate departments infiltrating every area of German life, such as radio, press, theaters, film, and culture (Taylor 214).

Note #2

In *Mein Kampf,* Adolph Hitler wrote, "The psyche of the masses is not receptive to anything that is weak. They are like a woman whose psychic state has been determined less by abstract reason than by an emotional longing for a strong force which will complement her nature. Likewise, the masses love a commander, and despise a petitioner" (qtd. in Taylor 213-14).

Note #3

According to Hitler, propaganda consisted of "attracting the crowd, and not in educating those who are already educated," and he saw the crowd as "brutal, violent, emotional, corrupt, and corruptible" (qtd. in Taylor 214).

Note #4

The medium that both Hitler and Goebbels were most interested in was film. They used newsreels more than anything else to drive forward the "glory" of

German military supremacy once the war started, with combat footage skillfully edited so that the film footage shown to the German audience would be effective for propaganda. The films were intended to make Germans believe that their armed forces were clearly superior to all others, and that this was the natural consequence of their racial superiority and the leadership of Hitler (Taylor 218).

Note #5

The British recognized the value of censorship as "negative propaganda," that is, persuasion through the restriction of information. The government tried to control access to information and prevent any information from reaching the public that might damage morale and pro-war spirit. At the beginning of the war, cameramen weren't even allowed to accompany troupes to France (Taylor 301).

Sample #2

Following is another sample student research information set. This one is on an article in a scholarly journal. This student also wrote a rhetorical précis for her annotation.

Research Information Set #1

Work Cited

Davidson, Emily S., et al. "The Effects of Television Cartoons on Sex-Role Stereotyping in Young Girls." *Child Development*, vol. 50, no. 2, June 1979, pp. 597-600. *Academic Search Complete*, doi: 10.1111/1467-8624.ep12428848.

Annotation

In their article "The Effects of Television Cartoons on Sex-Role Stereotyping in Young Girls" (1979), Emily S. Davidson, Amy Yasuna, and Alan Tower examine and analyze the results of their study on the assumption that female children ages five to six are influenced by the sex-role stereotypes that appear in popular children's cartoons. They highlight their findings by explaining how they carried out the study using three different cartoons, one with a female-positive message, one with a gender-neutral message, and one with a male-positive message. Their results show that girls who viewed the female-positive cartoon ranked significantly lower on the scale of sex-role stereotyping than the girls who viewed the gender-neutral and male-positive cartoon, which supports the theory that girls in this age range are highly impacted by gendered messages in children's media. This study paves the way for a discussion on how sexist messages in media impacts self-image in female children.

Evaluation

"The Effects of Television Cartoons on Sex-Role Stereotyping in Young Girls" was published in the 50th volume of *Child Development* in June of 1979. The Wiley Online Library website says that "*Child Development* has published articles, essays, reviews, and tutorials on various topics in the field of child development since 1930" and that the journal provides the latest research for child psychiatrists, specialists in early childhood education, psychiatric social workers, and other researchers. All articles in the journal are peer-reviewed to guarantee accuracy.

Note #1

Of the few studies of sex roles and television, most have been content analyses. Tedesco reports "Women are usually presented in a sexual context, in romantic or family roles. Male characters engaged in more activities and emitted more behaviors than females; they were more aggressive and constructive and were more likely to be rewarded for their activities" (qtd. in Davidson et al. 597).

Note #2

Davidson et al. point out that female characters do not receive the same treatment as male characters in children's programs, and when they are featured, they are only seen in matronly roles or as a romantic interest instead of as an independent character with their own storyline. This tells little girls that they are not the main characters in their own lives; they are only supporting characters in the lives of men (597).

Note #3

It is unclear on whether children will pick up on non-traditional gender roles in media if they are not overtly stated to be empowering for the female characters. Shows like the one used in the study are very clear in the message that girls can do anything that boys can, while some other neutral shows simply contain a plot in which the female characters are equal to the male characters without explicitly stating that they are equal (Davidson et al. 600).

Note #4

The present study has the characteristic of high clarity of message. The non-traditional program is particularly clear in showing females in unstereotyped roles and verbally labeling them. Friedrich and Stein (1975) have found that verbal labeling of prosocial content somewhat enhances learning, even of a program which is already rather explicit in its presentation. Most programs which are unstereotyped do not provide such labels; they show girls and boys in similar activities but do not emphasize the point (Davidson et al. 600).

Note #5

"The cumulative impact of watching many hours of stereotyped (or unstereo-typed) programs is unknown but would probably be greater than the impact of one program" (Davidson et al. 600). Children in the study would have already been exposed to many television shows with gendered messages before entering the study, and these years of influence may have affected their views on gender in the study. A more long-term study would be more effective in revealing how children are affected by the messages in television shows.

Name: _____ Section: _____ Date: _____

Part Three

Chapter 1 Workshop

The following section contains a series of ten tasks that, if completed, will help you gain mastery over the content in this chapter. Your instructor will assign some (or all) of them to you as a way to practice the material presented here. Notice that some of them are global and focus on the entirety of the skills laid out in this chapter, while others are more focused and explore only one or two sections of the chapter. Also notice that some are shorter, some are longer, but all are designed to flip the classroom and put the power of learning directly into your own hands.

Workshop One.

<u>Overview</u>: Summarize all of the major sections that you find in this chapter.

Each major section or heading should be clearly labeled and should have at least a one-sentence discussion. You might have a dozen or more headings and sentences here. Be thorough and accurate to show that you have read and comprehended this chapter's contents. Avoid the temptation to judge or add anything new (even critical discussion of the content); this is an act of pure summary. Tell your instructor exactly what came in this chapter and in what order.

Workshop Two.

<u>Overview</u>: This workshop has you examine all of the wrong answers from your chapter diagnostic and respond to them.
1. Make a list of each question from the chapter diagnostic that you got wrong.
2. Go through the chapter to look up the rules on each question. For every question you got wrong, do the following:
   A. Identify the page number where the rule was found.

    B. Discuss what the right answer should have been on the diagnostic test.

    C. Discuss how you can avoid this error in future writing and/or tests.

Workshop Three.

Overview: Write a short, personal essay explaining the content of this chapter. The point of this essay is to directly address what you have learned from the chapter and how it will impact your future academic writing. Consider some or all of the following:

1. What information was new to you?

2. How do you plan to incorporate some of this information into your own reading, thinking, and writing in the future?

3. What information did you already know about? Did you already practice the advice given, or do you ignore it for some reason? If so, what was the reason?

4. Your instructor will provide you with more details, such as the length of the piece, if you should use quotations from the chapter, if personal anecdotes and casual language are allowed, etc.

Workshop Four.

Overview: Choose an issue you have strong opinions about and write about the following:

    A. In a sentence or two, state exactly what you believe.

    B. Write a paragraph discussing why you believe what you believe.

    C. Do some research to come up with evidence and arguments *against* your own beliefs. List the evidence you find.

    D. Write a paragraph discussing how you feel about this evidence.

Workshop Five.

Overview: Practicing emotional self-management.

Copy the following on a piece of paper or on a computer document. Complete these three emotional self-management exercises:

1.

> **Reflection: Emotional Self-Management**
>
> For me, the emotions that are most difficult to manage when others disagree with me are
>
> I deal with these by

2.

> **Reflection: Challenging Opinions**
>
> For me, the things I find most difficult about challenging the opinions of other people are
>
> I deal with these by

3.

> **Reflection: Challenging My Own Opinions**
>
> For me, the things I find most difficult about challenging my own opinions are
>
> I deal with these by

Workshop Six.

Overview: Find a scholarly journal article on a topic you would like to write a research paper on and take notes using the "Double-Entry Note Taking" model.

Workshop Seven.

Overview: Find a different scholarly journal article on a topic you would like to write a research paper on and write a rhetorical précis of the article.

Workshop Eight.

Overview: Find a different scholarly journal article on a topic you would like to write a research paper on and take notes using the "SQ3R" model.

Workshop Nine.

Overview: Find a different scholarly journal article on a topic you would like to write a research paper on and apply the "CRAAP Test."

Workshop Ten.

Overview: What is your take away from this chapter? What did you learn and what questions do you still have?

1. Write a short response of several sentences that covers the most important things that you learned from this chapter.
2. Write out at least five questions you still have about the chapter. What things would you want to communicate to your instructor? What would you like to see discussed in class or handled with more depth to help you master this chapter's content?
3. What did you find most valuable about this chapter? What did you find most useful in the workshops asking you to implement different kinds of evaluation, summary, and note taking?

CHAPTER 2

How to Master All Steps of the Writing Process

In this chapter, you will learn about the following:

Part One: The Formal Writing Process
1. Step One: Prewriting
2. Step Two: Thesis Generation
3. Step Three: Academic Research
4. Step Four: Outline
5. Step Five: Draft
6. Step Six: Initial Proofreading
7. Step Seven: Revising
8. Step Eight: Editing
9. Step Nine: Final Proofreading
10. Step Ten: Publication of the Final Draft

Part Two: Workshop

Part One

Formal Writing Process

Mustafa has a paper due. He's not procrastinating. His professor only announced it in class today, and it's due in two weeks, but he's kind of freaking out. "It is only five or six pages," his professor told the class. "ONLY five to six pages!" Mustafa says to himself. Seems a little crazy to him since he's never written a college essay before. How is he supposed to string along enough words to come out to five pages, let alone six if he wants to make a good impression?! He has an idea for the paper. He thinks it's a solid topic. But getting started seems impossible. He now wonders if maybe his friends were right—maybe he should have waited to take English!

Many of you reading this chapter may have found yourself in a similar situation to Mustafa's. A paper is assigned. The topic is announced. You sit down. And you stare at a blank screen for hours. Getting from a blank screen to a fully formed, edited, polished, printed paper seems unmanageable. And that's the key word: unmanageable. Many college students possess the requisite skills needed to craft and compile a paper, but *managing* the process is the critical challenge.

Many people don't realize that writing is a process. It takes time. It takes thought—a lot of thought. It takes writing and rewriting your ideas down again and again. It takes failure. It takes small successes. It takes hard work before getting it right. No paper comes out as a good piece of writing in just one quick step like ordering something on Amazon Prime. Indeed, writing takes many iterative steps: edits, drafts, and revisions. And, often, other sets of eyes are required to make the paper good enough to turn in (well, to turn in and be proud of anyway). Professional writers of all types of texts—i.e., comics, news articles, textbooks, screenplays, you name it—all employ a writing process. They all realize one universal truth in writing: "The first draft is the worst draft." Professional writers—your professor included—take their time, think, plan, outline, and change their work. They change it a lot. This chapter shows you how to do what the pros do, and as you become aware of the writing process, unlike Mustafa, you will no longer fear a five- to six-page paper—you will approach it with confidence by knowing how to manage the process.

The formal writing process followed by composition students and instructors all through the nation includes specific steps although some writers may emphasize one step over another, and others may rearrange the order of the steps. One thing, however, is clear: in some way or another, the following ten steps define what we identify as the formal writing process:

TABLE 2.1. Steps to the Formal Writing Process	
Step One	Prewriting
Step Two	Thesis Generation
Step Three	Researching (if required)
Step Four	Outlining
Step Five	Drafting
Step Six	Initial Proofreading
Step Seven	Revising
Step Eight	Editing
Step Nine	Final Proofreading
Step Ten	Publication of the Final Draft

Though these steps may seem like a lot, some are quite quickly accomplished and incredibly rewarding, whereas some are more difficult and require more time, but are equally, if not more, rewarding. Remember, the process takes time. This process won't work if you're doing a Hail Mary Pass and trying to write the paper in one quick go the night before it's due. This is the path of the organized, prepared student, and honestly, if you don't think you're particularly organized or prepared, simply going through the steps discussed in this chapter will get you there.

1. Step One. Prewriting

Generating ideas serves as the first step for any organized writer. To accomplish this, simply use a series of prewriting techniques to help you dig deep and come up with fresh thoughts. Consider this: in your history class, your professor asks you to write an essay about World War II, which you've just covered. You first think about the major battles fought because you've seen them in movies and even played some in video games. The problem: most of the other students are thinking the same thing. Our solution: help yourself think outside the box and come up with some truly original paths to your writing by adopting some prewriting techniques. Try each of them out. Discover which ones work for you. And use the ones that help you generate the topics that interest you for your paper.

Generate a List

Start with the simplest prewriting technique of generating a list—an exhaustive list—of as many ideas on your topic that you can think of. Once you've been assigned your prompt, simply write down as many ideas as you can. Start with the biggest ideas and gradually move to the more specific, or start specific and then back off to think of the bigger picture items. Either way, making a list of the ideas helps manifest all the ideas in your head (and it is a great way to record them, so you don't forget any brilliant paper idea that may have entered your brain at three in the morning).

List-Making Tips

- **No grammar. No worries. No doubts.** Don't worry about grammar, sentence errors, spelling, or anything like that. Be creative. Let your stream of consciousness do all the work. This bit of the writing process is entirely for you, so it doesn't matter if there are blemishes. If you see an error, keep going; don't double back or try to correct it. Let the creativity flow through you.
- **Dig deep. Dig far. Dig wide.** Don't cheat yourself. You cheat yourself by writing a short list and stopping prematurely. The power of making a list really comes deeper down in the list. The first ideas will be the most obvious—to you and your professor. The ideas you come up with further down the list are where the true imagination and the "you" come out in the process. Set a goal of, say, a thirty or forty item list, even if it's a struggle to complete it.
- **Set a timer. Set a goal. Set a target.** One of the best ways to make sure you dig deep is to set a timer. Use an app on your phone and set a timer for, say, twenty minutes. You would never normally go that long—trust us—but the timer will keep you going. You may feel you've run out of ideas at ten minutes and be desperate at fifteen, but as you keep going, you'll tap into the reserves of your mind and stretch your imagination in ways that will invariably surprise you.
- **Use paper. Use a phone. Use napkins.** The key here is to create results of your thinking as your thinking happens and in a place where your thinking can be easily "written" down—the computer screen, however, often finds

itself in an inconvenient place, and the blank screen often intimidates rather than stimulates. In the end, a computer screen often restricts the creative portals of the mind. Some would argue the kinesthetic merits of putting pen on actual paper, being able to doodle on actual paper, and scratch things out on actual paper creates the best possible creative outcomes. Many newer-generation students, however, would argue that this same energy and creativity can be expressed on the phone or tablet. They use various apps such as Notes, OneNote, or Notability, for example, where a stylus or mobile keyboard allows for ideas, images, and doodles to be "written" down and stored. On the other hand, one of the authors of this book, who is not a millennial, used napkins at a restaurant to record the topic and direction that his undergraduate thesis would eventually take—he just had to ask the waiter for a pen.

Brainstorm with Others

An important variation on making a list is to brainstorm. What's the difference between a brainstorm and a list? A list is done in private and on a page. Brainstorming is done with other people, aloud, and written down as a record of your discussion. You're still making a list as you brainstorm, but the power of doing this with other people cannot be overstated. Different people will bring different backgrounds, college majors, and life experiences to the table. The best way to do this is to organize a group of students from the same class you're in. Set up a study group at a coffee shop or meet in the hall a few minutes before class and bounce ideas off one each other and record the list as you go. Using friends, roommates, co-workers, or anyone with imagination will help you at this stage. Finally, texting a classmate, a friend, or significant partner can generate great ideas as well, because texting can act as a recording device of sorts, to which you can refer as you begin to develop your ideas.

Freewrite within a Determined Amount of Time

Many students prefer this type of prewriting because they feel that freewriting gets their creativity fired up. Unlike making a list, in freewriting, you take a pen and paper (or fingers and a keyboard) and just…write—it's a one-time event each time. Use complete sentences and be thorough here. Write for the sake of getting words on a page, and don't stop to look at grammar or punctuation. Why do students often prefer this type? Because studies indicate the act of writing spurs your creativity and makes you able to write even more. By simply forcing yourself to write, you get your mind fired up and your imagination going.

Freewriting Tips

Time it: Set a timer and write for a pre-designated amount of time. Many students find that ten minutes is good, but others will dig deeper and go for twenty or thirty minutes to really get those valuable ideas rolling. Another good idea is to set a time limit and free write. Then, take stock of your best ideas, set another timer, and do a second (or third) session of free writing to narrow in on those ideas subtopics.

- **Say anything. Say everything. Say whatever.** If you feel stuck when you start your free write, just say anything at all. Write "I don't know what to say. I don't know what to say." Do this over and over, and eventually, you'll start to think of things and get going. Write for the pure sake of writing; if you stray off topic, so be it. Play around with language here and have fun.
- **No rules. No grammar. No corrections.** Don't worry about spelling or grammar. Most people gain more from free writing done by hand, but if you prefer the word processor, turn off the grammar and spell checking. Those little aggressive squiggly underlines will just tempt you go back and correct things. Free writing is all about content generation, not rules. Turn that part of your brain (and computer!) off, and turn on the imagination to generate as many ideas as possible.

Keep a Journal

Using a journal is different from the freewriting listed above in that it is not a one-time event. Instead, you do it as you go through the class. For example, if your professor gives you three weeks to work on a paper, start doing the steps of freewriting listed above, but on a regular basis. Sit down every day and keep a journal of your process, questions, concerns, thesis drafts, etc. The act of returning to this journal keeps your ideas flowing and roots you more firmly in the writing process. You won't forget deadlines or the urgency of your paper because you will be working on it every single day. It's just like a diary, but for your paper project.

Clustering (Visual Mapping)

Many professors will refer to the clustering style of prewriting as visual mapping, since a visual element dominates this method. For this, you ultimately create a list, but you don't write it in a column or row. Instead, you put each part of the list in a circle, and you branch these circles off to touch one another. This is a helpful technique because (1) it stimulates the visual and kinesthetic parts of your brain and (2) it shows connections between ideas by the lines you draw linking this each thought to another thought.

Here is an example of a cluster. Note that the main topic is in the larger circle in the center, and all other circles are sub topics (or even sub-sub topics) that spring from there:

Ask Questions Journalists Ask

The journalistic questions comprise those that start with *who, what, when, where,* and *why* (and let's throw in *how* while we're at it). Many journalists ask questions that start with these basic context questions in order to get to the truth of a story. Hence, you can you use these same basic questions to generate ideas for your paper topic.

For example, if you have a paper that is due on the topic of fast food, you can begin asking journalistic questions to generate new ideas:

- *Who* made the first fast food?
- *Who* eats fast food?
- *What* is the definition of fast food?
- *What* would be the effects of eating nothing but fast food?
- *When* was fast food invented?
- *Where* are most fast food restaurants located within a city?
- *Why* is fast food so popular?
- *Why* is fast food so unhealthy?
- *How* can we address the health crisis caused by the over-consumption of fast food?

Any research paper should answer all basic questions such as these. Use these types of questions to guide your database search queries—e.g., when using EPSCO*host* or *Academic Search Premier*. You can start to find books and articles that answer these questions, and you're off and running with your research component. Starting with a series of questions like these ultimately helps you to create a thesis statement that is clear, precise, and contextual.

Do Preliminary Research

Finally, the last type of prewriting discussed here involves the activity of fast and simple research. With the power of search engines and smart devices, you can find information in seconds that would have taken students of previous generations many, many hours. We call this "preliminary research" because you shouldn't think of it as the same type of rigorous research you include in the actual paper itself. Instead, this is much more casual, informal, and non-scholarly. Indeed, much of it may not be deemed trustworthy to include in your final paper, and that's fine for this stage of the process.

Your professor may tell you not to use Wikipedia or YouTube videos in your paper. Generally, that is a good call. However, while you are generating ideas, this type of source is a great place start. In fact, the authors of this book encourage you to seek out Wikipedia to get a sense of potential research topics. What does Wikipedia say about your topic? Usually, it provides a simple and extensive outline of major events from which you can begin further inquiry. Also, are there any "top ten" lists on YouTube that may push you in some significant direction. Remember, the goal here is prewriting and idea generation. Later on, you can do the staunch and refined research that will verify whether this more casual information is worthy of inclusion in your final manuscript.

2. Step Two. Thesis Generation

After you have finished prewriting, the next logical thing to do is to generate a thesis statement, something that grounds and puts boundaries around your idea. Your thesis is your guiding sentence that sums up your paper's main idea and intention. If you are writing an argumentative paper instead of an expository or analytical paper, it will advance your main argument. Note that your thesis will (and, indeed, should) change as you continue deeper down the writing process—research, outlining, even sitting down to write the rough draft will make you see better and better ways to make your thesis shine. Every single sentence in your paper has but one function—to support and prove your thesis statement. For a deeper and more nuanced understanding of a thesis, we invite you to read Chapter 3 of this book.

3. Step Three. Academic Research

To craft a complete, sophisticated thesis statement, research must come first. Research at this stage should represent the results of a deeper investigation into the literature on your topic than previously done during the earlier stages of prewriting. Here, you want to dig into peer-reviewed sources, particularly primary sources, and head to an academic library, usually at your college or university. Only by reading scholarly sources will you be able understand what the experts say on the topic—in effect, you start to become an expert yourself (After all, what percentage of the world's population has truly spent months researching your topic?).

We do recommend that you consult other texts for tips and tricks about academic research, as an exhaustive list is beyond the scope of our book. Our biggest advice, however, is to consult the librarians at your school's library. They may offer workshops or a class that will help you with formal academic research, and if not, they may be willing to set up a reserved block of time to cover the fundamentals with you. Remember: librarians are your friends.

4. Step Four. Outline

One of the most critical parts of the writing process for virtually all professional writers is creating an orderly, logical outline of your work before attempting to write a first draft. We often find that many college students think they can skip this critical step and still perform at the same level. This simply isn't true. One school of thought on how the brain physically works suggests that the various types of thoughts, such as imagination or logic, actually rely on different regions of the brain. Trying to be creative (writing the draft) and logical (thinking of the structure) at the same time is inherently difficult, since the neural energy in your brain is currently in one portion or the other, depending on the activity. Shifting between the two makes both types of thought too challenging for you since the brain is literally rerouting electricity to different neural paths and different areas of your brain. Even without this aspect of brain function, however, the need to have a plan before starting to draft is paramount.

Knowing your thesis, your introduction, your first body section, your second, etc. provides a firm but flexible foundation on which to start building your draft. One simple reason is that you won't need to write the paper in sequential order if you have an outline. Many writers struggle with the introduction until the body is complete, and the outline makes this easy to do. Similarly, you might have a major argument at the end of your paper, but you want to write it first simply to see the word count, so you stay within assignment parameters. The reasons for an outline are endless, but many people don't know how to construct a formal outline. We do want to highlight the various types of outlines that will help you during your academic life: formal outlines, sketch outlines, and topic and sentence outlines.

TABLE 2.2. Types of Outlines	
The Formal Outline	Traditional. Formal structure. Use of Roman numerals. Half-inch indents.
The Sketch Outline	Informal. Flexible indents and fonts. Your choice of heading and subheadings.
Variations within Formal and Sketch Outlines	
Topic Outline	Use of single word or phrases.
Sentence Outline	Use of complete sentences.

The Formal Outline

The traditional, formal outline must follow a very specific set of parameters. You set the major ideas out against the left margin using capital Roman numerals, such as I., II., III., IV., V., and so on. The next level of ideas will be details about the major ideas, and they are set off with capital letters, such as A., B., C., etc. Yet another level of detail fleshes out the secondary ideas with regular numbers, such as 1., 2., 3., 4. And a fourth level of detail uses lower case letters, such as a., b., c., etc. You will not always need all four levels; indeed, you will seldom need that much detail unless you are writing a particularly long paper. For shorter papers, the second or third levels of detail may be enough. Each level must have at least two components—if you can only think of an A., for example, that should probably be moved up to the next level.

Each level of detail gets indented a full one-half inch indent for effective and practical display of the content. Below is an example of an outline for a paper on fast food. Recall the sample and strong thesis statement discussed earlier: *Fast food is known to contain high amounts of saturated fats, sugar, and sodium; indeed, its consumption has led to a silent health epidemic for America's youth that includes premature high blood pressure, obesity, and diabetes.*

TABLE 2.3. Creating a Formal Outline

I. Introduction
    A. Interesting "hook"
        1. Quote from Eric Schlosser
        2. Discussion of quote
    B. Gradual build up of information used in the paper
    C. Thesis statement
II. Fast Food Contents
    A. Saturated fats
    B. Sugar
    C. Sodium
III. Health Epidemic
    A. Impact on youth
        1. Define youth
        2. Stats on rise in problems
    B. Premature high blood pressure
    C. Obesity
    D. Diabetes
IV. Conclusion
    A. Thesis reminder
    B. Gradual exit from paper
    C. Final reflection on the opening quote in the hook

Note that this outline could be made much longer if the author included several elements of a typical research paper: topic sentence, research and statistics, direct quotations, personal thoughts, transitions, thesis reminders, etc. The outline presented here is actually quite bare bones and brief; most professors may ask for longer outlines than this, but at least this example can get you started.

Sketch Outlines

If a formal outline like the one above isn't required as part of a writing assignment, you may want to create an informal or sketch outline. You can number these using different systems than the one specified above. You can use simple bullets or any other schema that will make logical sense for you later on in the process.

Topic versus Sentence Outlines

The formal outline example shown above represents a specific variation within the types of outlines explained. It is what we call a topic outline. You can build a successful topic outline with use of single words or short phrases. This means that only a single word or a simple phrase is written after each heading and sub-heading of the outline. The point is you do not concern yourself with writing out grammatically correct sentences with clearly defined subjects and verbs. However, some professors (and students) prefer the sentence outline. Subject outlines require you to use complete sentences for every element of the outline. For example, our formal outline above uses simply "Saturated fats" under section II.A. So, instead of using a phrase here, you would say something like "Saturated fats are much more prevalent in fast food than people think, and they are chemically very unhealthy." The benefit of this type of outline is that it forces you to think in more than merely quick sound bites, and it goes a long way toward your having a complete rough draft of the paper.

Software Troubles

As a final note about outlines, you should be aware that the word processor you use will include incredible time-saving built-in features to help automatically format your paper. You should also be aware that most people strongly dislike these automatic features, as they are hard to control. Be ready for software that indents numbers and letters for you and does plenty of other things to help you. However, these things may not be in proper outline format, not be properly indented for MLA format, and may create any number of issues that frustrate you more than help you. Be ready to tinker with settings a bit here, or turn those settings off.

5. Step Five. Draft

The next part of the writing process is the part you simply cannot do without— writing the first draft of the paper. This is where you let your creativity flow, and you set down the core of the paper. For most, using a word processor is easier than paper, due to the possibility for editing and saving as you go. For others, pen and paper is preferred since the software, auto-correct, spell checking and all the rest of it slow them down and take them out of "the zone." Either way, this part of the paper process is where you create the first iteration of what you will submit. It is stressful for many, a joy for others, and time consuming no matter what.

This is where we would normally tell you what steps to take to make your drafting process easier, but guess what? We already have. If you have done prewriting, generated a solid thesis, done preliminary research, and crafted a logical outline, you are ready to write this draft. If you have done that legwork, your draft should be much easier to write than if you avoided any of these steps. More to the point, you will have a draft of much higher quality and depth than students who skipped them.

For many rushed (or lazy) students, the draft is the entire writing process. Don't let this happen to you, and remember, the draft is not the end of the process. There are several more steps to take you from a rough draft to a polished, solid composition you can be proud of.

Saving Your Work

One final but critical note about rough drafts and the writing process is that you need to get in the habit of saving and making multiple backups as you go. While you are writing the draft, you should hit the save button after every single paragraph you write. Software auto saves every so often, but don't rely on that.

Save it yourself. More importantly, every time you are done with a writing session, make another copy.

Our advice is as follows: First, you should save it to the cloud. This can be done by emailing it to yourself or dragging it to a virtual drive (such as Google Drive or pCloud) as soon as you are done. If you are using Google Docs, it is already saved in the cloud, but then you should download a copy to make sure it is also saved on your computer in case your Net goes down. Second, make a physical backup on a thumb drive that you keep with you when you go to campus. If you do all this, you will always have a copy on your home computer, the cloud (which can be accessed almost anywhere), and on a thumb drive in case of Internet outages. Be paranoid and have multiple copies. Software fails. Hardware dies. Hard drives crash. The Net goes down. Don't let this stop you from turning in your work.

6. Step Six. Initial Proofreading

Once the draft is complete (or even partial if you regularly see a tutor or writing expert or study buddy to work out a draft as you go), you will want to get it proofread. Proofreading is one of the most beneficial steps in the process because it gets you out of your own head and lets someone else take a look at what you've done with a set of fresh, objective eyes. You may have a regular error you always make—you won't catch it. You may think a sentence flows a certain way, but it is awkward and confusing—you won't catch it. You may have completely missed a parenthetical citation—you won't catch it. But a skilled proofreader will.

Keep in mind that proofreading does not mean someone is there to correct all your mistakes. The goal of good proofing as a student is to get someone who knows more about writing than you do to go over your draft and point out what could be better and what is already solid. The goal here isn't to find a grammar Nazi who will simply mark everything for you; the goal is to find someone who will point out the errors and snags and help show you rules and techniques that will empower you to avoid them in the future.

So who should you turn to to proofread your paper? Here is a list that is ranked from more preferable to less preferable, but all will still help you.

- *Your professor.* If your professor is willing, you should visit or drop by during office hours to get feedback on the piece. Professors aren't likely to mark up all your punctuation errors, but they can let you know what they are after and if you hit the mark.

- *Writing expert/TA.* Your college probably has a writing center staffed by experts or possibly a teaching assistant or target tutor who sits in on the class and knows exactly what your professor is looking for. Make an appointment and sit down to work on your paper together.

- *Tutor.* Virtually every college has a tutoring center staffed by student tutors who major in different fields and who are paid to help other students. Your tutoring center will certainly have English or composition tutors who may not know your professor but will know good research and writing and will help. Such tutors are most effective as part of a regular tutoring regime in which you visit them weekly to keep building your writing skills all semester long.

- *Classmate.* Another good bet is to find a classmate in the same class as you and proof each other's papers. You could invite several to a coffee shop or reserve a study room in your library and meet up for peer critique session.

- *Roomie, parent, or friend.* If you have a relative or friend who is an English major, a journalist, or a good natural writer, consider visiting them with your paper. If you don't know anyone who is any of these things, such a person can still read your paper with fresh eyes and let you know if your ideas are clear.

- *Yourself.* Give yourself a break from the paper (several days is best!) and then revisit it with fresh eyes. You may be surprised at what mistakes and negative patterns you will find after taking a rest.

7. Step Seven. Revising

Revision means "re-visioning" your work. It is the "big picture" stage. In a revision, you rewrite your paper thinking of the content, rhetorical methods, and readers' needs. Don't worry about technical errors at this stage. Doing so will just distract you from the big picture. Does the paper flow well? Should some sections get moved around for greater impact? Would a specific rhetorical method (See Chapter 6) be helpful instead of what you used in the original draft? Will a reader understand what you're after in a particular argument? Do you need to add further evidence or support? Have you articulated the relationships between ideas? This type of global thinking about the "flow" of the paper and improving upon it is the revision process.

8. Step Eight. Editing

Many people refer to all stages of revision as "editing," but editing is what you do after you revise. Editing leads to improved style, coherence, and content. It can help for you to read the different sections of your paper out loud. Do you have a consistent sense of "voice"? Do your sentences connect logically with one another? Can you find any awkward passages to correct? Have you properly cited all of your sources? Editing is when you correct major problems that may have occurred in your revision. Revision is very helpful with the "big picture," but it may create problems within paragraphs. As with the revision stage, don't worry about technical errors here—that can distract you from noticing more important problems.

9. Step Nine. Final Proofreading

Since you will have made changes—often very significant ones—during the revision and editing stages, make sure to do a final proofreading of your paper because you may have made new errors at the technical level, in areas like spelling, punctuation, grammar, in-text citations, and so on. It is a good idea to have this very handbook out to look up rules as you do your final proofreading. Another good idea is to print your paper out and mark things up. If you know you have problems with commas, take a highlighter to mark every single comma, and then look up the rule for every comma to make sure they are correct. Is this time consuming? You bet. But it is also what separates professional-level writing from a quick and messy draft. Make sure your whole paper is in proper MLA format, with your identification information presented properly, and so on. As with the initial proofreading, it is very helpful to have someone else take a final look at your paper.

10. Step Ten. Publication of the Final Draft

Once you've done all of the above, congratulations! Hit print, throw a staple in the corner, and, if you have been diligent with the earlier stages of writing, you will have an impressive final draft of your paper that you (and your professor) will be proud of.

Name: _____ Section: _____ Date: _____

Part Two

Chapter 2 Workshop

The following section contains a series of ten tasks that, if completed, will help you gain mastery over the content in this chapter. Your instructor will assign some (or all) of them to you as a way to practice the material presented here. Notice that some of them are global and focus on the entirety of the skills laid out in this chapter, while others are more focused and explore only one or two sections of the chapter. Also notice that some are shorter, some are longer, but all are designed to flip the classroom and put the power of learning directly into your own hands.

Workshop One.

Overview: Summarize all of the major sections and/or bullet points that you find in this chapter.

Each major section or heading should be clearly labeled and should have at least a one-sentence discussion. You might have a dozen or more headings and sentences here. Be thorough and accurate to show that you have read and comprehended this chapter's contents. Avoid the temptation to judge or add anything new (even critical discussion of the content); this is an act of pure summary. Tell your instructor exactly what came in this chapter and in what order.

Workshop Two.

Overview: This workshop has you examine all of the wrong answers from your chapter diagnostic and respond to them.
1. Make a list of each question from the chapter diagnostic that you got wrong.
2. Go through the chapter to look up the rules on each question. For every question you got wrong, do the following:

    A. Identify the page number where the rule was found.

    B. Discuss what the right answer should have been on the diagnostic test.

    C. Discuss how you can avoid this error in future writing and/or tests.

Workshop Three.

<u>Overview</u>: Write a short, personal essay explaining the content of this chapter. The point of this essay is to directly address what you have learned from the chapter and how it will impact your future academic writing. Consider some or all of the following:

    A. What writing element(s) were new to you?

    B. How can you incorporate some of the elements into your own writing in the future?

    C. What writing element(s) did you already know about? Did you already use them in your writing, or did you ignore them for some reason? If so, what was the reason?

    D. If appropriate, use some of the techniques and language from the actual chapter in your paper to help illustrate mastery.

    E. Your instructor will provide you with more details, such as the length of the piece, if you should use quotations from the chapter, if personal anecdotes and casual language are allowed, etc.

Workshop Four.

<u>Overview</u>: Come up with a paper topic and a thesis statement both with and without conducting prewriting and compare the results.

    1. Establish something you can write a paper about with your instructor (ideally, something that will tie into your overall class). Now, set a timer for five or ten minutes. Without doing any prewriting, create a thesis and the major subtopics of this paper.

    2. Second, get a different idea about what you could write a paper about. Now, complete two of the types of prewriting listed in this chapter,

taking your time and being thorough. After that, generate a list of subtopics you can include in a paper and create a thesis statement.

3. In several sentences, discuss the two. Which one is better and more thorough? Which one has more innovative subtopics and ideas to include? Do you think the result could have been different if you used even more types of prewriting? Discuss.

Workshop Five.

<u>Overview</u>: Take a piece of someone else's writing and create an outline showing what it contains.

1. Agree upon a piece of writing with your instructor (it could a fellow student's work, a news article, a scholarly journal, a single chapter from a book you're reading in class, etc.). Reread this piece.

2. Now, create (or back-engineer) what you would consider to be the outline for the piece. Add at least three levels of details as discussed in this chapter, and make it a formal outline.

3. Add a quotation for each major section to show what type of evidence and support this piece uses to make its point.

Workshop Six.

<u>Overview</u>: Find a topic that you could write a paper about and then create a thorough, formal outline and thesis.

1. Go to the website procon.org. This is a storehouse of some of the hottest debate topics around right now. Pick one (for an extra challenge, randomly select one!) and consider what you would need to write a paper on one side of this topic. Alternatively, your instructor may supply you with a list of topics.

2. Create a thesis statement that you could use in a paper on this topic.

3. Create a formal outline with at least three levels of detail and that runs at least two full pages in length on this topic. Think about a format you could actually use for writing the draft of a paper.

Workshop Seven.

<u>Overview</u>: Revise and edit your paper to address a single significant problem you had.

1. Take a piece of writing you have done already and consider the markings your instructor made on the paper.
2. Edit and revise your paper on this one single problem only. The idea here is that if this is the biggest problem you had, it will yield the biggest results as you fix it.
3. Print the paper. Now, identify the biggest problem your essay had. On the top of page one in large handwriting, identify what this error is.
4. Take a highlighter and highlight every single change you made on your paper before you turn it in.

Workshop Eight.

<u>Overview</u>: Take a previous piece of your own writing and proofread it for practice in finding your own technical errors and awkward sentences.

1. Take a piece of writing that you have done already (ideally, a paper for a class that is at least several pages long). Print it out and then do a thorough proofreading of it, marking up everything from improper MLA format to punctuation, grammar, spelling, and syntax errors. Mark your paper up with different colored pens and highlighters. First, mark up grammar and sentence level errors in one color, next punctuation errors, and so on. Use different colors for all of the different types of errors.
2. Take a highlighter and highlight every comma. Now, go through the comma rules and make sure that they are each correct. If yes, put a C above the highlighted comma. If not, write down the rule broken.
3. Finally, using several well-developed sentences, discuss what you learned through this process. What strengths and weaknesses in your own writing did this proofreading reveal?

Workshop Nine.

<u>Overview</u>: Do a complete and thorough revision and editing of a paper you've already written.

1. Complete all the steps of Workshop Eight above. Alternatively, take your piece to a writing or tutoring center or share it with peers in class for a peer critique workshop, so you have a marked up draft that has been thoroughly proofread.

2. When you are done with that, read it again and go in with a highlighter and find sections you can re-write with an eye toward how you can improve your style, rhetoric, argument, presentation of evidence, logical transitions, flow, and tone. Make suggestions to yourself in the margins.

3. Now, go in and fix errors and follow all the suggestions you made on your paper. This should be a thorough and impactful rewriting of your piece.

4. Write a response of several sentences that discusses the changes you made. What problems did you see happening the most? What can you work on in the future? What rules did you learn that will change your writing? Discuss.

Workshop Ten.

<u>Overview</u>: What is your take away from this chapter? What did you learn and what questions do you still have?

1. Write a short response of several sentences that covers the three main things that you learned from this chapter.

2. Write out at least five questions you still have about the chapter and about the writing process. What things would you want to communicate to your instructor? What would you like to see discussed in class or handled with more depth to help you master this chapter's content?

3. What is one thing that you have taken away from this chapter and will use on your next writing task? Why is this thing important, and how do you plan to implement it?

CHAPTER 3

How to Craft Expository, Analytical, and Argumentative Thesis Statements

In this chapter, you will learn about the following:

Part One

College Essay Types & Thesis Statements

1. The Most Common Types of College Essays

Every essay that you write, including research papers, should have a main idea. The sentence that captures your position on this main idea is called a thesis statement. In order to craft a thesis statement, you need to first determine what type of college paper you are writing. The three most common types of paper are expository, analytical, and argumentative. All three of them are important to college-level writing, but at the same time are different types of college papers. Each has its place, depending on the class and the assignment, but some do include and require more critical thought than others.

Expository Essays

An expository essay, also called an explanatory essay, is designed to explain or describe something using factual information. It does not try to persuade readers to adopt a point of view or take an action. You only have to understand the topic and present it to readers in a clear, logical manner. If you were ever asked in earlier school years to write an essay on how you spent your summer vacation, that was an expository essay. On a more sophisticated level, if you have to write a paper in a history class on the causes of a specific war or the impact of a major event, that is also expository writing. Basically, you are showing what you know. You are presenting information in such a way that your readers will know what you know (and demonstrate to your professor what you have learned).

Analytical Essays

An analytical essay focuses on examination and interpretation in order to analyze something, such as a literary work or a historical or cultural event. To analyze something is to ask what that particular something means. This type of essay answers how something does what it does, or why it is as it is, or both. It is more sophisticated than an expository paper. It must also provide information, but it goes further, breaking something down into its component parts and presenting this breakdown and an evaluation to your readers. It may even involve presenting one or more arguments, but presenting an argument is not the main purpose of the essay.

Argumentative Essays

An argumentative essay is one crafted to persuade readers to believe that a theory, opinion, or assertion of policy or action is superior to other alternatives. You must take a stand on something. It also has to be informative and analytical, but it is the most sophisticated and demanding of the three main essay types. An argumentative essay can be a full research paper, which is the lengthiest essay you will be asked to write and which will require extensive research to find sources to back up your main argument. And yet an essay of this type can also be a short but critical five-page position paper on a debatable topic asking you to prove that your main conclusion is true at the same time as requiring you to prove a counter-argument false.

2. Thesis Statements

Think of your thesis statement as the guiding sentence that sums up your essay's key idea and intent. A good way to think of a thesis statement is to use the following formula: Topic + Assertion = Thesis. A topic is simply the subject your essay addresses. An assertion is a statement of fact or belief.

> *A good way to think of a thesis statement is to use the following formula: Topic + Assertion = Thesis. A topic is simply the subject your essay addresses. An assertion is a statement of fact or belief.*

Note that your thesis will (and, indeed, should) change as you move further along in the writing process—researching, outlining, and even sitting down to write the rough draft will make you see better and better ways to make your thesis shine. Think of your thesis as a contract between you and your imagined audience. What do we mean by an "imagined audience" and why is this important? After all, you know that your professor is your real audience, However, keeping an imaginary audience in mind of people who don't know as much about your topic as you do will help you to write a clearer essay with sufficient information, and that is part of what will determine the grade that your professor gives you. By presenting your thesis to an imagined general audience, you are agreeing to deliver on the major points you bring up there. It is a sophisticated statement that will take time and research to support.

Outside of college writing, an essay's thesis could be anywhere in the essay or even be implied rather than explicitly stated. However, in college writing, your instructors want a clearly stated thesis, and they want it early in the essay—the last sentence of the introductory paragraph is usually considered ideal. Why the last sentence and not the first, if the thesis is so important? The answer is simple: you need introductory material to set it up. The thesis is a distillation, in a sense—an extraction of the essential meaning or most important aspects of what you are going to say. As such, you need an introductory paragraph to set it up. That paragraph lets your imagined readers know what the scope of your paper is and why your topic is important. Provide background information. Move from the general to the particular, narrowing your focus. While some writers say that a thesis can be one or two sentences, we strongly advise keeping it to a single sentence to make it clearer and stronger. After all, you will be preceding it with other sentences where you present information that will help to set it up. An important point to remember is that a thesis statement must always be a declarative sentence. It states something. It does not ask a question or simply express emotion. Declarative sentences end with periods, not question marks or exclamation points. While your thesis itself cannot be a question, it can, however, be the answer to one or more questions that you pose earlier in the introductory paragraph.

Expository Essay Thesis Statements

A thesis statement for an expository essay should not express an opinion or take a position on a topic. It should be based purely on the factual information that you will present in the body of the essay. Following are three examples:

Example 1.

> Jane Yolen's novel *Briar Rose* addresses both the horrific effects of the Holocaust on targeted groups and how some of the attitudes that led to the Holocaust still exist today.

Example 2.

> Even though it has the most costly health care system, the United States ranks last among the eleven highest-income countries on measures of equity, access, administrative efficiency, care delivery, and health care outcomes.

Example 3.

> The Treaty of Versailles, which ended World War I, is considered by historians to be a major contributing factor in the outbreak of the World War II, as it forced Germany to disarm, to make territorial concessions, and to pay reparations to the Allied powers in the then staggering amount of $5 billion.

Each of these thesis statements lets readers know exactly what to expect in terms of factual information that will be presented in each essay.

As mentioned previously, a good way to think of a thesis statement is to use the following formula: Topic + Assertion = Thesis. A topic, if you remember, is simply the subject that your essay addresses and an assertion is a statement of fact or belief. *In an expository essay, you should be dealing just with facts, not beliefs.* As stated earlier, your thesis should change as you progress through the writing process. Very few authors start with a thesis that is clear or sophisticated enough for an A paper on their first go at it. It takes time, research, and more thought to get it to evolve to a place that will suit your essay's needs. Below, you can see the evolution of an expository thesis as it goes from bad to vague to decent to good.

Evolution of an Expository Thesis

Version 1: Is fast food really bad for people's health?

> Problem: This won't work as a thesis statement because it is a question, not an assertion.

Version 2: Fast food is bad for people's health.

> Problem: This thesis follows the formula of topic (fast food) + assertion (bad for people's health), but it is vague and leaves the audience wanting more information. More details would be helpful.

Version 3: Fast food is bad for people's health because of all the saturated fats.

> Problem: While this is getting more focused, it still leaves a lot of questions for readers to wonder about. What does the writer mean by bad for people's health? Is he or she targeting specific people or demographics? What specific health problems are going to be discussed? Are saturated fats the only health issue? What about sugar or sodium?

Version 4: Fast food is known to contain high amounts of saturated fats, sugar, and sodium; indeed, its consumption has lead to a silent health epidemic for America's youth that includes premature high blood pressure, obesity, and diabetes.

> This is a solid thesis statement for an expository essay that tells readers exactly what information to expect in the essay, and it answers more questions than it leaves the reader with.

Analytical Essay Thesis Statements

Since an analytical essay's purpose is to answer how something does what it does or why it is as it is, a thesis statement for an analytical paper should be answering a "how" or "why" question. Following are three examples.

Example 1.

> The *Quiet American* by Graham Greene exposes the questionable moral foundations of growing American involvement in Vietnam in the 1950s with its depiction of the interactions between the three main characters: a cynical English reporter, an American undercover CIA operative, and the Vietnamese woman both men fall in love with.

The thesis statement answers the question "How does *The Quiet American* expose the questionable moral foundations of growing American involvement in Vietnam in the 1950s?" The answer is "It does this with its depiction of the interactions between the three main characters: a cynical English reporter, an American undercover CIA operative, and the Vietnamese woman both men fall in love with."

Example 2.

> The rise in populism and nationalism in European democracies has occurred in part because of the steady decline of moderate and centrist parties that had dominated the continent since World War II.

The thesis statement answers the question "Why has populism and nationalism in European democracies risen?" The answer is "It has risen in part because of the steady decline of moderate and centrist parties that had dominated the continent since World War II."

Example 3.

> The Innocence Project was founded because, due to systemic defects, a significant number of innocent people have been convicted of crimes they did not commit, so it represents people seeking post-conviction DNA testing to prove their innocence.

The first question this thesis statement answers is "Why was the Innocence Project founded?" The answer is "It was founded because, due to systemic defects, a significant number of innocent people have been convicted of crimes they did not commit." The second question the thesis statement answers is "How does the Innocence Project help these people?" The answer is "It helps them by representing people seeking post-conviction DNA testing to prove their innocence."

Argumentative Essay Thesis Statements

Thesis statements for argumentative essays require debatable thesis statements, not simply assertions of fact. They must express stands that reasonable people can disagree with and that must be supported in the body of the essay with both logical arguments and factual (empirical) evidence. Also, many instructors require that an argumentative essay should explore potential solutions to the problem the paper explores. Following are five examples of argumentative thesis statements on two issues. They are clearly debatable because they take different stands on these issues.

Example 1.

> While hate speech is deplorable and may actually encourage acts of violence, we should not pass laws banning hate speech on social media because the Bill of Rights guarantees us freedom of speech.

Example 2.

> Because hate speech on social media has led to an increase in acts of violence against members of certain groups, we should support laws that require social media platforms to use rules, algorithms, and direct intervention to stop the spread of such speech.

Example 3.

> Making college free for all students would simply be too expensive for the federal and state governments to maintain long-term, and Americans might have to start paying much higher taxes, which would hurt them and the economy.

Example 4.

> Making college free for all students would help them and our economy as a whole because our current total student loan debt in this country is $1.48 trillion, and if people did not have such massive student loan debt, they could buy houses and more consumer items and contribute more to our economy.

Example 5.

> Many more jobs today than in the past are knowledge-based or require advanced technical skills to the extent that there are sometimes not enough qualified people to fill the positions, so making college free for all students would increase American economic growth and tax revenues.

3. Distinguishing between Debatable and Non-Debatable Thesis Statements

Sometimes students have trouble distinguishing between debatable and non-debatable thesis statements, and they create thesis statements that merely state facts.

Example of a non-debatable thesis statement:

> Eating huge quantities of fast food is bad for children's health.

This is not debatable by reasonable people. A person would have to be pretty unreasonable to advocate eating huge quantities of any kind of food, let alone fast food, which is known to be unhealthy.

Example of a debatable thesis statement:

> The United States should ban fast food marketing in both print and electronic media aimed at children under the age of thirteen.

This is an example of a debatable thesis because reasonable people could disagree with it. For example, some people might think that any restrictions aimed at limiting fast food advertisements to children would amount to a violation of corporations' First Amendment rights. Other people might disagree with them, pointing out that we already have laws designed to protect children regarding advertisements for alcohol and tobacco products. These are not the only two stands that people can take, but they are examples of ways that reasonable people can have different opinions.

Earlier, we presented an example of a clear and detailed expository essay thesis statement. We also mentioned how an introductory paragraph should lead up to and support your thesis statement. The expository thesis we presented could actually be used as part of an introductory paragraph leading up to a thesis statement for an argumentative essay.

> Fast food is known to contain high amounts of saturated fats, sugar, and sodium. Indeed, its consumption has lead to a silent health epidemic for America's youth that includes premature high blood pressure, obesity, and diabetes. Because of these serious health problems, <u>the United States should ban fast food marketing in both print and electronic media aimed at children under the age of thirteen.</u>

By the way, if you are going to argue in favor of legislation, you need to know the steps that people take. A fun and useful resource is the video "I'm Just a Bill," which first aired on an educational series called *Schoolhouse Rock* back in 1973. According to CNN, more than 30 million people have since watched the *Schoolhouse Rock* videos on YouTube, and "I'm Just a Bill" is one of the most popular. It describes how a bill can become a law by passing both houses of Congress and then going to the White House, where the president must sign it. There are other resources, but this is a fast and fun introduction. You should not simply state that "the government" should make something happen—discuss what ordinary people like you and your readers can do to help get laws passed.

4. Narrowing Argumentative Thesis Statements

Generally speaking, the narrower—that is to say, the more specific—your thesis is, the more effective your argument will be. You have to support your thesis statement with evidence, and that is easier to do when you limit it to something very specific.

Example 1. A Broad Thesis

> The United States should ban cruelty against the animals used for food production.

There are several reasons why this statement is too broad and too vague. What does "cruelty" mean? We know what words like this mean to us, but other people may have widely differing ideas on what is too cruel to be tolerated. Even "food production" may be too vague—does this include only animals raised to actually be food, or does it also involve animals used for producing eggs, cheese, and milk?

Example 2. A Narrower Thesis

> The Humane Slaughter Act of 1978 requires the humane handling of animals slaughtered in USDA inspected-slaughter plants except for chickens and other birds; it should be expanded to apply to all animals, including birds.

While agreeing on the definition of "humane handling" may seem to pose a problem, the thesis refers to a specific law, which actually does establish legal definitions, and these can be supplied in the body of the paper. This thesis could even be reduced to the following, as long as the introductory sentences leading up to it supply the necessary information:

Example 3. A Better Thesis

> The Humane Slaughter Act of 1978 should be expanded to require the humane handling of all animals, including chickens and other birds, which are currently exempted.

Think of the thesis statement you generate as tentative. Remember—while you need to have a thesis in mind as you do your research, you should be prepared to refine it or even make major changes to it as you conduct research and learn more about your topic. Keep an open mind—you may find that the evidence you uncover about your topic contradicts what you believed when you first visualized your essay. In Chapter 1, we discussed confirmation bias: the human tendency to favor, interpret, and remember information in a way that suits our pre-existing beliefs without being conscious that we are doing so. Learn to monitor how you look at evidence to guard against this. Otherwise, you may find yourself getting low, even failing grades on argumentative essays that you thought of as very strong because your instructor knows enough about your topic to recognize that you left out important evidence and misinterpreted the evidence you presented.

TABLE 3.1. A Quick Summary of Thesis Statements
1. A thesis is not simply a quick fact or a topic.
2. A thesis is not a question, but can answer a question.
3. A thesis is not typically the first sentence of your paper.
4. A thesis is one sentence or claim.
5. A thesis is your Topic + Assertion of fact or belief.
6. A thesis is a guiding statement that sums up your paper's main point.
7. A thesis is a claim that takes time to develop.
8. A thesis is usually found at the end of your introduction.
9. A thesis is a contract between you and the reader.

There are Three Types of Thesis Statements

Expository Thesis	Does not express an opinion or take a position on a topic. Does not present an argument. Instead presents assertions of facts.
Analytical Thesis	Answers the "how" and "why" questions: how something does what it does or why it is as it is, or both. Focuses on examining and interpreting something, such as a literary work or a historical or cultural event.
Argumentative Thesis	Requires a debatable statement, not simply assertions of facts. The main purpose is to present an argument.

Name: _____ Section: _____ Date: _____

Part Two

Chapter 3 Workshop

The following section contains a series of tasks that, if completed, will help you gain mastery over the content in this chapter. Your instructor will assign some (or all) of them to you as a way to practice the material presented here. Notice that some of them are global and focus on the entirety of the skills laid out in this chapter, while others are more focused and explore only one or two sections of the chapter. Also notice that some are shorter, some are longer, but all are designed to flip the classroom and put the power of learning directly into your own hands.

Workshop One.

Overview: Summarize all of the major sections and/or bullet points that you find in this chapter.
- Each major section or heading should be clearly labeled and should have at least a one-sentence discussion. You might have a dozen or more headings and sentences here.
- Be thorough and accurate to show that you have read and comprehended this chapter's contents. Avoid the temptation to judge or add anything new (even critical discussion of the content); this is an act of pure summary. Tell your instructor exactly what came in this chapter and in what order.

Workshop Two.

Overview: This workshop has you examine all of the wrong answers from your chapter diagnostic and respond to them.
1. Make a list of each question from the chapter diagnostic that you got wrong.

2. Go through the chapter to look up the rules on each question. For every question you got wrong, do the following:
   A. Identify the page number where the rule was found.
   B. Discuss what the right answer should have been on the diagnostic test.
   C. Discuss how you can avoid this error in future writing and/or tests.

Workshop Three.

<u>Overview</u>: Write a short, personal essay explaining the content of this chapter. The point of this essay is to directly address what you have learned from the chapter and how it will impact your future academic writing. Consider some or all of the following:
   A. What was new to you about the types of essays?
   B. How can you determine whether you should use analytical, expository, or argumentative approaches in your writing?
   C. What writing element(s) did you already know about. Did you already use them in your writing, or did you ignore them for some reason? If so, what was the reason?
   D. If appropriate, use some of the techniques and language from the actual chapter in your paper to help illustrate mastery.
   E. Your instructor will provide you with more details such as the length of the piece, if you should use quotation from the chapter, if personal anecdotes and casual language are allowed, etc.

Workshop Four.

<u>Overview</u>: Think of a topic that could be addressed in an expository essay, an analytical essay, and an argumentative essay.
   • Write three different thesis statements on the same topic. Each should be appropriate for only one of the three types.
   • When you are done with the thesis statements, write a two paragraph response. The first paragraph should explain which of the three you think is the strongest for you to write a paper about. The second

paragraph should explain why you think the other two are not as solid as the idea you selected as your favorite. Explain.

Workshop Five.

Overview: Create a PowerPoint presentation or a website that can be shared with your colleagues and professor that cover the ideas found in this chapter

1. Your presentation or website must cover the basics of analytical essays.
2. Your presentation or website must cover the basics of expository essays.
3. Your presentation or website must cover the basics of argumentative essays.
4. Your presentation or website must show examples of how to narrow a thesis from being broad and vague to narrow and specific.
5. Your presentation or website should cover any other ideas you found to be especially important.

Workshop Six.

Overview: A key skill in writing a solid paper is the ability to craft a specific and powerful thesis statement. This workshop will help you practice that process. Revise the following broad thesis statements using the techniques discussed in this chapter. Feel free to use some quick web-based research to give you more information on the topics if your instructor allows.

- Thesis One: Many big corporations are responsible for the health epidemic in the nation.
- Thesis Two: Many problems come from stray animals, and something must be done to stop the problem.
- Thesis Three: The United States government is wasteful in its spending; this is something that costs the tax payer.
- Thesis Four: Social media has both good and bad elements, but the bad elements are sometimes thought to outweigh the good.
- Thesis Five: Politics in America have gotten really bad due to differences in political views.

Workshop Seven.

<u>Overview</u>: Often, teaching something can be the best way to learn it yourself on a deeper level. Therefore, write a quiz for future students that covers the basics of the three types of essays discussed in the chapter.

1. This quiz should include various styles of questions, including multiple choice, short answer, and true/false. Check with your instructor on specifics.
2. This quiz should be designed to show mastery of the skills from another student at your own level.
3. You must write an answer key starting on a new page after the quiz. This answer key must include the page numbers from *Flipping English* where students can find the answer. It must also include a complete sentence for each quiz question you generated to explain to the instructor why you thought this question targeted a critical skill discussed in this chapter.

Workshop Eight.

<u>Overview</u>: Often, teaching something can be the best way to learn it yourself on a deeper level. Therefore, write a quiz for future students that covers the basics of how to narrow a thesis statement.

1. This quiz should include various styles of questions, including multiple choice, short answer, and true/false. Check with your instructor on specifics.
2. This quiz should be designed to show mastery of the skills from another student at your own level.
3. You must write an answer key starting on a new page after the quiz. This answer key must include the page numbers from *Flipping English* where students can find the answer. It must also include a complete sentence for each quiz question you generated to explain to the instructor why you thought this question targeted a critical skill discussed in this chapter.

Workshop Nine.

Overview: Create a PowerPoint presentation or website that can be shared with your colleagues and professor that cover the ideas put forth in this chapter.

1. Your PowerPoint or website must define and give examples of analytical essays and thesis statements.
2. Your PowerPoint or website must define and give examples of expository essays and thesis statements.
3. Your PowerPoint or website must define and give examples of argumentative essays and thesis statements.
4. Your PowerPoint or website must define and give examples of how to narrow a strong thesis statement.

Workshop Ten.

Overview: What is your take away from this chapter? What did you learn and what questions do you still have?

1. Write a short response of several sentences that covers the three main things that you learned from this chapter.
2. Write out at least five questions you still have about the chapter. What things would you want to communicate to your instructor? What would you like to see discussed in class or handled with more depth to help you master this chapter's content?
3. What is one thing that you have taken away from this chapter and will use on your next writing task? Why is this thing important, and how do you plan to implement it?

CHAPTER 4

How to Properly Organize an Essay

In this chapter, you will learn about the following:

Part One: Organizing Your Paper
1. Paper Length
2. The Introduction
3. The Body of the Paper
4. The Conclusion

Part Two: Workshop

Part One

Organizing Your Paper

Becky has a paper due in a few days and is having a hard time getting started. She tries to begin, feels no creativity, no flow, nothing but an urge to get back on her cell phone and make posts about how much she hates writing. She has an idea of what she wants to say in the paper; she even has what she thinks is a decent thesis. She knows that she should do some prewriting and come up with an outline to work from, but even that seems like walking on an alien planet.

She's written papers before and actually kind of got into it, but she can't even imagine how she ever got started. She knows she needs to write an introduction, but what goes into one of those, anyway? Where should she place the thesis? Of all the arguments she has thought up, which one should go first, and how exactly should she set up her body arguments? As for the conclusion, that's a million miles away, so forget it!

If you are like Becky, you might be stumped when the time comes to write the draft because you don't yet have a clear idea of your paper's structure. Once you understand what needs to go in a typical academic paper, it is easier to start writing and let the words flow from you. If you have a solid understanding of the component pieces necessary for a good introduction, a good body argument, and a good conclusion, then writing them becomes more like a formula, a set of steps to complete in an orderly manner. In fact, believe us when we say it becomes somewhat easy.

1. Paper Length

Before going into detail about what you should include in your introduction, body, and conclusion, a discussion about differing paper lengths is worthwhile. Since the major project of a college-level composition class is usually an argumentative research paper, that will be our focus, but we will also discuss the other two most common types of college essay (see the previous chapter). Your instructor may have you start with an expository essay, move to an analytical essay, them move on to argumentative papers. Other professors may demand only argumentative essays. And professors in other disciplines may focus only on expository or analytical papers. Argumentative research papers, however, tend to be the ones that are longest. Someone can take the same thesis and turn that thesis into a three-page, six-page, ten-page, or twenty-page essay. This seems mind boggling, but it's true. This chapter will show you how to write varying paper lengths even with the same thesis and the same outline, depending on what your instructor asks for. Let's see how this is possible.

If you have to write a short expository essay of just a couple of pages, you might have a one-paragraph introduction that outlines the information you are going to present in detail in the body of your paper. Each paragraph will focus on specific facts, and you will finish with a concluding paragraph that sums up what you have "taught" your imagined audience—what you have learned about your topic. Expository essays tend to be shorter than analytical and argumentative essays because all you are doing is sharing information. It is unlikely that you will be asked to write an expository essay that matches the length of a research paper.

As stated in Chapter 3, an analytical essay focuses on examination and interpretation in order to analyze something. To analyze something is to ask what that something means. This type of essay answers how something does what it does, or why it is as it is, or both. English professors in literature classes may ask you to explain a poem, short story, play, or novel. Unlike what you do in an expository essay, an analytical essay will require you to come up with your own ideas. You interpret what the literary work means, and you explain how the writer conveys meaning. You will also look at aspects of writing style, such as symbolism, point of view, plot, and characterization, depending on the genre of the work. History professors may ask you to explain the "how" and "why" of an important event or movement or how a noted historical figure made an impact on our country or world. There are other disciplines, including those in the behavioral sciences, where instructors ask for analysis. An analytical essay may involve presenting one or more arguments, but presenting an argument is not the focus of the essay. This type of essay is more complex than an expository essay, so such essays are often lengthier—it all depends on the assignment's topic.

If you have to write a short analytical essay, for example, on a poem, you may have a one-paragraph introduction where you tell your readers the features of the poem that you will focus on and what you feel to be the poem's theme, which should probably be expressed in your thesis statement. Each body paragraph will address one of these aspects. A short essay of four body paragraphs might focus on rhyme scheme; other sound effects from words, such as alliteration; meter; and theme. A longer essay might also explore the speaker and whom the speaker is addressing; mood and tone; structure, such as a type of fixed form versus free verse; and so on. No matter what the length, your concluding paragraph will sum up the impact of the features of the poem that you have discussed.

If you have to write a short argumentative essay of just a few pages, you might have a one-paragraph introduction, and then each argument in the body will be a paragraph presenting one of your arguments and its supporting evidence, or, if the essay presents only one argument, each paragraph will introduce different evidence. You can end with a one-paragraph conclusion that sums up your main points in support of your thesis. If you are writing a research-based term paper of ten pages or longer, you can expand by adding more evidence and elaborating on your arguments. You will have an introduction that might be a full page or a page and a half long—after all, if you have that many more arguments, you need that much more time to introduce all of them to your audience. Your first body argument that was a single paragraph in the shorter paper may now be a page and half, and so forth.

For example, if you were making an argument about the potential health dangers of high fructose corn syrup in sugary children's drinks, you could simply throw out a brief paragraph about diabetes in a shorter essay. In the longer essay, you may have a paragraph about diabetes (or two if you found plenty of statistics and information to now include), a paragraph about the glycemic index and how different sugars affect the human body, and a paragraph about obesity. You are making the same overall argument—high fructose corn syrup is bad in high quantities—but you are simply using a sliding scale of detail level.

So consider all the upcoming information in this chapter as completely variable in length. From an in-class essay as part of a midterm exam to a personal essay to a fully developed research paper, the same content needs to be there—an introduction, a body, and a conclusion. The only thing that changes is the depth of your discussion.

2. The Introduction

The first part of any paper is, of course, the introduction. Potential paper topics are extremely varied, for example, Abraham Lincoln, monarch butterfly migration patterns, fast food, video games, drunk driving, or the Fibonacci Sequence. Outside of a well-crafted title (Avoid titles like Essay One or Research Paper), the introduction provides the first clue, the first context, as to what content is to come. The introduction, then, lets your audience know what to expect and does this by slowly taking readers through the various parts of your paper. Let's put this another way: when your imagined audience picks up your paper, they are more or less concerned about their own lives and the world in which they live. Your task is to create an introduction that invites and brings your readers into your world, into your way of thinking. You need to consider your argument and help the readers come on board with your stance. You must be mindful of how you present the ideas you intend to include in your paper.

That can be an overwhelming task for many writers. Don't worry, however. Below is a list of all the elements that can be included in an introduction. The first element (the opening hook) is optional, but the other elements should be present in all good introductions.

TABLE 4.1. Elements of a Good Introduction

Opening Hook (*optional*)	Use opening quote, interesting fact, or compelling statistic.
Background Information	Add relevant information that contextualizes your topic.
Humor	You may briefly use humor to make your reader smile or laugh, but then move into a more formal, academic tone. Avoid vulgar language.
Rhetorical Question	Ask a question related to a profound situation or deep implication used to wake up your readers.
Personal Anecdote	If your instructor allows it, you could include a personal story to show you have a personal stake in the topic. Use the story, but then avoid using anecdotes for the rest of the paper.
Gradual Buildup of Ideas	Consider introducing ideas by building up from the general to the specific.
Thesis Statement	End the introduction with your well-crafted, single-sentence thesis statement. This must be a declarative sentence, not a question.

Opening Hook

The opening hook is a way to grab your readers' attention (or "hook" them) and get them interested in your paper. Instead of using a generic opening that any paper would use, you would come up with something unique, interesting, and possibly even funny or personal to start your paper. You should keep two audiences in mind. The most important one, of course, is your professor. Professors will read dozens (if not hundreds) of compositions alongside yours, and after a while, they all start to blend together. But it is useful to also keep an imaginary audience in mind as you write your paper—people who don't know as much about your topic as you do. Many papers open with a very bland statement, such as "In today's society…" or "In the modern world…." When a professor reads these back to back, no papers stand out, so from the very start, these papers are something they *have* to read, not something they *want* to read. However, if you come up with a way to be creative and hook your audience from the first sentence, you are off to a much better start than many other students.

Types of Hooks
Below is a brief list of some ways you can hook your audience in the opening sentences of your essay.

Opening Quote.
You can open your paper with a powerful or insightful quotation. This shouldn't be some familiar quotation from a typical article or book you've found in your research. Instead, it should be something very powerful that sets the stage for your entire discussion. Look for perfectly crafted, crisply phrased sentences by people like Mark Twain, Martin Luther King, Jr., Jane Goodall, Mahatma Gandhi, Winston Churchill, George Orwell, Harriet Tubman, or Sojourner Truth. Or, if you hope to open with a quotation that specifically deals with your topic, look for the absolute best expert who is writing in the field. This quotation should be pithy, bold, and a real attention grabber—otherwise, it isn't going to hook your readers. Of course, you still need to do something with your quotation; don't just quote someone and leave it at that. Discuss the

themes in the quotation and tie them to your own themes. And don't forget the parenthetical citation.

Interesting Fact or Statistic.
A good way to set the stage in your writing is to open up with a fact that might blow your readers' minds or really make them think. If you're doing a research paper, this is a natural way to open a paper. If you're writing about childhood obesity rates, and you ran into some statistics that really shocked you, the odds are they will shock others, as well. Lead with them. If you are writing a history paper, and you can't believe how many people died on the beaches of Normandy on D-Day, start there. Paint a picture of the importance of your topic through evidence like this, and you are much better off than the writer of a typical generic paper.

Background Information

As you advance in your studies, you will find yourself becoming an expert in your field and major. However, an imagined general audience might not be. If this is the case, start your paper with background information needed to even begin a conversation about your thesis. If you are writing about the dialogue between two published philosophers, you might want to start by summing up the conversation so far before you add your own insights. Giving a little history on your topic is never a bad idea.

Humor

Though most professors will want your essay to be written in a straightforward, academic tone, you can often get away with something funny or quirky in the opening hook of your paper. This might come from a great famous quotation (see above), or it could just be something you've come up with on your own. Don't use vulgar or shocking humor in a typical paper, but something that will make your readers smile or even laugh is a great way to pull them into your paper. Of course, as soon as you hit your punch line, you should go back to more formal language (but try not to sound pompous).

Rhetorical Question

You could also begin your essay by asking some questions that are meant to draw your readers in by making them immediately think of a profound situation or a deep implication. The opening question could also be funny or shocking, something used to wake readers up. Remember that the goal of an opening hook is to make your readers want to read your paper. A clever question can do so.

Consider these opening questions:
- What if Abraham Lincoln was not the "good guy" history makes him out to be?
- If you were desperate enough for money, would you work a job that you knew could physically maim you for life?
- If robots are so great for the economy, why do I feel like they are going to become self-aware and murder me?

These questions range from intriguing to ponderous to quirky. Each of them should serve to pull your readers in and make them curious to see exactly what your paper is about.

Personal Anecdote

An anecdote is a personal story about something that happened to you or someone else. While many writing tasks will ask for research only and no personal evidence as support, this can be a great way to grab someone's attention if your professor allows it. Suppose you work at a fast food restaurant and have had a miserable experience because your manager has exploited you. If you are writing a paper about the problems with fast food restaurants, this might be a catchy way to open your paper. It shows your readers that you have a personal stake in this discussion and that it is important to you. However, if you are not asked to write a personal essay (but a research paper instead, for example), you should do two things. First, ask your professor if this is an acceptable way to open your paper. Second, as soon as you are done with your personal story as an opening hook, leave all personal stories out of the rest of your paper. Go back to empirical, research-based evidence in your body.

Gradual Buildup of Ideas

Once you hook your readers and grab their attention, the bulk of your introduction will be dedicated to one thing: introducing your ideas. This may seem self-evident since it is called an introduction, but you'd be surprised how many students fail to introduce key parts of their ideas in the paper. One way to look at this is to consider your paper's outline once you have written it. Think about every major heading in the outline (part I, II, III, etc.). For an argumentative (as opposed to an analytical or expository) paper, each of these is a major argument and major section of your paper. Therefore, each of these should be introduced to your audience in the paper's introduction.

Another way to look at this is to consider your thesis statement. Nothing presented in your thesis should come as a surprise after the preceding information in your introduction. The point of the introduction, in fact, is to introduce the key elements of your thesis, so your readers are conversant with key ideas before they see how they are all put together in the thesis statement.

As indicated earlier, many successful writers take the standard approach of moving from the general to the specific in their introduction. If your paper is on the assassination of Abraham Lincoln, and you plan to discuss the politics that may have pushed his assassin to do the deed, you have a lot of information that you need to present to your readers. Begin with a basic discussion of Lincoln, his freeing of the slaves, his political legacy, and so on. Then, get more specific and discuss how he made political enemies and how while many people in the nation loved him for his bold actions, many people hated him for them. Then talk about John Wilkes Booth (his assassin) and whatever political ties you plan to argue about his killing Lincoln. Start with general information and slowly narrow your focus down to the specifics in the thesis.

One way to look at this is as an inverted pyramid with the point at the bottom. The top of the upside down pyramid is a flat plane that is wide open and free to be filled with a general discussion. As you go through the introduction, you should get more and more specific as the triangle narrows. Eventually, it all moves to a single point at the bottom of the pyramid, and this is the paper's thesis.

Miniature Outline: Some writers look at their introduction as a way to put their entire outline in one place for readers to see (since the outline isn't typically read by most readers). If you are writing about problems with slave labor in third world countries, you might have an outline that includes the following:

    I.   Introduction
   II. Definition of Slave Labor
  III. Health Problems/Repetitive Stress Injuries From Work
  IV. Lack of Worker Safety in Sweatshops
   V. Mental Health Issues/Suicide of Slave Laborers
  VI. Conclusion

A way to construct your introduction would be to begin by mentioning what slave labor is (part II). Then, introduce readers to the idea of injuries and health problems from their jobs (part III). Then give a sentence or two on worker safety (part IV). Next, discuss mental health issues and suicide in your introduction (V), and then give the thesis that ties it all together. This may seem monotonous to you since you're thinking of the paper's plans, but your audience has no idea what is coming, so establishing all these key paper components in the introduction (in the same order you will present them in your paper) gives them a nice mental framework as they proceed to your paper's body.

Thesis Sentence

The final element of the paper's introduction is the placement of a well-crafted, single-sentence thesis statement. We have a lot to say about thesis statements, so to find out more about how to write one, refer back to Chapter 3.

Thesis Placement

In the humanities, most professors advocate that you should place your thesis at the very end of the introduction. After all, if you put it at the start of the introduction, your thesis may not be entirely comprehensible to your imagined readers. The introduction is supposed to introduce your readers to every major idea you plan to cover. The common wisdom here is that you need to do all this in a strong introductory paragraph (or several) and then let information culminate in a clean thesis that brings all these ideas together. Note that in some disciplines, most notably the sciences, you may be expected to put the thesis first and then spend your introduction discussing the scientific or statistical methodology you used to get to your conclusion. Understand your discipline's specific quirks in this regard, and, as always, if you aren't sure, ask your professor.

Should you begin your thesis with the phrase "In this essay, I will…"? Many students use phrases such as this. For example, they may write, "In the following pages, I will argue that fast food workers are exploited." Indeed, you will read scholarly articles and books that do this very thing, and in some disciplines, such as philosophy, this may very well be what is expected of you. However, many professors don't like this approach. They believe in "Show, don't tell." If you have a strong thesis, it is perfectly clear what you plan to do, so saying so is just a waste of words. Don't find yourself being just one more of the student writers who uses phrases like "In this paper I will…." and "My essay will show that…." Frankly, such tired, over-used phrases are clunky, unnecessary, and bore your professors to dearth. If you write a clean introduction following all the steps outlined here, and you have a solid, complex thesis statement, then announcing what you plan to do becomes superfluous.

3. The Body of the Paper

The body is the bulk of your paper and follows your introduction. All your evidence for supporting your thesis goes here. You share your ideas and research that you've worked so hard to gather and organize. However, many people freeze up when confronted with the idea of how to write the sections of the body. Indeed, many questions come to mind: When do I know a body paragraph is too short or has gotten too long? For an argumentative paper, is it best to provide the other side of an argument as well as my own? How do I weave research and other people's ideas into my own work? These and many other questions can slow a writer down. However, once you get the hang of some basic concepts on developing your paper's body, it should get easier.

Individual Body Paragraphs

The core of the body is of course body paragraphs that supply individual ideas, research data, concepts, or facts. One thing that many student writers struggle with is the idea of how long to make a paragraph. While there is no actual set definition on how long a paragraph should be, here are a few guidelines.

First, whereas most people expect a paragraph to be at least three sentences long to fully develop an idea, this is not a rule set in stone. That said, however, this is an expectation of many readers and professors—so it's good to keep in mind, even if you break this rule. How much can you really develop an idea in just three, four, or even five sentences? You can, however, use a short body paragraph to emphasize a point developed in a longer preceding paragraph.

Second, the most important thing to consider with paragraph length is that a paragraph should be the vessel for one single idea. For example, if you are planning to write an essay on types of tea, you might decide to write about black tea, green tea, and herbal tea. A logical division system would be to give each type of tea its own paragraph, so that readers can clearly see your thought process in easily digestible blocks of text. However, if you plan to write about the problems of black and green tea (say, too much caffeine), and then the problems of herbal tea (it's too expensive to buy the good kinds) and the reason that herbal tea is superior (health factors), you will want to split the discussion on different types of tea into two or more paragraphs. Logically, for example, the discussion of the problem of herbal tea will be a different idea (therefore a different paragraph) than the discussion of why it is the best tea to drink.

Finally, another key concept about length goes back to what was expressed earlier in this chapter. The length of what you call an argument should be based on the size of the overall paper. In a two-page essay, you can easily convey a body argument or concept in a single paragraph. With a ten-page paper, your argument may be stretched over several pages with half a dozen examples. It's a good idea to make each of those examples its own paragraph, so you don't end up with a confusing three-page paragraph that overwhelms readers. Even with expository and analytical papers, where the point is not to present and support arguments, you want your body paragraphs to be coherently organized.

Paragraph Structure

Now that you have an idea of how long to make a body paragraph, you may be wondering about the best way to actually construct one. Whereas a common format for body paragraphs exists in academic writing, other acceptable ways to construct a paragraph exist as well. The common format we show you here will serve you well for any academic paper you will most likely be asked to write at this stage in your writing development—it's almost like a formula, where you add the constituent parts, and before you know it, you have yourself a powerful body paragraph. The common formula for a body paragraph includes the following components: topic sentence, primary content, critical discussion, thesis reminder, and transition.

TABLE 4.2. Constitutive Parts to Each Paragraph in the Body of the Paper	
Topic Sentence	First sentence, which guides content of individual paragraph.
Primary Content	Includes research, argument/counterargument, personal anecdotes, and rhetorical modes.
Critical Discussion	Shows how your content supports your thesis and shows advanced level of thought.
Thesis (*sometimes*)	Does not have to be in every paragraph, but useful to help remind readers what your thesis is and how the content of a paragraph relates to it.
Transition	Rhetorical strategy to help readers know that you have finished one idea and are ready to move to the next.

Topic Sentences

Every paragraph needs a topic sentence that identifies its main idea. A topic sentence indicates the point the writer wishes to make about that subject. Typically, the topic sentence appears at the beginning of the paragraph. Its job is to tell readers what the paragraph will be about. A paragraph without a topic sentence can be confusing and slow your readers down—you don't want them to have to fight through several sentences of confusing information before they finally figure out what point you are trying to make. The topic sentence announces your point in advance, and then you can get to the more important job of proving the point to be correct. Many writers think of the topic sentence as a miniature thesis statement. While a thesis guides the content of your entire paper, the topic sentence guides the content of your individual paragraph.

Going back to the example of the paper about tea, here are some sample topic sentences for those different paragraphs.

Topic Sentence 1. While black tea is one of the most popular teas in America, many people consume too much caffeine every day as a consequence.

Topic Sentence 2. Another tea that is often touted as having health benefits is green tea; however, it has more caffeine than most people are aware of.

Topic Sentence 3. Herbal tea, though free from the caffeine that plagues the other two types, is often too expensive for a typical consumer.

Topic Sentence 4. Once a consumer gets past the high price point, the important thing to note about herbal teas is the vast range of health benefits they provide.

Each of these sentences clearly tells readers what to expect that paragraph to be about. If in paragraph one, the paper discusses that there is too much caffeine in black tea and then also discusses that people drink it with too much sugar, then the idea of the sugar needs to be included in the topic sentence (or, more effectively, you might add the sugar discussion to a totally different paragraph about black tea).

Primary Content

Once you have established the content of your paragraph with your topic sentence, you will now move on to what is often the bulk of the body paragraph, and that is the primary content that your paragraph delivers. There are several types of content and rhetorical techniques you may want to include in your paragraph. The following discussion of content imagines an argumentative research paper:

- *Research*: One thing to base a body paragraph on is some outside research you may have done. This will come in the form of a direct quotation, a paraphrase or summary, some data, statistics, dates, or even graphs. The ideas of an expert will be presented to support your thesis in such a body paragraph (even if the expert is simply information from your professor presented during lectures in the case of an in-class essay).

- *Argument/Counter Arguments*: Another thing to base a paragraph on for an argumentative paper is providing your own original argument and then proving its worth by discussing a counter argument to your claim. It can be very effective to anticipate what the opposition will think and then prove them to be wrong in advance. Since there may be several counter arguments, you may have several different paragraphs. If done properly, this can make readers more easily agree with your side; if done poorly, however, you simply bring up a point better than your own and weaken your own stance. Just keep in mind intellectual honesty when you are presenting counter arguments in an argumentative paper—don't "cherry pick" information and ignore arguments and evidence that are inconvenient. Your professor will catch this. In fact, keep an open enough mind that you are willing to revise your own thesis as you further your research. You will learn more and get a better grade.

- *Personal Anecdotes*: If the paper is more casual or personal in nature, personal stories and anecdotes can be used to make points in your paper. If you are writing a paper about the dangers of texting and driving, and you use an example of a time your friend was texting while driving with you in the car and the accident you got in, this will move people. However, be sure that your professor is okay with such a rhetorical approach since it is still too informal for some writing tasks.

- *Rhetorical Modes*: See Chapter 6 for more on rhetorical modes and other strategies to employ while developing the body of your paper.

Critical Discussion

Once you deliver your content, your next goal is to practice critical thought and discuss the content of your body paragraph. Simply presenting a fact, quotation, or story alone does nothing to advance the thesis of your paper. The most important part of an argumentative essay is where you prove how your content supports your thesis and shows an advanced level of cognition. Even with expository essays, most professors don't want you to simply regurgitate facts. Google can do that for us in a few seconds. The interesting part of a piece of writing is what the author does with those facts; that's where imagination, academic writing, and critical thinking merge in a meaningful way.

Here are some suggested ways to critically examine the types of content you may have included in a body paragraph:

- *Research*: Once you give your facts, statistics, or quotations, you need to interpret them for your readers. For example, if you presented a statistic revealing that a survey of 800 parents revealed that in 2016, 91 percent of them reported purchasing at least one meal a week for their children at one of the four largest fast food chains in the country: McDonald's, Burger King, Wendy's, and Subway, a number that was up from 79 percent doing so in 2010, this alone isn't meaningful enough. Until you demonstrate to your readers that this increase is related to increasing health problems for children, they don't know what to do with this information. Statistics alone can be interpreted in various ways by everyone who reads them, so your job is to do that heavy lifting for them.

- *Arguments/Counter Arguments*: In argumentative papers, once you give your argument or you show a counter argument, your job is still to tie it all back to your thesis. If you simply make a point, say what the other camp says about the point, and move on, then you haven't done very much with your argument. Until you really drive home how much your camp is correct and point out the flaws in the opposition, your readers have no context for what you've done.

- *Personal Anecdotes*: If your professor allows personal anecdotes, you will want to go from the personal back to the academic in your discussion. If you have a story about how your little brother eats too much fast food, the story is just a short narrative with no context. Once you discuss it in an objective voice and show that this event is commonplace and important, you are exhibiting the critical thought that a professor will want to see. This might include a shift from a more informal, personal tone that uses first person pronouns such as "I" to a more formal, academic tone.

- *Rhetorical Modes*: This discussion will vary greatly depending on the rhetorical mode you have selected, but again, the goal is to connect the content to your thesis

Thesis Reminder

The thesis reminder is one of the most important parts of the body's content, but it may be something that doesn't happen in every single paragraph. It is important to understand the context of your paper to fully understand the need for a thesis reminder. First, you should be writing a sophisticated argument or an expository or analytical essay with multiple points that all connect in specific ways to support your reasoning. However, your readers will not always see how a single example (or single paragraph) ties into the bigger picture. Indeed, your professor may read dozens of essays on the same topic, each with subtle differences in the thesis. It's easy for readers to forget the specifics of your thesis when they are midway through a long paper.

The thesis reminder is typically a sentence that will remind readers what the thesis is and also show how this particular paragraph is connected to it. In a shorter essay, you might do a thesis reminder in each paragraph, but in a longer research paper, you might do it at the end of each complete argument, not after each single idea. This means that the thesis reminder may come after a page or more (often, when you finish a major point of your paper's outline such as II, III, VI, etc.).

The goal of a thesis reminder is not to simply cut and paste the thesis and keep saying the same thing over and over. Ideally, you have a complex thesis with many parts. The reminder just shows the audience how your ideas are connected to that thesis. It helps to improve your critical thinking as well as your sense of transition if done properly. Toward the end of this section on the body, there is a sample paragraph. Refer to it to see an example of a good thesis reminder.

A Transition

An important rhetorical strategy is a transition. It is important to let your readers know that you are now done with one part of your paper and moving on to something new. Of course, the topic sentence helps establish the details of your new section, but you need to close out the point you've just finished to make the shift in ideas smooth. You don't want your readers to be gobsmacked by a new point or idea and wonder how it ties to what you've been talking about.

<u>Transition Words:</u> You can get in the habit of good transitions by using some key transition words. There are many more than those listed here, but this is a good start:

- *Examples*: for example, specifically, one example is, another example of, to illustrate this

- *Contrast*: on the other hand, conversely, however, on the contrary, in the way of a contrast, whereas, nevertheless

- *Addition*: in addition, consequently, furthermore, (first, second, third, etc.), next, moreover, similarly, also, what is more, not only (this) but also (that), alternatively, further

- *Comparison*: similarly, similar to this, in a like manner, likewise, in a similar fashion, another, in the same way, equally

Sample Body Paragraph

The following is a sample body paragraph that puts all of these pieces together. We have numbered each sentence to show each part of the paragraph. This paragraph is for a research paper. The thesis is as follows: "Workers at fast food restaurants are exploited by the companies they work for by being manipulated to work off the clock, doing dangerous jobs, and being underpaid; the United States needs new legislation to improve working conditions."

TABLE 4.3. A Sentence-by-Sentence Breakdown of a Sample Body Paragraph
[1] Aside from working off the clock, another problem for the fast food worker is that they do dangerous jobs. [2] Indeed, the rates of injury for fast food workers is very high, according to a study done by Carla Vasquez, director of food studies at the University of Linlo. [3] She says that 43% of all fast food workers are injured doing dangerous jobs they are not properly trained for (Vasquez 18). [4] The study suggests that things such as changing hot fryer oil and using fast-moving machinery can be done safely, but that workers are not given the right training to do so. [5] Because the overturn rate for employees is so high, workers are seldom there long enough to know the ins and outs of doing all the aspects of the job. [6] This type of danger is one of the reasons that the United States needs to pass new legislation for worker safety in fast food. [7] However, another reason is the fact that the workers are underpaid.

Breakdown of the Individual Body Paragraph Sentence by Sentence

[1] This is the topic sentence. It announces that the paragraph is about the dangers faced by fast food workers, and it also does double duty by adding transition words "Aside from…" In this manner, it sets itself off from what was done in the previous paragraph. [2] This sentence establishes the credibility of the author being cited in the paragraph to let readers know her expertise and to gain trust in the statistic. [3] This sentence provides the statistic that makes the core of the paragraph. [4 and 5] These sentences give a critical discussion of the citation. Here, the student discusses what this information proves in this context. [6] This sentence is the thesis reminder. You can see that the student points back to the overall message of the thesis, situates this paragraph as part of the larger argument, and even looks forward to what will come next. [7] This is the transition. Note that it uses the phrase "another reason" to tell the audience that they should be ready for a change in topics as we go from the danger faced by workers and shift to a new paragraph about workers being underpaid.

Conclusion

Finally, after the introduction and the body, the last part of any essay is the conclusion. Many people imagine the conclusion to be a relatively unimportant part of the essay, but that couldn't be farther from the truth. The conclusion is where you are able to tie

> *A popular way to structure your conclusion is the opposite of how you constructed your introduction.*

together any lose strings you had in your essay and put some final polish on your thoughts. Note that you should no longer be presenting evidence or arguments in your conclusion—that should all be done by the end of your body. Don't include new information in the conclusion. If you come up with new ideas, create new body paragraphs.

The conclusion does the opposite of what the introduction did. It walks readers out of your essay and lets them go back into the world having learned some perspective specific to you. A popular way to structure your conclusion is the opposite of how you constructed your introduction. In the introduction, remember, you started with a hook to draw your readers in, moved to a gradual buildup of facts about the paper, and then end with a compelling thesis. The sample conclusion structure below discusses how you do the opposite of that to conclude your work.

Final Thesis Discussion

In this type of conclusion, you open with a final discussion and reminder of your thesis. For an argumentative essay, tell the audience exactly what you intended to prove and remind them that you finished doing just that. Don't simply paste the thesis there again, verbatim, but remind your readers of the major points you planned to argue, or, in the case of an expository essay, the information you planned to cover. In the case of an analytical essay, summarize the "how" and the "why" of your major points. Show your readers that you accomplished your stated purpose. This helps them remember exactly what your intentions were (and it helps remind professors of your specific take on your topics, so your work doesn't just blend in with hundreds of other compositions they grade).

Gradual Exit

Your introduction involved a gradual buildup of key ideas you planned to include in your paper. This is designed to gradually walk your readers into your paper and immerse them in the major ideas in your topic. Now, you do the opposite and sum up how you used the key ideas in your paper. End with a discussion that reminds readers of the different parts of your paper that tied all of your ideas and information together.

Closing Hook

Finally, end your essay in an interesting manner. If you started with a personal anecdote, it may be a good idea to end with a reflection on the same story. If you hooked your readers in the introduction with statistics that were startling, refer back to them. In light of what you've just said, are they even more impressive? Or you can end with rhetorical questions that leave readers wondering about deeper implications of your writing and maybe even call on them to take action.

Regardless of the format you use for your conclusion, remember that it has one job: to remind readers of your thesis and how you supported it. Do this by reflecting back on your main points or by connecting your main points to potential future areas of exploration. This is your final chance to share your thoughts with the audience before they get to your works cited page, and it is often a place to make significant points, final judgments, and deep musings.

What to Avoid in Conclusions

1. *"In Conclusion," "In Closing":* While some disciplines may teach you to use "In conclusion…" or "In closing…," most disciplines in the humanities prefer you to avoid these phrases. They come off as trite and stale in the conclusion. They are just as obvious and boring as "This essay will be about…" When readers see they are at the end of your paper, and they see a nice turn on the thesis that ties everything together, it's quite obvious they are in the conclusion. Stating it so obviously seems lazy and obvious to many readers.
2. *New Evidence/Arguments:* As noted earlier, the conclusion is not a place to bring up new evidence, research, or arguments to support your thesis.

All of these things belong in the body. This is not to say you can't have a new quotation in your conclusion; a good quotation can really make your conclusion pop; however, don't include a quotation that introduces brand new ideas at this stage in your composition.

3. *Don't Repeat Yourself:* While it is important to remind readers of your thesis and even the major body points from your paper here, you don't want to just copy and paste. Don't repeat yourself word for word. Every point you bring up—including the thesis—needs to have a new light shining on it. What have you, and therefore your audience, learned about these thoughts by the end of your paper?

Name: _____ Section: _____ Date: _____

Part Two

Chapter 4 Workshop

The following section contains a series of ten tasks that, if completed, will help you gain mastery over the content in this chapter. Your instructor will assign some (or all) of them to you as a way to practice the material presented here. Notice that some of them are global and focus on the entirety of the skills laid out in this chapter, while others are more focused and explore only one or two sections of the chapter. Also notice that some are shorter, some are longer, but all are designed to flip the classroom and put the power of learning directly into your own hands.

Workshop One.

Overview: Summarize all of the major sections and/or bullet points that you find in this chapter.

Each major section or heading should be clearly labeled and should have at least a one-sentence discussion. You might have a dozen or more headings and sentences here. Be thorough and accurate to show that you have read and comprehended this chapter's contents. Avoid the temptation to judge or add anything new (even critical discussion of the content); this is an act of pure summary. Tell your instructor exactly what came in this chapter and in what order.

Workshop Two.

Overview: This workshop has you examine all of the wrong answers from your chapter diagnostic and respond to them.
1. Make a list of each question from the chapter diagnostic that you got wrong.
2. Go through the chapter to look up the rules on each question. For every question you got wrong, do the following:

A. Identify the page number where the rule was found.
B. Discuss what the right answer should have been on the diagnostic test.
C. Discuss how you can avoid this error in future writing and/or tests.

Workshop Three.

Overview: Write a short, personal essay explaining the content of this chapter. The point of this essay is to directly address what you have learned from the chapter and how it will impact your future academic writing. Consider some or all of the following:

a. What writing element(s) were new to you?
b. How can you incorporate some of the elements into your own writing in the future?
c. What writing element(s) did you already know about? Did you already use them in your writing, or did you ignore them for some reason? If so, what was the reason?
d. If appropriate, use some of the techniques and language from the actual chapter in your paper to help illustrate mastery.
e. Your instructor will provide you with more details, such as the length of the piece, whether you should use quotations from the chapter, if personal anecdotes and casual language are allowed, etc.

Workshop Four.

Overview: Write an introduction to an essay that explores multiple opening hooks discussed in this chapter. By the end, you should see how powerful a hook can be as well as which one you prefer.

1. Write a paper introduction that uses all of the elements discussed in this chapter. Focus on a strong opening hook.
2. Write a second version of the introduction that uses a completely different type of opening hook than the first. The second half of the

paragraph may be identical to the first version you wrote, but the hook needs to be completely different.

3. Write an answer of several sentences that critically explains which hook you think is better and more appropriate for a college paper. Why do you feel this way? Was this a surprise? Discuss.

Workshop Five.

Overview: Practice writing an introduction that uses all of the elements discussed in this chapter and that clearly labels them. To do so, write a single introduction that identifies each step laid out in the process in square brackets. These areas are the opening hook, gradual buildup of ideas, and thesis sentence. Each sentence of your introduction should be doing one of these steps, so each sentence should self-identify with one of them in square brackets. This means, before each sentence in this intro, you should have the following [opening hook], [gradual buildup of ideas], or [thesis statement] to identify it.

Workshop Six.

Overview: Practice writing a body paragraph that uses all of the elements discussed in this chapter and that clearly labels them. To do so, write a single body paragraph that identifies each step laid out in the process in square brackets. These areas are the topic sentence, primary content, critical discussion, thesis reminder, and transition. Each sentence of your paragraph should be doing one of these steps, so each sentence should self-identify with one of them in square brackets. This means, before each sentence in this paragraph, you should have the following [topic sentence], [primary content], [critical discussion], [thesis reminder], and [transition] to identify it.

Workshop Seven.

Write a conclusion that identifies each step laid out in the process in square brackets. These areas are the same as the introduction, but would be accomplished in a backward order. They are the final thesis discussion, gradual exit, and closing hook. Each sentence of your conclusion should be doing one of these steps, so each sentence should self-identify with one of them in square brackets. This means, before each sentence in this conclusion, you should have the following [final thesis discussion], [gradual exit], or [closing hook].

Workshop Eight.

Overview: Write two paragraphs that practice use of transitions in your essay.
1. Write two body paragraphs and produce a several-sentence transition that clearly shows that one idea is concluding and another is about to start. Use one of the sample transition phrases listed in this chapter.
2. Then, part two is to use the same paragraphs, but to build a transition out of different phrases and words.
3. Now, write a brief reflection of a couple of sentences that explains the logical and rhetorical difference between these two transitions as well as which one you believe would be better for a college essay and why.
4. Before turning this in, take a highlighter to the transitions to show your instructor what parts you consider to be transitions.

Workshop Nine.

Overview: Revisit the primary content section of this chapter. Now, write two similar body paragraphs using all of the key elements of a body paragraph (topic sentence, content, transition, etc.) as well as a reflection of which you think is stronger.
1. The first paragraph you write will make a point using a personal anecdote. Select a topic that your instructor approves of and write a body paragraph that could be used in a college essay, but the primary content is a personal story that happened to you.
2. Now, rewrite the paragraph making the same point, but avoiding any personal anecdote at all. Instead, use either research, argument/ counter argument, or a rhetorical mode to make the same point in the paragraph.

3. When you are done with both paragraphs, write a short reflection of a couple of sentences that explains which one you think will be stronger to an audience and why.

Workshop Ten.

Overview: What is your take away from this chapter? What did you learn and what questions do you still have?

1. Write a short response of several sentences that covers the three main things that you learned from this chapter.
2. Write out at least five questions you still have about the chapter. What things would you want to communicate to your instructor? What would you like to see discussed in class or handled with more depth to help you master this chapter's content?
3. What is one thing that you have taken away from this chapter and will use on your next writing task? Why is this thing important, and how do you plan to implement it?

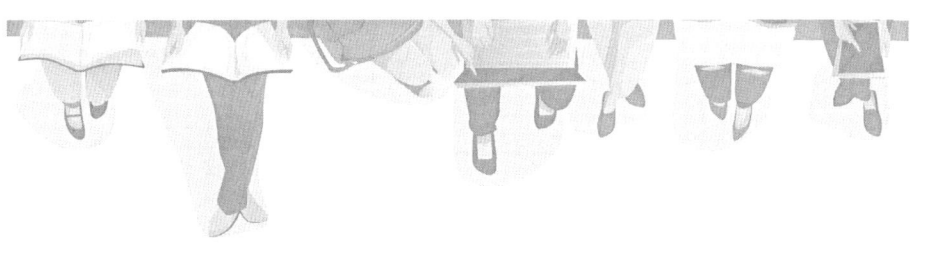

CHAPTER 5

How to Breakdown
the Components of Arguments

In this chapter, you will learn about the following:

Part One: Understanding the Elements of Arguments
1. What is an Argument?
2. The Three Essential Parts to an Argument
   a. An argument must contain at least one premise
   b. An argument contains only one conclusion
   c. An argument must have a relationship of support or proof
3. Additional Elements of Arguments
   a. An argument must have more than one sentence
   b. An argument comprises declarative sentences
   c. An argument is not to be confused with non-arguments
   d. Indicator words identify premises and conclusions
   e. Standardizing an argument into its parts

Part Two: Workshop

Part One

Understanding the Elements of Arguments

1. What is an Argument?

Simply put, an **argument** is *a set of statements whereby at least one statement [called a premise(s)] attempts to support or prove another statement [called a conclusion].* This definition provides us with clarity in its simplicity, which makes it easy to remember and easy to unpack. Yet do not be

> An **argument** is *a set of statements whereby at least one statement [called a premise] attempts to support or prove another statement [called a conclusion].*

fooled. Arguments are complex and require a lot of work to develop—but a simple definition helps us break down the basic structure and components so you know what to work on. Arguments are either short or extended, distinctions referring only to the level of support provided. When you develop argumentative essays, know that you are most likely dealing with extended arguments, i.e., arguments that have more than one level of support. We will begin our discussion using only short arguments, arguments that have only one level of support:

Example 1.

> [1]Steel-cut oats ranks high among the healthiest of most breakfast foods. [2]With 23 grams of net carbs and 8 grams of protein, but also 5 grams of fiber, steel-cut oats provide a more balanced set of nutrients than, for example, French toast, which has 36 grams of net carbs and 18.8 grams of fat but only 5 grams of protein and 3 grams of fiber.

Example 2.

> [1]Smith should win the presidential election in 2020. [2]Smith was a successful governor for three years, and [3]her compassionate message resonates with the people. [4]She also has experience successfully running a multinational company.

Notice what each of these arguments has in common: Each has more than one sentence. Each provides some type of supporting evidence, also called **premises**. Each has a **conclusion**, or one sentence or claim that is being proven true by the supporting evidence, the premises. In other words, **a relationship of support or proof** exists between the sentences. And each of the pieces of evidence directly links to its respective conclusion. Each also has sentences that relate to the topic and assertion being made. These are all critical ingredients of an argument.

For example, the first argument has two sentences (or statements), and we can clearly see that the first statement must be the conclusion because it is being supported or proven true by the second statement. This second statement must be the premise because it provides the evidence for believing the claim that steel-cut oats rank high among the healthiest of all breakfast foods. All statements are also making a reference to steel-cut oats. In the second example, we see that there are four sentences, the first of which must be the conclusion because it is being supported by the other three. Smith should win because of the three reasons outlined in statements [2], [3], and [4]. This argument has three premises and one conclusion. Moreover, all statements relate to the topic of Smith and the election and the assertion of Smith winning.

2. The Three Essential Parts to An Argument

The two argument examples mentioned contain at least three essential components that comprise arguments: 1) a **premise** (or premises), 2) a **conclusion**, and 3) **a relationship of support or proof**. Let's define each of these terms and then highlight the remaining elements of an argument:

An Argument Must Contain At Least One Premise

DEFINITION OF A PREMISE

A premise is a declarative sentence that attempts to provide evidence, proof, or support for the truth of another statement, namely a conclusion. [There can be one or more such sentences just as there may be main or subpremises that support a main or subconclusion.]

An argument may have only one premise as in Example 1 above, or it may have several premises as in Example 2 above. Premises provide the essential evidence for why anyone should believe what you want to claim or prove true. Evidence or premises need to be consistent, reliable, and factual. The truth of your conclusion is only as strong and reliable as the evidence that you provide in its support. Bad evidence=unsupported and unreliable conclusion. Good evidence=supported and reliable conclusion.

A conclusion is not true because everyone just believes it without any good evidence—e.g., many of us believe that soap or shampoo is only effective if it generates a bunch of small bubbles when mixed with water. Not enough lather, then our belief is that soap doesn't work. It turns out that if we asked for evidence, well, *good* evidence, our belief would be proved wrong. Most companies add foaming agents to make the product appear more effective. And so premises attempt to round out your set of beliefs, keep you honest, so to speak, so you hold on to the ones that have good evidence and eliminate those for which you do not have good evidence. Any beliefs you may have that are not supported by good premise(s) have no business being used in academic writing. Beliefs supported by good evidence=what we call knowledge.

Should your premises contradict common knowledge, things we call facts, then your responsibility is to prove to your reader that the evidence you are presenting, albeit not common knowledge, is, in fact, reliable. That is your job. If you fail to make your premises reliable and believable to the reader, your reader will have no interest or need to accept your conclusion.

Every set of premises must lead to one conclusion (or a subconclusion).

An Argument Contains Only One Conclusion

DEFINITION OF A CONCLUSION
A conclusion is a declarative sentence that is being supported or proven to be true by a premise or series of premises. [There is only one main conclusion in any argument although there could be several subconclusions. Another term for a conclusion is an argumentative thesis, or a debatable statement. See Chapter 3 for a quick review on this type of thesis.]

In a strict sense, an argument has only one conclusion to which all other statements lead, as they do in both examples above. However, you may come across a set of declarative sentences, or just one, from which two independent and separate conclusions are drawn. While some may reduce such an argument structure to a single argument but containing multiple conclusions, we do not. We call any argument that has one premise, or a set of premises, leading to two separate conclusions, two independent arguments:

Example 3. Argument with one premise supporting two separate conclusions

[1]Life is sacred. Therefore, [2]do not waste your life away by doing drugs, and [3]euthanasia must be wrong.

In this example, there are three statements, the first of which, "Life is sacred," is being used to support statements [2] and [3] separately. The structure of this argument pattern creates two entirely different arguments, and each argument should be separated because an argument can only have one conclusion:

Independent Argument 1.
    [1]Life is sacred. Therefore, [2]do not waste your life away by doing drugs.

Independent Argument 2.
    [1]Life is sacred. Therefore, [3]euthanasia must be wrong.

When crafting a conclusion as your main conclusion or argumentative thesis, do not include two independent statements that are not related. As you can see from the argument above, statement [2] is totally unrelated and separate from statement [3].

When trying to identify a conclusion of an argument, ask yourself, what is the *main point* that the passage is trying to make or what is the author trying to *prove*? A conclusion must be the statement toward which the other statements are pointing. Just as an argumentative thesis must provide support to persuade us to believe the thesis is true, a conclusion must have other statements outside of it that *support or prove* the conclusion true in some manner. How do we know if a series of statements provides this support? Let's turn to that topic next.

An Argument Must Have a Relationship of Support or Proof

DEFINITION OF SUPPORT OR PROOF
Support or proof in an argument is the reasoning process of the argument and involves the presence of a logical (inferential) relationship between statements such that one or more statement(s) attempt to provide reasons for the truth of another statement. [Stated differently, by support, we mean that some inference, or new piece of information, can be drawn or inferred from the given premises.]

An argument must attempt to support or prove another statement, i.e., it must make an inference from a premise or a set of premises. An **inference** is this *attempt to derive the truth of a logical conclusion from stated evidence or premises assumed or known to be true.* We call this the "reasoning process" expressed by the argument. The reasoning process is an objective logical part of an argument, and it is often challenging to identify. The reasoning process is also rational, though.

Whereas we tend to only think reasoning is present when the premises are true, it turns out that reasoning may also be present even when the premises provided are known to be false. In other words, reasoning is less concerned with the truth value of the provided premises than it is with attempting to establish reasons for believing the conclusion to be true.

Example 1. An argument with *support* but false premises, false conclusion

> [1]All doctors are from Wisconsin. [2]Congresswoman Tulsi Gabbard is a doctor. Therefore, [3]Congresswoman Tulsi Gabbard is from Wisconsin.
>
> **Analysis**: Statements [1] and [2] are clearly false premises, and in this case, statement [3], which represents the conclusion, is also false. Yet since reasoning concerns the presence of *support*, not the truth value of the supporting premises, we see that *support* is nevertheless provided, and this passage represents an argument: Should we assume statements [1] and [2] are true (even though we know they are not)? They do, in fact, attempt to provide reasons to *support* statement [3], the conclusion. Stated differently, if we assumed statements [1] and [2] to be true (even though we know they are false), then statement [3], which is the conclusion and is inferred from the evidence, tells us something new based on that given evidence.

Example 2. An argument with *support* and true premises, true conclusion

> [1]John Lennon was one of the lead singers for the Beatles. [2]All members of the Beatles were millionaires. Therefore, [3]John Lennon must have been a millionaire.

Analysis: Statements [1] and [2] are clearly true premises, and in this case, statement [3], which represents the conclusion, is also true. While reasoning concerns the presence of *support*, not the truth value of the supporting premises, we see that *support* is provided, and this passage represents an argument: Should we assume statements [1] and [2] are true (and here we know they are), they do, in fact, attempt to provide reasons to *support* statement [3], the conclusion. Stated differently, if we assumed statements [1] and [2] to be true, then statement [3], which is the conclusion and is inferred from the evidence, tells us something new based on that given evidence. We learned that John Lennon must have been a millionaire.

Example 3. A passage without *support* – a non-argument

> [1]Social medicine is the future. [2]Socialism is good for everyone. [3]Medicare for all is the best, and [4]supporting open borders is the right way to run our country.

Analysis: Notice that none of the four statements provides any support for another. In fact, each statement exemplifies a separate opinion unrelated to any of the others. To this end, this passage represents a set of opinions only, none of which proves any other statement true. Thus, no support is here, and thus this is not an argument. [See Table 5.5 for more examples of non-argument types.]

The first two examples highlight a reasoning process that is taking place, the linking process between the premises and the conclusion. The third shows what a passage may look like when there is no support or reasoning process present.

In logic, the relationship of support is often, but not always, made more concrete by connecting the argument's reasoning process to a type of common argument pattern. Let's look at one of these types of argument patterns:

Table 5.1. Argument Based on Authority – A Common Argument Pattern

Definition

An *argument based on authority* involves drawing upon an authority to create the support, the logical inferential link, required to establish the truth of the conclusion.

Logical Structure (The Reasoning Process)

[1]Person A is claimed to be an authority on subject B.

[2]Person A makes a statement C about subject B.

Therefore, [3]statement C is true.

Argument Example

[1]Dr. John Cook is a research assistant professor at the Center for Climate Change Communication at George Mason University and co-author of *Climate Change Science: A Modern Synthesis.*

[2]He claims that "among papers expressing a position on anthropogenic global warning (AGW), an overwhelming percentage (97.2% based on self-ratings, 97.1% based on abstract ratings) endorses the scientific consensus on AGW."

Therefore, [3]the majority of authors on AGW endorse the factual reality of anthropogenic global warning.

Analysis

Since this argument appeals to the authority of Dr. John Cook to establish the truth of the conclusion (see statement [3]), an inferential link is being presented, and this is an argument. Moreover, since we know the conclusion is only proved to be true based on the relevance of the authority of the person appealed to, we can say that the reasoning of this appeal is strong, meaning the authority of Dr. John Cook is *appropriately* linked to the conclusion claimed in the argument. Obviously, if Dr. John Cook was a non-degreed bartender at Sandrini's Public House without any experience or studies in the field of Climate Change, there would be good reason not to trust or rely on his authority.

There are plenty of other argument patterns identified in logic that help us identify whether a reasoning process is present in a given passage. Some include, for example, arguments of probability, such as analogy, predictions, and cause and effect, whereas others are arguments

> If both *the reasoning process is effective* and *the premises are true*, then you are on your way to creating an argument that will earn you high marks.

of necessity, such as hypothetical syllogism, categorical syllogism, and math. While we could list them all, our purpose in the chapter is a) to make you aware that a reasoning process must occur in an argument for there to be an argument and b) provide you with an introduction to what that reasoning process might look like. Reasoning, interestingly, does not care about the truth of your premises, only that the premises, in fact, do what they are supposed to do, namely support the conclusion. And evidence can show this support in a myriad of different ways, just as the evidence may or may not actually succeed in supporting the conclusion.

A final note on support or reasoning: A necessary condition for any good argument must go beyond just establishing the presence of support. The reasoning process must be good before considering the truth value of the premises. Don't be fooled by an argument just because all the evidence sounds true or good because while you can have all true evidence, there is no guarantee that the conclusion is sufficiently being supported by that evidence. A conclusion is only as strong as the strength of the premises. This is why understanding reasoning is critical to your success when you create your own arguments and when you learn how to critique other people's arguments. *If both the reasoning process is effective and the premises are true, then you are on your way to creating an argument that will earn you high marks.*

3. Additional Elements of Arguments

Table 5.2. Additional Elements of Arguments
Definition: an **argument** is *a set of statements whereby at least one statement [called a premise] attempts to support or prove another statement [called the conclusion].*
✓ An argument must have more than one sentence.
✓ An argument comprises declarative sentences.
✓ An argument is not to be confused with non-arguments.
✓ Indicator Words Identify Premises and Conclusions
✓ Standardizing an Argument and Its Parts

An Argument Must Have More Than One Sentence

An argument must contain more than one sentence, or statement. This represents the most basic feature of any argument: single statements, even if they are opinions or beliefs, are not arguments. So single statements like "Steel-cut oats are the best breakfast food" and "The directors of the latest Marvel movie series did the right thing to include a cameo by Stan Lee in each of the films" are not by themselves arguments. All arguments per se must include at least two statements—or, put another way, all arguments must have two or more statements.

An Argument Comprises Declarative Sentences

An argument uses only declarative sentences. Refer back to Chapter 3 for reinforcement of this point. Declarative sentences, also known as statements, end in periods and refer to sentences that present a fact, an opinion, or a piece of information, or they may explain or declare something. Examples include "the world is round" or "vegetarians are unhealthy."

In some way or another, statements also carry with them the potential of being proven right or wrong (or true or false), or more likely right or wrong (or more likely true or false). For example, if I state that "the world is round," I can use certain types of scientific or mathematical evidence to prove or support the truth of this declarative statement. Whereas sometimes the truth-value is obvious, other times the truth-value is less obvious.

Table 5.3. Declarative Sentences with Obvious Truth Value
Bob Kane and Bill Finer created the DC comic fictional hero Batman in 1939.
Washington Irving's novel *History of New York* (1809) created a picture of Santa Claus as wearing a green, not red, winter coat.
Santa Claus is a legendary figure that traces back to St. Nicolas, a monk born around 280 C.E. in Patara, Turkey.

Each of these statements is true. They are facts. A simple Google search or research at your local library will result in confirming the truth of these statements. These statements are more likely to act as your premises, or evidence.

Some declarative statements, however, are less obvious and would require that we provide a more sophisticated case to make us believe that a certain statement is more likely or less likely true. These statements are more likely to be your conclusion in an argument.

Table 5.4. Declarative Sentences with Less-Obvious Truth Value
The Harry Potter literary series by J.K. Rowling is the most creative set of adolescent fantasy novels of the 21st century.
Ignoring the effects of climate change will result in the end of the world in 12 years.
God is love.

None of these statements is simply true or false. No Google search or trip to the library research center can help you quickly determine the truth value of these declarative sentences. For example, can we really agree on what is or what is not "the most creative set of adolescent fantasy novels"? Can we determine the future in "12 years"? Or can we ever prove that "God is in fact love"? The truth value for these statements is more sophisticated and requires you to provide other declarative statements to help show or convince the reader that your statement is, in fact, more likely to be true than false.

Arguments contain declarative statements that fall somewhere on the scale from obviously true to less obviously true. And when creating your own arguments, you want the declarative sentences acting as your premises, or evidence, to lean toward the side of the scale of more obviously true than less obviously. And if your premises are not obvious to the reader, then you will want to prove that the evidence you are using is, in fact, true. Your declarative statement acting as your conclusion, however, will most likely be less obviously true at first because, by definition, it will require other statements to prove to others that your claim is true, or more likely true than false.

Avoid Questions, Exclamations, Imperatives, and Rhetorical Questions
In the end, arguments only use declarative sentences. Should you come across **questions**, **exclamations**, or **imperatives**, you must seek to do one of two things: either 1) eliminate them from the argument you are trying to make or 2) restate the sentence in such a way as to create a declarative sentence.

Often times, people will rely on **rhetorical questions** in an argument. A rhetorical question is a figure of speech in the form of a question designed to create a particular effect: it might be used to persuade the reader, to emphasize a critical point, or to create a literary mood. Whatever the reason, rhetorical questions are discouraged in arguments and may deflect from the real evidence or declarations you want to make.

Some examples of rhetorical questions
  What is the meaning of life?
  Doesn't everyone strive for success?
  Isn't abortion murder?
  Isn't an Iman Muslim by definition?
  Don't you value life?
  Are you really that naïve?
  Isn't a terrorist a criminal?

A caveat: You may find yourself wanting to use questions as a way to draw your readers into your line of reasoning. Stylistically, this may be okay if used as a hook in the introduction, but know that the question is not part of your argument, and it cannot be used as evidence. You cannot rely on the reader to answer the question in the same way that you intend to answer it. As a rhetorical device, any question must eventually be declared in the form of a declarative sentence if you want to use the strategy in your argument.

An Argument is Not To Be Confused with Non-Argument Patterns

We have learned that arguments occur only if support is given, regardless of whether the support successfully proves the conclusion true or not. As we learned in the previous section, some passages may look like arguments but are, in fact, not arguments—we call these non-arguments. Non-arguments are a set of sentences that do not meet the criteria of having a reasoning process. Non-arguments do not make conclusions and do not provide evidence for those conclusions. Here is a list of common non-argument patterns:

Table 5.5. A List of Common Non-Argument Patterns	
Definition: A non-argument represents a set of statements that lacks a relationship of support or proof and thus does not contain any inferences.	
Descriptions	A set of sentences describing things, people, or events.
Opinions	A set of sentences expressing a series of unrelated and independent opinions, none of which provides evidence for another.
Reports	A set of sentences providing information about people, places, things, or events.
Expositions	A set of sentences developing a topic, theme, or idea, but lacking any reasoning process.
Explanations	A set of sentences explaining the "why" or "how" of an accepted fact or event.
Suggestions	A set of sentences implying or suggesting an action or feeling.
Conditional Statements**	A "single" sentence comprising the form "if x, then y" or some variation thereof, like "x only if y" or "y, if x."

** Conditional statements are treated as single statements, but they are complex and can, if additional statements are added, serve as premises or conclusions. Suffice it to say, since a conditional statement acts like one statement, it cannot be by itself sufficient to represent an argument. So if I say to you "If Freddy Mercury were alive today, then he and Elton John would be best friends," you now know that in itself I am not making an argument.

Whereas there might be some utility to providing examples for each of these non-argument patterns, there are two in particular that cause students the most trouble that we would like to cover in this primer of a book: expositions and explanations. Maybe in the next edition we will add a section about conditional statements, but for now, we just wanted to introduce them to you in the chart.

Expositions

Expository passages represent a set of declarative sentences that provide information, usually facts, about a given topic, theme, or idea, often in terms of developing that given topic, theme, or idea. But no support or reasoning is being used.

Example 1. Expository passage as non-argument

> [1]Morro Bay is a town of about 10,000 overlooking the Pacific Ocean. [2]It has only one main street, and [3]it has a few stoplights.

This set of sentences provides bits of information about Morro Bay, namely it's "a town of about 10,000," "it overlooks the Pacific Ocean," "it has only one main street," and "it has a few stoplights." Four statements. Four pieces of information about the topic, Morro Bay. Notice that no claim supports or is supported by any of the other statements. It turns out that all sentences are statements of facts. No statement is debatable or is in need of "support." For this reason, this series of statements cannot be an argument, and since it only provides factual pieces of data about one topic, namely Morro Bay, this is an expository passage.

Interestingly, all non-argument patterns can, however, be used in an argument if we add a related but debatable statement that the given information acts to support or prove, or provide reasons or evidence for, this new debatable statement. In other words, if you can add a debatable conclusion that is supported by the already given facts in an expository passage, then you have created an argument:

Example 2. Turning an expository passage into an argument

> [1]Morro Bay is a town of about 10,000 overlooking the Pacific Ocean. [2] It has only one main street, and [3]it has a few stoplights. [4]Morro Bay is a wonderful place to get away from all the pressures of everyday life.

With this additional debatable statement (statement [4]), we have created an argument, because the other three statements, [1], [2], and [3], attempt to provide the specific factual reasons supporting the conclusion (statement [4]): "Morro Bay is a wonderful place to get away from all the pressures of everyday life."

In other words, most arguments rely heavily on expository passages that insert critical background information about a setting, a character's history, key plot events, or historical or actual contexts. Many of your premises or evidence will come in the form of expository passages. You now know, however, that by only providing key facts, e.g., about a novel you are reading in class, this is not sufficient to establish an argument. You need to use these key expository pieces of information and facts to support what you really want to say to your reader—and what you really want to say is what your thesis articulates.

Explanations

Like expositions, explanations often play a key part in an argument that you eventually make, but in and of themselves, they are not arguments. They are not arguments precisely because, like explanations, nothing is being argued—explanations explain things; they do not prove things. They explain why or how something occurred. Explanations are a bit trickier than expository passages because they often look like arguments. When we see or hear them, it appears "reasoning" is occurring and an argument is being made.

Both explanations and arguments start out with information that is known, a known fact, for example. Explanations, however, explain why or how this known fact occurred, while arguments prove something new based on the known facts. For example,

Example 1. An explanation – explaining known fact

> [1]The Duffer Brothers, authors and directors of the American science-fiction TV series *Stranger Things*, were fascinated with the potential negative impact that other dimensions can have on this world. So [2]in *Stranger Things*, we see that opening up the mysterious portal using Russian technology unleashes the ability of the evil interdimensional Mind Flayer to wreak havoc upon the people of Hawkins, Indiana.

> **Analysis**. In this example, we have two declarative statements, each representing facts—however, of the two facts, statement [2] tells us something we already know. Neither of them is debatable. It says "… *we see* that opening …" (italics mine). Perhaps, in this scenario, I didn't know that the Duffer Brothers were fascinated with interdimensional contact, but based on the language of the passage, I should know about the evil interdimensional Mind Flayer (and if I didn't, I just have to watch *Stranger Things* to "see" it). And of the two sentences, I might imagine statement [2] is the information being proved by statement [1], and, thus, making it an argument. The problem, however, is that an argument infers new information from known facts. And if what I think is the conclusion here, namely statement [2], is already a known fact, then statement [2] by definition cannot be a conclusion, as a conclusion by definition is something to be proven true, or inferred from known facts. If I already know statement [2] to be true, then I don't need prove it, and thus Example 1 cannot be an argument.

Here we have a fact and another fact. No debatable claims. And the relationship between the two facts is one of explanation, where one fact, statement [1] is explaining why "we see" an example of an interdimensional beast wreaking havoc in our world. Why do we see it in *Stranger Things*? Because the Duffer Brothers were fascinated with the negative impact that other realities might have on our world.

Example 2. An argument – proving something new with known fact

> [1]In *Stranger Things*, we see that opening up the mysterious portal using Russian technology unleashes the ability of the evil interdimensional Mind Flayer to wreak havoc upon the people of Hawkins, Indiana. So [2]we can infer that using technology irresponsibly leads to serious and negative consequences in our everyday lives, even possibly opening up interdimensional portals unleashing evil into our world.

Analysis: In this example, we have two declarative statements, where one (statement [1]) represents a fact and another (statement [2]) that represents something new—something to be proven, something debatable. When we read statement [1], we all nod our heads in confirming this piece of information. When we read statement [2], however, we may not all agree—it's debatable. But, statement [2] becomes more likely to be true given the evidence, the known fact, provided in statement [1]. In this sense, we have an argument.

To analyze this a bit further, we can identify the structure of this argument as using a plot line from a science fiction television series to try to convince you that irresponsible use of technology can have devastating consequences, maybe interdimensional consequences. In this sense, the series plot would more likely have any authority if the series was nonfiction, which provided other expert witnesses on the subject of technology and interdimensional realms. Given the series is science fiction, we can all agree that more authoritative evidence would be needed before convincing us of the conclusion. In this case, using a fictional plot may serve as an interesting way to hook your readers into a fascinating topic, but in and of itself it will need other expert scientific research and knowledge to provide authenticity to the plot line.

Explanations, while they may appear to be arguments, are not arguments. Explanations invert the relationship between the evidence and conclusion, and in doing so, we must give each of the two parts different names so that we do not confuse the parts with each other.

Table 5.6. Distinguishing Explanations from Arguments	
Explanations	A set of statements that provide unknown factual statement(s) (called *explanans*) in an attempt to explain a previously known fact (called *explanandum*).
Logical Structure	Known fact X (*explanandum*) because of unknown fact Y (*explanans*).
Arguments	A set of statements that provide accepted and known fact(s) (called *premises*) in an attempt to prove a previously unknown statement (called a *conclusion*).
Logical Structure	Unknown debatable statement C (*conclusion*) because of known fact X (*premise/evidence*).

Where arguments have a structure with two parts, a *premise* and a *conclusion*, an explanation has a structure with two parts, *explanans* and *explandum*. *Explanans* represents the statements that do the explaining, while *explandum* is the fact to be explained.

Indicator Words Identify Premises and Conclusions

Key words often present themselves in arguments, indicating which statements present premises and which point toward the conclusion. Distinguishing between premises and conclusions is one of the most important skills you need to learn when constructing your own argument or reading one in a text. Without this skill, you will never succeed in understanding someone else's argument or knowing when you are making an argument in a paper. This is just a fact.

To this end, we have identified indicator words for both premise and conclusion statements. Consider these indicators words and phrases as serving as signposts in an argument, pointing you toward the premises or the conclusion. However, you do not want to be overly reliant upon indicators because many arguments will lack indicators entirely. In those cases, it is often helpful to put one of these indicator words in front of the statements to help your brain "see" the structure and movement of the argument. In this sense, indicator words can be used to confirm your analysis. If indicators are present, however, you should use them and trust them unless further analysis suggests otherwise.

Overlooking the presence of indicators is one of the most common mistakes students make. To this end, let's identify each set of indicator words, starting with conclusion indicators.

Conclusion Indicators

Conclusion indicators are words and phrases that occur right before a conclusion in an argument. They provide a clue that the statement following the indicator is the conclusion:

Example 1.

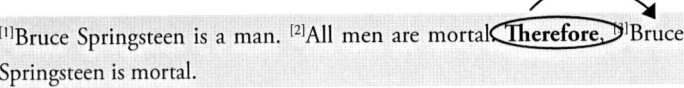

[1]Bruce Springsteen is a man. [2]All men are mortal. **Therefore,** [3]Bruce Springsteen is mortal.

Obviously, when we read this argument, we all recognize that statement [3], "Bruce Springsteen is mortal," is the conclusion, and statements [1] and [2] are premises serving as support for [3]. We know this so easily because of one word, "therefore." "Therefore" is an indicator word, and its presence directs you to the conclusion, which means the other statements [1] and [2] must be operating as the premises. As such, there are other examples of conclusion indicator words:

Table 5.7. A List of Conclusion Indicator Words		
accordingly	hence	therefore
as a result	it follows that	thus
consequently	it must be that	we may conclude
entails that	so	we may infer

Whenever a statement follows one of the indicators, trust that the statement will be operating as a conclusion—again, unless some deeper analysis suggests otherwise. Here are other examples:

Example 2.

> [1]Bruce Springsteen makes good music. Since [2]all people who make good music have won Grammy awards, (it follows that)[3]Springsteen won a Grammy Award.

Example 3.

> [1]No man who would defraud his mother is fit to hold public office. [2]Congressman Sleaze did that (Consequently,)[3]he is not fit for office.

Example 4.

> (We may infer that)[1]Batman is not afraid of the dark because [2]he operates exclusively at night.

Premise Indicators

Just as there are indicator words for conclusions, there are ones for premises. Like conclusion indicators, premise indicators are often placed immediately before the premise; however, in other cases, you may find a conclusion indicator placed between the premise indicator word and the statement to which the premise indicator refers. Also, you may find a premise indicator word slipped in immediately after a conclusion indicator word but before the actual statement representing the conclusion. We will look at all three variations after we list the various premise indicator words. Memorize these:

Table 5.8. A List of Premise Indicator Words		
as	for the reason that	owing to
as indicated by	given that	provided that
because	in that	since
for	inasmuch as	seeing that

The location of indicator words is important—the following are examples of a premise indicator placed immediately before the actual premise statement [examples

1-3] and examples where both premise and conclusion indicators are presented [Example 4-5]:

Example 1. Premise Indicator [1 premise]

[1]Bolivia lost its struggle for access to the sea **because** [2]its army was smaller than those of Chile and Peru.

Example 2. Premise Indicator [2 premises]

[1]There is no life on Venus **since** [2]the temperature is too high **and** [3]the circulating winds are too powerful.

Example 3. Premise Indicator [2 premises]

As indicated by [1]the story in the *Daily Planet* **and** [2]the articles written by Lois Lane, [3]Clark Kent is really Superman.

Example 4. Premise and Conclusion Indicators

premise

[1]Mike Trout hits many homeruns. **Since** [2]all hitters who hit many homeruns get elected into the Homerun Derby, **it must be that** [3]Mike Trout was elected into the Homerun Derby.   *conclusion*

Example 5. Premise and Conclusion Indicators

premise   *conclusion*

[1]The talented neurosurgeon Dr. Stephen Strange was in a tragic car accident. **Therefore, since** [2]he couldn't use his hands, [3]Dr. Strange could only regain his identity by seeking comfort in the secrets of a hidden world of mysticism.

Standardizing an Argument and Its Parts

Finally, just as indicator words help you identify the two parts of any argument, namely the premises and conclusion, another technique we use to unpack the structure of an argument is called standardizing. **Standardizing** is simply a method by which we break down an argument into its parts in order to simplify the argument's structure and put it in outline form. Many times an argument looks quite convincing and elegant when written in prose form; however, after breaking the argument down into its parts, the argument's flaws (or strengths) are easier to spot. Presenting arguments in standard form is a simple way for you to help identify your main point and the evidence you are using to support it.

Example 1. Given argument passage written in prose form

> For millennia, academics, scholars, and leaders of the world have debated certain issues that are specifically important to humanity. One such topic is God's existence. Let's settle this debate now. God is all that is perfect. Since nothing is perfect unless it exists, we conclude that God must exist.

Step One. Number each statement in the entire passage.

> [1]For millennia, academics, scholars, and leaders of the world have debated certain issues that are specifically important to humanity. [2]One such topic is God's existence. [3]Let's settle this debate now. [4]God is all that is perfect. Since [5]nothing is perfect unless it exists, we conclude that [6]God must exist.

You may have noticed that throughout this chapter, every time an argument has been presented, numbers were placed next to each sentence. Numbering your statements, especially your premises and conclusions, saves you a lot of time over the long run. Let me explain: The reason for adding numbers is to show you that each argument has two parts: a conclusion and premises. However, when you write an argumentative essay, which presents your argument over many pages, you will come across many sentences that do not operate as one of those two parts of an argument.

Some of those sentences that do not operate as premises or conclusion include, for example, topic sentences, hooks, transitions, questions, imperatives, etc.; yet they are important for clarity and presentation and possibly for persuasion, often being used for stylistic and/or rhetorical purposes. Numbering helps you easily identify these with the goal of removing them—to reduce any essay or paper down to its simplest elements: 1) statements representing premises and 2) statements representing the conclusion. The other statements or sentences, while important, as we said, do not represent per se your specific evidence and conclusion or main point.

Key point: When numbering each statement, avoid indicator words, placing the number at the beginning of each sentence, not in front of an indicator word. Indicator words act to show direction of support, but they are not part of the evidence or statement themselves. They show the reasoning process, not the actual evidence. So, in Example 1, we see two indicators, one for a premise ("since") and one for a conclusion ("we conclude that").

Step Two. Identify indicator words.

> [1]For millennia, academics, scholars, and leaders of the world have debated certain issues that are specifically important to humanity. [2]One such topic is God's existence. [3]Let's settle this debate now. [4]God is all that is perfect. (Since)[5]nothing is perfect unless it exists, we conclude that[6]God must exist.

Notice that immediately, when taking a quick look at the passage, we see that statement [5] must be the premise and statement [6] must be the conclusion. Whew! That helps us already. And I may not have even read the passage. This helps immeasurably, because, based on this preliminary analysis, the odds are that statement [6] is the main point of the entire passage and thus is the conclusion of the argument that this person is making.

Once numbered, list all the statements in a vertical fashion. Interestingly, while we remove all premise indicator words, we like to include any conclusion indicators and always place the conclusion at the bottom of the vertical list. Fortunately, our example locates the conclusion in the last statement. If the conclusion is not the last statement, expect to make adjustments and move that concluding statement to the bottom. To this end, our standardization of the argument initially looks like this:

Step Three: Standardizing the argument in outline form.

> [1]For millennia, academics, scholars, and leaders of the world have debated certain issues that are specifically important to humanity.
> [2]One such topic is God's existence.
> [3]Let's settle this debate now.
> [4]God is all that is perfect.

[5]Nothing is perfect unless it exists.
Therefore [6]God must exist.

Important: no matter what conclusion indicator is used in prose, when standardizing an argument, we always use "therefore" in lieu of any other conclusion indicator. This keeps our visual presentation simple, consistent, and clear. Thus, we replaced the original conclusion indicator phrase "we conclude that" with the standard "therefore."

Step Four: Remove any statements not acting as premises or conclusions.

[4]God is all that is perfect.
[5]Nothing is perfect unless it exists.
Therefore, [6]**God must exist.**

We removed statements [1], [2], and [3], because they were not essential to the argument—they were important for composition only. They were acting as topic and general sentences designed to introduce the topic and guide you to the next steps in the paper.

Sometimes you may be able to quickly identify which statements are unnecessary and not essential to the argument, and so you can skip this step and jump to step five.

Step Five: Renumber statements and arrange premises in a natural order.

[1]God is all that is perfect.
[2]Nothing is perfect unless it exists.
Therefore, [3]**God must exist.**

Fortunately, the argument we have chosen to standardize already presents its ideas in a logical order, and we did not need to adjust them. Really, in this example, whether we placed statement [2] above under Step Five as statement [1] and vice versa, the logical flow of reasoning would be unaffected. Thus, for us, there was no reason to switch them. Sometimes arguments are not stated in a natural logical order, and you will have to rearrange the statements to create a more logical sense of order.

Name: _____ Section: _____ Date: _____

Part Two

Chapter 5 Workshop

The following section contains a series of ten tasks that, if completed, will help you gain mastery over the content in this chapter. Your instructor will assign some (or all) of them to you as a way to practice the material presented here. Notice that some of them are global and focus on the entirety of the skills laid out in this chapter, while others are more focused and explore only one or two sections of the chapter. Also notice that some are shorter; some are longer; all are designed to flip the classroom and put the power of learning directly into your hands.

Workshop One.

Overview: Summarize all of the major sections and/or bullet points that you find in this chapter.

Each major section or heading should be clearly labeled and should have at least a one-sentence discussion. You might have a dozen or more headings and sentences here. Be thorough and accurate to show that you have read and comprehended this chapter's contents. Avoid the temptation to judge or add anything new (even critical discussion of the content); this is an act of pure summary. Tell your instructor exactly what came in this chapter and in what order.

Workshop Two.

Overview: This workshop has you examine all of the wrong answers from your chapter diagnostic and respond to them.
1. Make a list of each question from the chapter diagnostic that you got wrong.
2. Go through the chapter to look up the rules on each question. For every question you got wrong, do the following:

A. Identify the page number where the rule was found.

B. Discuss what the right answer should have been on the diagnostic test.

C. Discuss how you can avoid this error in future writing and/or tests.

Workshop Three.

<u>Overview</u>: Create at least five short arguments that contain three premises or more supporting a conclusion. The point of this assignment is to directly address what you have learned from the chapter and how it will impact your future ability to generate arguments for your classes. Consider some or all of the following:

A. You can choose from a variety of topics from which to derive your argument, some of which may derive from material you have already read in class or be separate entirely, such as taking a stance on euthanasia, border walls, capitalism, socialism, human nature as good or evil, etc. Consult your instructor as to which topics may be more appropriate for your course.

B. Be sure to standardize your argument and place the conclusion at the bottom after the conclusion indicator "therefore."

C. When you finish all five arguments, write a paragraph explaining your confidence in coming up with supporting evidence for your positions.

D. Your instructor may ask you to complete more or less than five short arguments.

Workshop Four.

<u>Overview</u>: Create a PowerPoint presentation or website that can be shared with your peers and professor that cover the basic elements of an argument.

1. Your PowerPoint or website must cover the essential elements of an argument, including but not limited to premise(s), conclusion, and relationship of support.

2. Your PowerPoint or website must explain the basics of what type of sentences you can use and which ones you cannot as well as give examples of some of each.

3. Your PowerPoint or website must explain why an argument has only one main conclusion, instead of more than one.

Workshop Five.

Overview: Often, teaching something can be the best way to learn it yourself on a deeper level. Therefore, write a quiz for future students that covers the basics of understanding the components of an argument.

1. This quiz should include various styles of questions, including multiple choice, short answer, and true/false. Check with your instructor on specifics.

2. This quiz should be designed to show mastery of the skills from another student at your own level.

3. You must write an answer key starting on a new page after the quiz. This answer key must include the page numbers from *Flipping English* where students can find the answer. It must also include a complete sentence for each quiz question you generated to explain to the instructor why you thought this question targeted a critical component of an argument.

Workshop Six.

Overview: Often, teaching something can be the best way to learn it yourself on a deeper level. Therefore, write a quiz for future students that covers the basics of how to tell the difference between an argument and non-argument.

1. This quiz should include various styles of questions, including multiple choice, short answer, and true/false. Check with your instructor on specifics.

2. This quiz should be designed to show mastery of the skills from another student at your own level.

3. You must write an answer key starting on a new page after the quiz. This answer key must include the page numbers from *Flipping English* where students can find the answer. It must also include a complete sentence for each quiz question you generated to explain to the instructor why you thought this question targeted a critical skill in telling the difference between an argument and non-argument.

Workshop Seven.

Overview: Often, teaching something can be the best way to learn it yourself on a deeper level. Therefore, write a quiz for future students that covers the basics of identifying premises from conclusions.

1. This quiz should include various styles of questions, including multiple choice, short answer, and true/false. Check with your instructor on specifics.
2. This quiz should be designed to show mastery of the skills from another student at your own level.
3. You must write an answer key starting on a new page after the quiz. This answer key must include the page numbers from *Flipping English* where students can find the answer. It must also include a complete sentence for each quiz question you generated to explain to the instructor why you thought this question targeted a critical skill in reasoning.

Workshop Eight.

Overview: Take a previous paper you have written (for this class or for another if you haven't written one yet) and identify the argument and its components by pulling out the premises and conclusion.

1. Make sure to pull out the premises and conclusion.
2. Outline this argument in standard form.
3. Try to identify whether the support you provided was strong or weak and explain why.

Workshop Nine.

Overview: Identifying an author's argument is one of the most important critical thinking skills you can develop. For this exercise, watch the news, take a commercial, read the newspaper, or take a reading from your current course and identify an argument that is being posed to you.

1. Identify a total of four arguments from any of the listed sources or from a source your instructor suggests to use.
2. Write each of the arguments in standard form.
3. Write a few sentences about whether you think the evidence provided is sufficient to support the conclusion. Explain your reasoning.

Workshop Ten.

Overview: What is your take away from this chapter? What did you learn and what questions do you still have?

- Write a short response of several sentences that covers the three main things that you learned from this chapter.
- Write out at least five questions you still have about the chapter. What things would you want to communicate to your instructor? What would you like to see discussed in class or handled with more depth to help you master this chapter's content.
- What is one thing that you have taken away from this chapter and will use on your next writing task? Why is this thing important, and how do you plan to implement it?

CHAPTER 6

How to Use Rhetorical Techniques to Persuade an Audience

In this chapter, you will learn about the following:

Part One: Various Rhetorical Techniques or Modes
1. Description Mode
2. Definition Mode
3. Cause and Effect Mode
4. Division and Classification Mode
5. Example and Illustration Mode
6. Process Analysis Mode
7. Comparison and Contrast Mode
8. Narration Mode
9. Argument and Persuasion Mode
10. Problem and Solution Mode

Part Two: Workshop

Part One

Various Rhetorical Techniques of Modes

André has been assigned a research paper, and he has spent several days in the library gathering and reading sources. He's confident that he has the information he needs in order to construct a good paper. He did some work gathering information on the background of his topic, and he spent a lot of time finding out who the best people in the field were, so he could find their works. André did what his composition instructor showed him to do: he took good notes, gathered statistics and information, found relevant quotations, and even worked up an outline of the order in which to everything. The only problem . . . how does he say it all?

He can't just write paragraph after paragraph of boring statistics and quotations. That would be factual, but nobody would want to read the darned thing. André remembers that some of the sources he read did some interesting things in order to make their points. There was some narrative storytelling in one article, and another one did a good job of explaining all the working parts of an economic system. Another book spent a lot of time comparing two of the experts in the field and discussing how they differed. André knows he needs to do more than just lay out a bunch of boring facts, but he needs help in order to make his paper not just factual, but interesting. He will ultimately write a successful paper because he will learn to use different rhetorical modes in his writing.

Rhetorical Modes

Rhetoric is the art of effective and persuasive writing or speaking. In a communications class, studying rhetorical strategies may include examining verbal and nonverbal cues, audience reactions, and different communications environments to make effective presentations. In composition classes, however, rhetoric emphasizes techniques used in written work. These techniques are called rhetorical modes or rhetorical strategies.

Rhetorical modes are different strategies or types of writing you can employ to make your writing more interesting and effective. Formally, these are usually divided into the following categories: *description, definition, cause and effect, division and classification, illustration, process analysis, comparison and contrast, narration, argument and persuasion,* and *problem and solution.* You may use some of them every day without even realizing it when you talk to people.

For example, if someone asks you how your bus ride was, you'll use the rhetorical mode called description to give sensory details of the trip. Similarly, suppose you invited friends over for lunch, and they were blown away by your split pea soup, so you wrote down the recipe for them. In breaking down each step of the recipe, you engage in process analysis. This chapter focuses on several of these rhetorical modes, shows examples of how to use them in your papers, and provides writing tools you can put into your tool chest and use to craft the best papers you can.

One final thing to consider before looking at the individual rhetorical modes is the frequency, length, and variations of their use. In other words, some professors may ask you to write an essay that uses one and only one of these modes for the whole composition. It is not uncommon to write a paper that is solely argumentative, one that is solely illustrative, or one that is solely cause and effect, for example, in a science class. However, you are more likely to encounter paper prompts that don't stipulate which rhetorical techniques to use. This is why some professors call them paragraph patterns. You can write one body paragraph which focuses on definition, then move on to an example, and then move on to argument and persuasion. If you are writing a paper that is basically argumentative, you might repeat this pattern or add other patterns as appropriate, such as cause and effect and comparison and contrast. Use them as you see fit and toggle between them to be the most effective writer you can.

For each of the rhetorical modes discussed in the following pages, we include a short writing sample to show you how they would look if used in a paper that was a mix of different rhetorical techniques. They are all on a paper that covers the topic of poverty in America. Hopefully, you can see how each different rhetorical mode could be used to support a paper's thesis.

1. Description

What It Is

We all describe things on a daily basis. We might describe how a friend's car looked after a fender bender, what a slice of pizza tastes like, how the house smelled after you burned your microwave dinner, or how a funny meme you saw on social media made you laugh. To successfully use description, you want to appeal to the senses of your readers: explore the sight, sound, feel, smell, touch, and taste of the thing being described.

When to Use It

This type of writing won't come to play much in a research-based paper, but as a rhetorical tool, description is powerful and used to show things vividly to your readers. You can describe, for example, a) the materials needed for a project in your art class, b) the equipment you will use in a physical education class, c) the results of a science experiment involving mixing different chemicals together, or d) any number of other types of things or events. In literature classes, describing a scenario, event, or character as you see it plays a critical role.

When professors want you to avoid any personal anecdotes or narratives in research writing, description can play a paramount role by simply focusing your writing on providing sensory input on the scene or items you are discussing. Do this and you can avoid talking about yourself. For example, if you were asked to write an essay that critiqued some element of your college campus, you would rely heavily on description to avoid a simple narration of a sequence of events. Instead, you could objectively and accurately describe the litter in the trashcan and do so without giving a narrative of how disgusted you personally were.

TABLE 6.1. Sample of the Description Rhetorical Mode

Sample of Description Mode

The following is a sample paragraph written for a paper on the topic of poverty in America that uses the description rhetorical mode. Note the words in bold that add to the sensory description of the passage.

*When it comes to poverty in America, one of the people who it affects the most is the typical K-12 student, both physically and psychologically. These students can be **seen** in the hall of their schools, often **showing** a lack of confidence. **Their eyes may not meet the eyes** of their colleagues as they walk down the halls wearing their **second hand shoes** they got from older siblings. Their backpack is blazoned with **images** of a cartoon character who was popular several years ago, and the **images** are a contrast with those of the students who can afford newer, currently fashionable clothing. Since they don't have the money for haircuts, they have **hair that is haphazard**, cut by a mother or a father at home. When they **talk**, they may be **quiet**, embarrassed to hear their own voices, and when they pass people in the hall, they may even emit the distinct **smell of body odor** or **poorly washed clothing** since they might live in a car or a shelter where laundry facilities and basic showers are absent.*

2. Definition

What It Is

In its most formal sense, you may think of the rhetorical mode of definition as being something simple—you break out a dictionary to look up what a word means or simply ask your phone, and Google churns out a simple definition. While this is helpful for you to understand a single word, the rhetorical mode of definition is more complex. Instead of your defining a single word in your essay (something you seldom need to do since your instructors are perfectly capable of looking up any vocabulary words they don't know), you may be defining a complicated concept. If you are writing a paper about poverty, you may want to define what *you* mean by poverty, for example. Poverty in the United States is radically different than that in a third world country, and poverty is radically different in New York City than in a small farming town. Giving a definition is crucial to get your readers to be on the same page with you and understand your version of the concept you are presenting.

When to Use It

You will want to use definition to appeal to a layperson with lingo that is specialized in your discipline, such as clarifying a tricky biological term you learned in an advanced anatomy class. In a philosophy class, you may be asked to give your own personal definition of something (say, a soul or a mind or what love is) since it will vary from those of other people in the room—your definition is important to establish before you can theorize about it. In a cultural anthropology class, you may be asked to define your version of a winter holiday to people in the class who celebrate a different one (or the same one in a different way).

You may rely heavily on definition in a writing project that requires you do a lot of research on a complex subject. If you are discussing Artificial Intelligence (AI) for a general audience, you may need to define different types of AI, such as Broad AI, Strong AI, Weak AI, AI+, and other distinctions that the experts in the field make. (Note that doing enough of this can lead to a different rhetorical mode called division and classification, discussed later in the chapter.) Without defining them in your paper, your audience will not see a meaningful distinction between things with very similar names.

TABLE 6.2. Sample of the Definition Rhetorical Mode

Sample of Definition Mode

The following is a sample paragraph written for a paper on the topic of poverty in America that uses the definition rhetorical mode. Note that the paragraph begins with a simple definition of the term and then goes into how the term varies by family size and even location.

TABLE 6.2 *continued*

Before discussing the impact of poverty on American children, it is important to define what is meant by poverty. At the most basic level, poverty simply means that someone is extremely poor. However, the definition gets more tricky than this. For example, several government groups define poverty differently based on how many people are in a family or how many children they have. This definition usually involves a set amount of money per year (say, less than $25,000 for a family of four), but even this changes based on the state in which someone lives. Regardless of the amount of income or what one considers "extremely poor," for the purposes of this discussion, poverty will be defined as not having enough money to guarantee the basic necessities of life, such as food, shelter, water, and medicine, regardless of locale.

3. Cause/Effect

What It Is

Cause and effect is one of the hallmarks of science, and it is also one of the basic levels of cognition for a young child. If you have a child or a little brother or sister, you may find yourself growing tired of answering an endless stream of questions. Why is the ocean blue? Why does the dog dig a nest on the blanket? Why do things fall when you drop them? Why did I get burned by touching the stove? These questions are the result of a young mind grappling with the concept of cause and effect.

The cause and effect mode provides a way to look at the world and start to understand patterns that affect behaviors. It is the ability to find connections between things that may not seem related and to tie them together in a logical and meaningful way. While using the cause and effect mode in your writing, you won't want to spend a lot of time in your writing on basic notions of cause and effect (such as gravity makes things fall to the ground, in response to the earlier child's question). Instead, you'll save it for complex issues. Why is America so interested in the politics of the Middle East? Or you may ask yourself some hard questions about your own life: Why am I not doing so well in my math class? Why is my girlfriend or boyfriend leaving me? What am I doing wrong, so I know not to do it again?

When to Use It

In an economics class, you may be asked to explore why Amazon.com has become the largest retailer on the globe, which would require a discussion of the cause of its success and additionally an examination of the effect Amazon has had on brick and mortar retailers. In a literature class, you may have to wrestle with questions like why Hamlet delayed before getting his revenge. In this scenario, the effect would in fact be Hamlet's delay, but theories about the cause could involve cowardice, madness, lack of certainty about whether the Ghost really is his father (not a malevolent spirit), and even ethical scrupulousness against murder. A history class would require you to use this rhetorical mode the most—e.g., what was the cause of the Civil War? What finally got American involved in World War Two? Why did Spain and Britain war against each other for so long? An effect, such as the Civil War, will have dozens of complex causes, and your job as a writer would be to make these connections as a way to clarify the history of this unfortunate war.

TABLE 6.3. Sample of the Cause and Effect Rhetorical Mode

Sample of Cause and Effect Mode

The following is a sample paragraph written for a paper on the topic of poverty in America that uses the cause/effect rhetorical mode. You will note that while the terms cause and effect are seldom used in this sample, there are plenty of examples of the cause (hunger) leading to the effect (inability to concentrate).

Doing well in school and being able to maintain mental focus is contingent upon having plenty of sleep and good nutrition; in fact, students who lack one of these will not learn as much because they will not be able to concentrate as well as students who do have these things. This is one of many unfortunate truths about schoolchildren living below the poverty line—hunger equals bad grades. When students wake up to

TABLE 6.3 *continued*

nothing of any nutritive value in their cupboard and go to school hungry, waiting for their state-paid free lunch program at midday, they will not do well in any of their morning classes. This lack of breakfast will cause them to be distracted and even have spikes and crashes in blood sugar, making them feel ill throughout the morning. What all of this means is that the impoverished, hungry students will have lower grades and lower test scores than their well-fed counterparts. Being a bad student may simply be the effect of poor nutrition, not a lack of capability or intelligence.

4. Division/Classification

What It Is

Division and classification are two opposite skills. With division, you look at one large object or group and then break it down into different types or categories. With classification, you do the inverse—you take seemingly unrelated items but put them together in one class of thing. For example, with division, let's take a class of police officers: we realize that they are one group, but you can divide them into several types, such as "beat cops," detectives, highway patrol officers, undercover police officers, vice officers, etc. With classification, however, you take things and put them in the same "class" as each other. You can do this even though they may represent radically different types of items. For example, a list of your favorite things might include a Corvette, an Xbox, a bean burrito at Chipotle, and a pair of Chuck Taylor's sneakers. These items have nothing in common on the surface, but you classify them as your favorite things, and now they belong together.

When to Use It

In writing, there are many reasons to use division or classification. If you are writing an essay for a biology class, you may need to explore the animal kingdoms and divide and classify animals based on certain traits. In an English class, you might have to classify various types of authors (poets, playwrights, novelists, essayists, journalists) based on a certain ethnicity, period of time, or style. In a communications class, you may need to look at different types of speeches and divide them into impromptu, memorized, manuscript speeches, and so forth.

TABLE 6.4. Sample of the Division and Classification Rhetorical Mode
Sample of Division and Classification Mode
The following is a sample paragraph written for a paper on the topic of poverty in America that uses the division rhetorical mode. Note that the different groups of the division are in bold.
*There are many reasons why Americans may become poor and fall below the poverty line, and these reasons are as varied as the people they affect. The first type is people losing their jobs due to a **change in the business climate**; for example, autoworkers may find themselves unemployed due to automation or foreign outsourcing and suddenly find themselves in poverty. A second type is being unable to work due to **mental illness**. It may be that some people's mental condition has gotten worse to the point that they can no longer work, or a sudden injury or trauma may cause them to be unable to find sustainable employment. Yet another type is **addiction to drugs**. At first, money may be hard to keep because of the cost of maintaining the addiction, but, eventually, the impact of the drug on the mind, body, and even physical appearance can keep someone from finding meaningful employment and ultimately fall below the poverty line.*

5. Example and Illustration

What It Is

Examples and illustrations are provided when you use evidence of some sort to explain, clarify, or justify a point. This can come in the form of a formal, outside voice, such as when you use evidence like a quotation, a date, or a statistic to help prove the point you are making. It can also come from a more personal example or even data you yourself have gathered. As a rhetorical mode, this is one of the most important for writing a research paper, since your overall thesis will need to be supported by the experts you have researched; their information provides the illustrations and examples that make your arguments hold up to examination.

When to Use It

This mode is used in almost any discipline, especially when you are tasked with writing a research paper instead of a personal essay (though there are plenty of reasons to use it in a personal essay, as well). You will use it, of course, in your standard research paper for the transfer/freshman level English class at your college. You might find yourself using it in a paper for a statistics class since each statistic you gather will be one specific example that you will use to craft a bigger picture. You can use it in an engineering class to explain specific times a design has failed. This mode will be used in the most casual of papers to the most scholarly, so it is worth investigating and mastering.

TABLE 6.5. Sample of the Example and Illustration Rhetorical Mode

Sample of Example and Illustration Mode

The following is a sample paragraph written for a paper on the topic of poverty in America that uses the example and illustration rhetorical mode. The specific examples are listed in bold; note that after the examples, the author then takes time to discuss what the examples prove. That's perhaps the most important part of an example: not just providing it, but critically examining it.

*Even **welfare and food stamps** have traditionally failed to help those who live below the poverty line in America. This is in fact something that Kathryn J. Eden (professor of sociology and public health at Johns Hopkins) and H. Luke Shaefer (professor at the University of Michigan School of Social Work) tackle in their book about living poor in America called $2.00 A Day. In it, **they claim of welfare***

TABLE 6.5 *continued*
that in 1996, "a family of three couldn't live solely on the $360 or so the program provided on average. Just prior to welfare reform, it took roughly $875 to meet such a family's monthly expenses. But families could generally get only about three-fifths of that amount" (97). With this, Eden and Shaefer prove *that the government's allotment of food stamps and cash welfare is woefully short of what someone needs to survive.* They show this *$500 gap between income and need; indeed, that money is where things like healthy food, warm clothes, and medicine would come from, leaving these poor people with a budget of only $2.00 a day to survive.* Clearly, that is not enough, and something better can be done by the government to help diminish poverty in the United States.

6. Process Analysis

What It Is

Process analysis is a rhetorical mode you use almost every day. You get instructions at your job; you get directions for a homework assignment at school; you may even go online for a video game walkthrough or a quick recipe to watch being made on YouTube. The need to break down a process into individual steps that can be followed is a critical skill. In college writing, you will need to communicate the steps of a process as clearly as possible in order to let your readers know the specific details of the individual tasks that make up an overall activity. A successful process analysis typically provides all the steps in the order they are accomplished, from the start of the process until it is completed.

When to Use It

Process analysis will be used regularly in any of the sciences; you will need to follow the process of others who did an experiment before you, or you will need to detail the steps of your own experiment, so it can be duplicated in the future by your peers. If you are in a nutrition class, and you have been asked to provide a healthy recipe, this is a chance for process analysis. You will break down each step, measurement, type of cut, temperature, and ingredient in order for someone else to create the same dish as you. In computer science, you might have to write a computer code that others can use, and writing it out using process analysis will allow others to create the same program on their computers later.

TABLE 6.6. Sample of the Process Analysis Rhetorical Mode
Sample of Process Analysis Mode
The following is a sample paragraph written for a paper on the topic of poverty in America that uses the process analysis rhetorical mode. More specifically, this is from a section of the paper that covers some solutions of how to be poor and still eat good food.
One of the challenges of being poor is learning how to eat food that is inexpensive, nutritious, and also tastes good—in this case, a ramped up version of ramen noodles. Ramen noodles are a staple for all college students and most people struggling with poverty because they can typically be bought several packets per dollar. However, they need to have some work done on them in order to be more healthy and still inexpensive. The first task is to gather ingredients, ideally at a dollar store. Get as many packets of ramen as possible for a dollar and then also get some other ingredients; in this case, get mushrooms, green onions, and tofu. Take them home, add a quarter of the package of mushrooms, a quarter of the onion, and a quarter of the tofu to water along with the spice packet of one pack of ramen. Boil until the mushrooms are close to tender and then add the noodles. Cook until the desired texture is reached, and then dig in. Instead of a high sodium, low nutrition meal, you've added protein, minerals, and fiber with the other ingredients, and, for the price of four dollars, you have purchased enough for four or five meals. That is a lot cheaper than fast food, and meals like this can save money to help people get back on their feet financially..

7. Narration

What It Is

Narration is a rhetorical mode that tells a story or creates what we call a narrative. When you read a novel, a short story, or even a comic book, you are encountering a narrative. Some narratives are fictional, and others are biographical or personal anecdotes. While more advanced classes and more formal professors will not want narrative in their essays since they are a more casual mode of writing, there is still a place for it in academic writing. You might open a strong paper's introduction with a personal anecdote about yourself that shows in a palpable way why you are interested in the subject matter. You might also use it to give background on a person you are writing about—for example, a short paragraph describing Martin Luther King, Jr.'s childhood and education may be a good lead up to more formal discussion of his work a civil rights leader.

When to Use It

First off, be advised that you should always check with your instructor before you use too much narration (especially something you make up) in your essay. It is a strong rhetorical mode, but it dips into the realm of being quite informal at times, so some people may not like its use in a standard college essay. That being said, in a film-studies class in which you are exploring a particular piece of cinema, narration may come to play as a type of summary of a crucial part of a story line. In a history class, you may provide a formal bit of narration to explain how and why King Henry VIII established the Church of England (mainly because Pope Clement VII refused to grant him annulment of his marriage to Catherine of Aragon). In a philosophy paper, you may need to use narration to tell a story that will set up a particular philosophical issue that you then do a deep, critical exploration of.

TABLE 6.7. Sample of the Narration Rhetorical Mode

Sample of Narration Mode

The following is a sample paragraph written for a paper on the topic of poverty in America that uses the narration rhetorical mode.

This is a tale of two students. They are both college students who attend the same school and even take the same classes, but one is homeless, and the other is not. Albert is homeless and attends the same introduction to philosophy class as Ernest. Their typical Mondays look very different. Albert wakes up at 5:00 in the crowded bustle of the homeless shelter, takes a cold shower, and sets out for the 6:00 bus after a meager shelter breakfast. He does his best to finish his reading on the ride to school since he works odd jobs in the evenings trying to get enough money to make it through the week. When he gets to class, he is given a reading quiz on Kierkegaard, and it blows him away. He is not ready and did not properly digest the material due to his work schedule and the hectic nature of bus transfers. Ernest's Monday is different. He sleeps in until 7:45, takes a hot shower, and eats a hearty meal of hash browns and eggs. He leaves home at 8:30, grabs a mocha at Starbucks, and gets to campus by 8:50. He is well prepared since he was able to finish his Kierkegaard last night after dinner and before some Netflix. He takes the quiz, aces it, and finishes his mocha.

8. Comparison and Contrast

What It Is

Comparison and contrast are the opposite of each other, but both are useful, either on their own or in concert together. Comparison is the act of taking different things and discussing ways in which they are similar. Contrast is the act of taking different things and pointing out what distinguishes each from the other. You have probably encountered in-class essay questions with this term in the prompt before, such as the following: "Compare and contrast the characters of Hamlet and Ophelia in regards to how they feel about each other" or "Compare and contrast President Lincoln with President Obama." Whether you use these two techniques together or apart, they are helpful modes of discourse to build a paragraph with.

When to Use It

You will often use comparison and contrast in midterms or final exams in virtually all disciplines when you have to write an essay or short answer response. (When you read a prompt for such a test, pay close attention to whether it says compare, it says contrast, or it says compare and contrast because each of these will require a rather different type of response). In literature classes, you will use this mode frequently to compare and/or contrast everything from characters to death scenes to authors to entire novels. In a nursing class, you may compare and contrast the treatments of different types of illness—it is important to know how the treatments are alike and how they differ, such as in cost, side effects, and efficacy of treatment.

TABLE 6.8. Sample of the Comparison and Contrast Rhetorical Mode

Sample of Comparison and Contrast Mode

The following is a sample paragraph written for a paper on the topic of poverty in America that uses the comparison and contrast rhetorical mode. Note that it is the paragraph immediately following the sample paragraph in the narrative sample above. Also note that the first half of the paragraph is a comparison, and the second half shows contrast.

Both Ernest and Albert had one goal that Monday morning, and that was to do well on their reading quiz. Though they don't really know each other, and they live far across town from each other, they both have more in common than one would think. They both want to excel in the class, both want to transfer to a major university, and both put all their attention into success. Aside from these similarities, the differences between them are stark. Albert gets less sleep, is less prepared, and spends hours a day getting to campus by bus. Ernest gets plenty of sleep, is very well prepared, and takes a short ride to campus, complete with a stop at Starbucks. The contrast in their lives shows a baseline unfairness in their situations, as well as a baseline difficulty in the daily life of people dealing with poverty and homelessness in America.

9. Argument and Persuasion

What It Is

You may typically think of an argument as being when you and someone else exchange heated words, often getting mad at each other or even screaming and using choice swear words. Argumentation in writing is a totally different beast. In college classes, sciences, and other disciplines, Argumentation means the process of reasoning systematically in support of an idea, theory, or action. Technically, argument and persuasion are related but not identical. To distinguish between them, you need to ask the following question: "Is the writer primarily presenting evidence to prove something or primarily trying to convince you of something?" By answering that question, you are able to identify the author's primary purpose in writing the piece. A writer's purpose in creating a purely argumentative essay is not to convince you to adopt his or her opinion about something, but rather to present strong evidence for readers to accept acknowledge the truth of the evidence and the strength and validity of the argument. However, writers rarely present arguments without also trying to persuade people of something, such as a course of action, and people whose primary goal is to get people to accept their point of view know that they should present actual evidence to help to sway them. This is why the two concepts are typically linked together in one rhetorical mode. However, in an economics class, for example, your professor may want you to stick entirely to argumentation and not bring in persuasive devices; you may be asked simply to provide a strong summary of your evidence and finish with a statement emphasizing the strength and validity of your claim.

When to Use It

Argumentation is a common rhetorical mode for research papers; indeed, if your research paper requires an argumentative thesis, think of argument and persuasion as an "umbrella rhetorical device" that could work along with other rhetorical modes. You will almost certainly use argument and persuasion in a philosophy or

English class. If you are in a religious studies class, you may have to argue how a certain historical event or series of events led to a the adoption of behaviors now practiced by people in that religion. In an art class, you may have to argue that one artist set the stage for a whole movement of art that followed.

TABLE 6.9. Sample of the Argument and Persuasion Rhetorical Mode

Sample of Argumentation and Persuasion Mode

The following is a sample paragraph written for a paper on the topic of poverty in America that uses the argument and persuasion rhetorical mode. Note that there are several bits of evidence that build up in this paragraph until the final sentence that drives the argument home.

Even though many people are tempted to give money to the poor and homeless that sit on street corners asking for spare change, this is not the best way to help those who are truly needy. Indeed, the first problem with those who are begging for money is that many of them don't actually need the money. The amount of money some pull in on a busy street corner is better than a minimum wage job. Second, those with mental health issues may not be able to actually ask for money, or if they did, their illness may prevent them from actually getting any. Third, the people who ask for money may very well be using it for drugs or alcohol, not basic needs like food, water, and shelter; a kind donation may end up supporting a drug habit and making the person's lot in life worse, not better. This doesn't mean you shouldn't consider giving money to the homeless and impoverished. However, you should give to a homeless shelter. The shelter organizes the donations in a type of triage that will see more go to the most needy. It will also make sure that the money goes to food and shelter and even classes on how to apply for jobs or improve the lives of the residents. It is, quite simply, the only sure way to help people with your donation. Do not give on street corners.

10. Problem/Solution

What It Is

Another rhetorical mode is one in which you present a problem in order to provide a solution that is satisfactory. Many professors and rhetoricians classify this as a subtype of argument and persuasion, but we thought that presenting distinguishing characteristics would he helpful. In one paragraph, you may use this rhetorical mode to set up a problem (say, the suffering and death of stray cats near a freeway) and give a solution (a spay and neuter program that targets that neighborhood). Of course, you can scale this up and use the same exact problem and solution as the topic of an entire essay, but one in which you give many more examples than those found in a single paragraph. The problem and solution format is an offshoot of the argument and rhetorical mode because at the heart of it, this is suggesting a solution (we need more spay and neutering, for example) after making an argument that there is, indeed, a problem. It's just that the problem may be a significant portion of the paper before you get around to the solution, which could be presented in a relatively shorter section.

When to Use It

If you were in a nutrition class, you may discuss the problem of a fast food diet and then propose a solution of a tax on fast food to fund education for parents. In a finance class, you may discuss the problem that local businesses face against the juggernaut that is Amazon.com, only to propose a solution of a day that celebrates local shops in your town to get people to support your community. In a communications class, this format may be a good one to base a speech on, regardless of the subject.

TABLE 6.10. Sample of the Problem and Solution Rhetorical Mode

Sample of Problem and Solution Mode

The following is a sample paragraph written for a paper on the topic of poverty in America that uses the problem and solution rhetorical mode.

*While college students who live far below the poverty level face many **problems** that keep them from having the same chance of success as financially stable college students, one **solution** is for colleges to adopt global tuition fees that would help support programs for the very poor. Many people look back on their college days as some of the funniest of their lives, but a great many also laugh through horror stories of being the typical poor college students. There are a number of college students who are significantly poorer than the average student, however, and they face hard disadvantages compared to these other students. These impoverished students have difficulty finding transportation, making them miss class or arrive late. They also face a caloric disadvantage and are often forced to go hungry all day, unable to even afford the cheapest of meals. Poor students may not even have basics like pens and paper, much less ridiculously expensive college textbooks. One way to help **solve** this **problem** is to do what some colleges have done and add a small fee of a couple of dollars per student per semester to help. This money goes to buy book vouchers, provide food from donation pantries, subsidize meals from the school cafeteria or commons, and even pay for monthly bus passes. If everyone was willing to give the price of a cup of coffee, it could help the very poorest of us actually be able to afford a cup of coffee.*

Name: _____ Section: _____ Date: _____

Part Two

Chapter 6 Workshop

The following section contains a series of ten tasks that, if completed, will help you gain mastery over the content in this chapter. Your instructor will assign some (or all) of them to you as a way to practice the material presented here. Notice that some of them are global and focus on the entirety of the skills laid out in this chapter, while others are more focused and explore only one or two sections of the chapter. Also notice that some are shorter; some are longer; all are designed to flip the classroom and put the power of learning directly into your hands.

Workshop One.

Overview: Summarize all of the major sections and/or bullet points that you find in this chapter.

Each major section or heading should be clearly labeled and should have at least a one-sentence discussion. You might have a dozen or more headings and sentences here. Be thorough and accurate to show that you have read and comprehended this chapter's contents. Avoid the temptation to judge or add anything new (even critical discussion of the content); this is an act of pure summary. Tell your instructor exactly what came in this chapter and in what order.

Workshop Two.

Overview: This workshop has you examine all of the wrong answers from your chapter diagnostic and respond to them.

1. Make a list of each question from the chapter diagnostic that you got wrong.

2. Go through the chapter to look up the rules on each question. For every question you got wrong, do the following:
   a. Identify the page number where the rule was found.
   b. Discuss what the right answer should have been on the diagnostic test.
   c. Discuss how you can avoid this error in future writing and/or tests.

Workshop Three.

Overview: Write a short, personal essay explaining the content of this chapter. The point of this essay is to directly address what you have learned from the chapter and how it will impact your future academic writing. Consider some or all of the following:

   A. What writing element(s) were new to you?
   B. How can you incorporate some of the elements into your own writing in the future?
   C. What writing element(s) did you already know about. Did you already use them in your writing, or did you ignore them for some reason? If so, what was the reason?
   D. If appropriate, use some of the techniques and language from the actual chapter in your paper to help illustrate mastery.
   E. Your instructor will provide you with more details such as the length of the piece, if you should use quotations from the chapter, if personal anecdotes and casual language are allowed, etc.

Workshop Four.

Overview: Practice writing a narrative of someone famous.
   1. Identify someone famous whom you could write about. This could be someone from history (good practice for a history class) or someone who is alive today, such as a musician, author, or politician. Learn about his or her life through some research online.
   2. Craft a sample piece of writing of at least two paragraphs using the narrative rhetorical mode. Don't just give a summary of major points

about this person's life, however. Tell it as a story that will engage the audience, so that you can practice narrative.

3. At the end of the second paragraph, leave the narrative mode and switch to a more formal academic mode and provide some critical thought. Why was this story important? What point are you making with this narrative? How did this person have an impact on the world?

Workshop Five.

Overview: Write a short essay that practices two different rhetorical modes.

1. Agree upon a topic with your instructor, and write a short essay.
2. This essay must use two of the different rhetorical modes discussed in this chapter.
3. When you are finished with the essay, add one more short piece of writing in which you discuss the two rhetorical modes you used. First, why did you chose these out of all of them you have to select from? Second, which one do you think worked out better and why?
4. Check with your instructor for details such as word count, format, etc. for the essay.

Workshop Six.

Overview: Find two articles or other pieces of writing that use different rhetorical modes to discuss the same topic and think critically about which one worked better.

1. Go online and find two pieces of writing about the same topic (or find some in a local newspaper or even a class anthology). Make sure they each use a different rhetorical technique Alternatively, you can find one longer piece that uses multiple rhetorical modes and discuss the difference within the one piece.
2. In a couple of sentences, discuss which rhetorical mode each of these pieces used.
3. Write a response of at least a full paragraph which critically examines the two pieces. Which rhetorical mode worked best? Was one radically

better or radically worse? Which would you select in the future? Why do you think the author may have chosen the mode he or she chose?

Workshop Seven.

<u>Overview</u>: Complete a process analysis of something you know how to do.

1. Consider something you are good at doing. This could be working on a car, playing a video game walkthrough, performing a skateboarding trick, painting nails, following or even creating a recipe, even potty training a dog.

2. Now write directions for other people to follow if they were attempting the do the thing you are good at. These directions should be at least two paragraphs long, and they will explore the process analysis rhetorical mode.

Workshop Eight.

<u>Overview</u>: Complete a short piece of writing using the rhetorical mode of description by describing something on your campus.

1. Take a tour of your college campus and find something there that is interesting enough to describe. It could be an art installation, a cool piece of architecture, a dirty trashcan, the stadium when it is empty (or full), even the cafeteria or commons.

2. Write a piece that is several paragraphs long that describes the thing you selected. You should focus on at least three different senses, and you should devote a full paragraph to each sense.

3. In your piece of writing, don't ever name the actual thing you are describing; simply let the sensory description do the work for you.

4. Before turning this piece in to your instructor, give it to someone else familiar with your campus and see if he or she can identify the thing you are describing and jot down a response at the bottom of the paper.

Workshop Nine.

<u>Overview</u>: Visit and revise a previous essay you have written by adding at least one of the rhetorical modes above that you didn't use in the first draft.

1. Select an essay or paper you have written previously. Reread it.
2. First, write out a list that says exactly which rhetorical modes you have used so far in the paper. It is fine if it is all one mode so far. In this list, number each paragraph of the original and identify which mode each paragraph uses.
3. Find a rhetorical mode you didn't use the first time, and write an additional paragraph (or more) using this mode. It should seamlessly blend into the old paper and support your thesis, just as all the other body paragraphs do.

Workshop Ten.

Overview: What is your take away from this chapter? What did you learn and what questions do you still have?

1. Write a short response of several sentences that covers the three main things that you learned from this chapter.
2. Write out at least five questions you still have about the chapter. What things would you want to communicate to your instructor? What would you like to see discussed in class or handled with more depth to help you master this chapter's content.
3. What is one thing that you have taken away from this chapter and will use on your next writing task? Why is this thing important, and how do you plan to implement it?

CHAPTER 7

How to Learn and
Use College-Level Vocabulary

In this chapter, you'll find the following sections:

Part One: Build a College-Level Vocabulary
1. Seven Tips for Expanding Your Vocabulary
2. The Academic Word List
3. Thirty-Five Key AWL Definitions
4. Terms That Are Commonly Confused

Part Two: Workshop

Part One

Building a College-Level Vocabulary

Xochitl has always been proud of her vocabulary. She was above average in her K-12 classes whenever she and the other students were given vocabulary quizzes, and she never had any trouble at all understanding the material in her textbooks. She enjoyed reading for fun when she was a child, but once she was in high school, she didn't do a lot of outside reading since she

> *Research indicates that it could take as many as seventeen exposures for a person to learn a new word, and using the word yourself counts as exposure.*

got very involved in sports and some campus clubs. She only had time for the assigned readings in her classes. Still, she didn't have any trouble understanding what she needed to.

When she enrolled in college, she was confident that reading college textbooks would be just as easy for her as reading her high school textbooks had been. She was in for an embarrassing surprise. She found herself really struggling while reading the textbooks in her first semester of college classes. She tried guessing words by their context, like she had been taught to do in grammar school, but it just didn't work well. She lost points on tests and writing assignments when it turned out that she had frequently guessed wrong. On top of that, she discovered that some words that she had thought she was using grammatically and correctly in her high school assignments were words that she wasn't using correctly at all. Her high school teachers apparently hadn't thought it was important to let her know—or maybe they just didn't have the time.

Xoxhitl's experience with baffling vocabulary is by no means unusual. However, developing college-level vocabulary need not be difficult or painful. Building your vocabulary is one of the best ways to improve the power of your reading and writing and to make any writing task that much easier, as you will have a greater and more specific number of terms in your repertoire to pull from every time. This chapter is designed to help you develop the vocabulary that you need to become an accomplished wordsmith.

1. Seven Tips for Expanding Your Vocabulary

1. **Write Down New Words.** Keep a notebook, or a section of a notebook, or a list on your computer, tablet, or phone where you can write down unfamiliar words. If you don't encounter new words every day in your college reading, try to diversify your reading. To improve your vocabulary quickly, make an effort to learn at least one new word a day. You can scan the Academic Word List (AWL) later in the chapter for a list of 570 words considered crucial for college and university students.

2. **Look up Words You Don't Know.** Students often just gloss over words they don't know or assume they can figure them out in context. The latter practice worked a lot better in grade school than it will in college, where there is a good chance that what you try to infer from context isn't what the word means at all. Take the time to look new words up, and if you don't have the time right then, write them down to look up later.

3. **Use New Words.** Try to use a word right after you learn it. You can even make a game out of using new words. Every day, try to use a new word in a conversation, a journal entry, an assignment, or a text or email. Research indicates that it could take as many as seventeen exposures for a person to learn a new word, and using the word yourself counts as exposure. We all have two types of vocabulary: *comprehensive vocabulary*, which is composed of the words we understand, and *expressive vocabulary*, the words we use to express ourselves. People's receptive vocabularies are much larger than their comprehensive vocabularies. Moving words from your comprehensive, but passive, vocabulary to your active, expressive vocabulary improves your writing skills tremendously.

4. **Learn Word Roots, Prefixes, and Suffixes.** Most words in English are built from a common root, prefix, and suffix, usually with an origin in the Greek or Latin language. Once you learn roots, prefixes, and suffixes, you'll be better able to understand and remember more words that use the same root. Be careful, though. Greek and Latin words with the same sounds but different meanings are found in many English words. For example, the Greek word "homos" means "same." It is found in words like "homogeneous," which means "consisting of parts all of the same kind." The Latin word "homo" means "man," and it is used in terms like "homo sapiens," which refers to the human species. The Greek word "anti" means "against," and it is combined with words to indicate opposition, like "anticlimax," which means "a disappointing end to an exciting series of events." The Latin word "ante" means "before," and is found in words like "antecedent," which means "a thing or event that existed before or logically precedes another."

5. **Use a Thesaurus.** Keep a thesaurus handy. As you write, keep a thesaurus handy and use it when you find yourself using a word too often, or using a word that you know doesn't quite convey the right meaning. This will help you better express yourself, and you'll also learn a new word in the process.

6. **Have a Study Buddy.** Studying vocabulary with a friend makes a task that can feel very tedious feel more fun. The two of you can take turns saying the word aloud and having the other person define it. Or you can say the definition out loud and ask for the word.

7. **Sign up at "Word of the Day" Internet Sites**. These sites will send you a new word every day. The *Oxford English Dictionary* is generally regarded as the ultimate reference site for vocabulary. (The print version of the *OED* is twenty volumes long.) The *Merriem-Webster Dictionary* is less expansive, which means it may be even better for college-level students. It also provides audio pronunciation guides. You can choose to receive daily emails or listen to it as a podcast.

2. The Academic Word List

Dr. Averil Coxhead developed the Academic Word List (AWL) as her MA thesis at the School of Linguistics and Applied Language Studies at Victoria University of Wellington, New Zealand. The AWL was created to be used by teachers to help prepare students for college and university level classes and also to be used by students working alone to learn the words they most needed for college and university coursework. There are 570 "headwords," or stem words, namely the part of a word that is common to all its variants. For example, "normal" is a stem word, and "normalize" (verb) and "abnormal" (adjective) are just two examples of its variants. The 570 words are divided into ten sublists, which are ordered with the most frequently used words in sublist one and the least frequently used words in the last sublist. The AWL does not include words that are in the list of the most frequently-used 2000 words of English, nor does it include Latin terms and abbreviations, such as "et al."

In the following lists, we have used **bold font** to identify some of the words most important for students in English classes writing essays and research papers. Test yourself by scanning these lists and seeing which words you know. Do you know the exact meaning, or do you have only a general idea, or is the word totally unfamiliar to you?

Following the sublists, we have defined thirty-five terms that we have identified as especially important for expository and argumentative essays and research papers.

TABLE 7.1. Sublist One: Important Terms

analyze	contract	export	legal	**research**
approach	create	**factor**	**legislate**	respond
area	**data**	finance	major	role
assess	**define**	**formula**	**method**	section
assume	derive	**function**	occur	**sector**
authority	distribute	identify	**percent**	**significant**
available	economy	indicate	period	similar
benefit	environment	individual	policy	**source**
concept	establish	**interpret**	principle	specific
consist	estimate	involve	proceed	**structure**
constitute	evident:	**issue**	**process**	**theory**
context	[**evidence**]	labor	require	vary

TABLE 7.2. Sublist Two: Important Terms

achieve	chapter	construct	**evaluate**	item
acquire	commission	consume	feature	**journal**
administrate	community	credit	final	maintain
affect	**complex**	culture	focus	**normal**
appropriate	compute	design	**impact**	obtain
aspect	**conclude**	distinct	injure	participate
assist	conduct	**element**	institute	perceive
category	**consequent**	equate	invest	positive

TABLE 7.3. Sublist Three: Important Terms

alternative	**deduce**	**justify**	remove	purchase
circumstance	**demonstrate**	layer	scheme	**range**
comment	**document:**	link	sequence	region
compensate	[the verb]	locate	sex	regulate
component	dominate	maximize	shift	**relevant**
consent	emphasis	minor	specify	reside
considerable	ensure	negate	sufficient	**resource**
constant	exclude	**outcome**	task	restrict
constrain	framework	partner	technical	secure
contribute	fund	philosophy	technique	seek
convene	**illustrate**	physical	technology	**site**
coordinate	immigrate	proportion	**valid**	**strategy**
core	**imply**	publish	volume	survey
corporate	initial	react	potential	text
correspond	instance	register	previous	tradition
criteria	interact	rely	**primary**	transfer

TABLE 7.4. Sublist Four: Important Terms

access	confer	hence	occupy	promote
adequate	**contrast**	**hypothesis**	option	regime
annual	cycle	**implement**	output	resolve
apparent	**debate**	implicate	overall	retain
approximate	despite	impose	**parallel**	series
attitude	dimension	**integrate**	**parameter**	**statistic**
attribute	domestic	internal	phase	**status**
civil	emerge	investigate	predict	stress
code	error	job	**principal**	subsequent
commit	ethnic	label	prior	sum
communicate	goal	**mechanism**	professional	summary
concentrate	grant	obvious	project	undertake

TABLE 7.5. Sublist Five: Important Terms

academy	decline	**facilitate**	monitor	revenue
adjust	**discrete**	**fundamental**	network	stable
alter	draft	generate	notion	style
amend	enable	generation	**objective**	substitute
aware	energy	image	orient	sustain
capacity	enforce	**liberal**	perspective	symbol
challenge	entity	license	precise	target
clause	**equivalent**	logic	prime	transit
compound	evolve	margin	psychology	trend
conflict	expand	medical	pursue	version
consult	expose	mental	**ratio**	welfare
contact	external	modify	reject	whereas

TABLE 7.6. Sublist Six: Important Terms

abstract	cooperate	fee	instruct	**presume**
accurate	**discriminate**	flexible	intelligent	**rational**
acknowledge	display	furthermore	**interval**	recover
aggregate	**diverse**	gender	lecture	reveal
allocate	**domain**	ignorant	migrate	**scope**
assign	edit	incentive	minimum	subsidy
attach	**enhance**	incidence	ministry	tape
author	estate	incorporate	motive	trace
bond	exceed	**index**	**neutral**	transform
brief	expert	inhibit	nevertheless	transport
capable	**explicit**	initiate	overseas	underlie
cite	federal	input	precede	utilize

TABLE 7.7. Sublist Seven: Important Terms

adapt	decade	foundation	**media**	somewhat
adult	definite	globe	**mode**	submit
advocate	deny	grade	**paradigm**	successor
aid	**differentiate**	guarantee	**phenomenon**	survive
channel	dispose	**hierarchy**	priority	**thesis**
chemical	dynamic	identical	prohibit	**topic**
classic	eliminate	**ideology**	publication	transmit
comprehensive	**empirical**	**infer**	quote	**ultimate**
comprise	equip	**innovate**	release	**unique**
contrary	extract	insert	reverse	visible
convert	file	intervene	simulate	voluntary
couple	finite	isolate	sole	

TABLE 7.8. Sublist Eight: Important Terms

abandon	**complement**	exhibit	minimize	**revise**
accompany	conform	**exploit**	**nuclear**	schedule
accumulate	**contemporary**	**fluctuate**	offset	tense
ambiguous	contradict	guideline	paragraph	terminate
append	crucial	highlight	plus	**theme**
appreciate	currency	implicit	practitioner	thereby
arbitrary	**denote**	induce	predominant	uniform
automate	detect	inevitable	prospect	vehicle
bias	deviate	**infrastructure**	radical	via
chart	displace	inspect	random	virtual
clarify	drama	intense	reinforce	visual
commodity	eventual	manipulate	restore	widespread

TABLE 7.9. Sublist Nine: Important Terms

accommodate	concurrent	found	**norm**	route
analogy	confine	**inherent**	overlap	scenario
anticipate	**controversy**	insight	passive	sphere
assure	converse	integral	portion	subordinate
attain	device	**intermediate**	preliminary	**supplement**
behalf	devote	manual	**protocol**	suspend
bulk	diminish	mature	**qualitative**	team
cease	**distort**	**mediate**	**refine**	temporary
coherent	duration	**medium**	relax	trigger
coincide	erode	military	restrain	unify
commence	**ethic**	minimal	revolution	violate
compatible	**format**	mutual	rigid	vision

TABLE 7.10. Sublist Ten: Important Terms

adjacent	conceive	incline	nonetheless	pose
albeit	convince	**integrity**	notwithstanding	reluctance
assemble	depress	**intrinsic**	odd	so called
collapse	encounter	**invoke**	ongoing	straightforward
colleague	enormous	**levy**	panel	undergo
compile	forthcoming	likewise	persist	whereby

3. Thirty-Five Key AWL Definitions with Sentences

We have supplied the definitions for some of the words that we think are most relevant to you. Many of these words have even more definitions than what we have supplied, but we are giving you the ones we think you will most need for reading and writing in college English classes, where you are asked to write research papers.

1. **Abstract:** (adjective) existing only in thought or as an idea but without a concrete existence; dealing with ideas instead of events; theoretical. *We discussed the issues in an abstract fashion.* (Noun) a summary of a book,

article, or speech. *Scholarly journal articles are usually preceded by abstracts written by the authors.*

2. **Ambiguous**: (adjective) open to two or more interpretations; equivocal; unclear because a choice between alternatives has not been offered. *The Mona Lisa has fascinated viewers for centuries, in no small part due to the ambiguity of the subject's smile. She was frustrated by the ambiguous answer to her question.*

3. **Analogy**: (noun) a comparison between two things, usually in order to explain or clarify; something comparable to something else in important respects. *There are various versions, but an analogy comparing a field of study to a black cat in a dark room has been around since at least the 1890s; one example is "Philosophy is like being in a dark room and looking for a black cat."*

4. **Analyze**: (verb) the process of breaking a complex topic or work into smaller parts to reach a better understanding. *"Close reading" refers to analyzing specific passages in a literary text in order to determine how it works and what it means.*

5. **Assess**: (verb) evaluate or estimate the quality, ability, or nature, of something; calculate the price or value of something. *The students were asked to assess the relative merits of opposing arguments.*

6. **Bias**: (noun) prejudice for or against a person, group, or thing , typically in an unfair manner; (verb) cause to feel or demonstrate prejudice for or against someone or something. The adjective is formed by adding "ed" to the end; for example, you can say that a person "is biased"; don't write that a person "is bias." *Media that are biased in favor of particular political stances may present factual information; however, they may favor facts that support their biases and not report facts that undercut them.*

7. **Civil**: (adjective) relating to ordinary citizens and their concerns; courteous. *Civil liberties, such as freedom of the press and freedom of speech, are personal guarantees and freedoms that the government cannot abridge, either by law or judicial interpretation, without due process.*

8. **Classic**: (adjective) after a period of time, judged to be outstanding and of the highest quality; instructively typical; (noun) a work of art or literature of established value. *While a lot of people associate the name Frankenstein only with horror movies, Mary Wollstonecraft Shelley's novel is considered a classic of nineteenth century literature.*

9. **Coherent**: (adjective) (of an argument, theory, or policy) clear, logical, and consistent; (of a person) able to speak logically and clearly. *The candidate failed to develop a coherent political strategy.*

10. **Comprehensive**: (adjective) complete; of large scope; including most or all elements or aspects of something. *A comprehensive plan is an important tool for planning the future growth of a community.*

11. **Comprise**: (verb) consist of; be made up of; constitute. *The committee comprised five members.* (Note: since "of" is an implied part of the meaning of comprise, it is technically incorrect to say that something is "comprised of" something.)

12. **Contrast**: (noun) comparison of similar people or things to call attention to their dissimilarities; the juxtaposition of dissimilar elements in something; the action of calling attention to notable differences; (verb) differ strikingly. *The article contrasted totalitarian regimes with other types of authoritarian regimes.*

13. **Criterion**: (noun) a standard or principle by which a decision or judgment can be arrived at. The plural form is "criteria." *One of Robert A. Dahl's criteria for a democracy was that each citizen's vote must be counted as equal in weight to the vote of any other citizen.*

14. **Data**: (noun) factual information, such as statistics and results of scientific research, used for calculation and reasoning; in computing, information in digital form. The singular form is "datum." However, some style guides classify data as a collective noun when—and only when—the data comprise a single unit. *A carefully crafted experiment allows researchers to identify the variables that influence their data.*

15. **Differentiate**: (verb, with object) recognize or ascertain what makes a person or thing different from another; make a person or thing (verb, no object) differentiate between; identify differences between two or more people or things. *We need to differentiate facts from opinions.*

16. **Discrete**: (adjective) individually distinct; constituting a separate entry. *In statistics, a discrete distribution is one in which the data can only take on certain values, for example, integers.* Note: Do not confuse "discrete" with "discreet," which means showing good judgment in one's conduct and behavior, particularly to avoid causing offense.

17. **Discriminate**: (verb, no object) recognize a distinction; (verb, with object) perceive or mark the distinguishing feature of something; make an unjust or

prejudicial distinction in the treatment of different categories of people or things. A common mistake is to write a sentence like "They discriminated against a group of people." "Discriminate" can't stand alone like this; it needs to be followed with against. *Many people boycotted the restaurant after it discriminated against some members of the community.* Note: "discriminate" is not always a negative term (see initial part of definition). *Researchers concluded that cats can discriminate the content of some human speech, including their own names, from other words based on phonemic differences.*

18. **Document**: (verb) record something in written, photographic, or other form; furnish documentary evidence of. *When people are bullied in the workplace, they should document the bullying in order to make their personal experience less abstract for those who need to weigh in on the decision making about what to do*; (noun) an original or official piece of written, printed, or electronic matter relied upon as the support or proof of something; *the document was notarized after it was witnessed and signed.*

19. **Empirical**: (adjective) originating, based on, concerned with, or verifiable by observation or experience rather than theory or speculation. *The students were told that they needed empirical data, not just assumptions, to support the arguments in their research papers.*

20. **Evaluate**: (verb, with object) form an idea of the value of, number, or amount of something; assess. *When searching the Internet, it's important to critically evaluate your search results.*

21. **Evidence**: (noun) proof; body of facts or information indicating whether a belief, proposition, or hypothesis is true or valid. *In college papers, students need to offer concrete evidence, not just suppositions, quotations, and guesses.*

22. **Explicit**: (adjective) stated clearly and in detail; fully expressed or demonstrated. *Their boss's criticism was scathingly explicit.*

23. **Hypothesis**: (noun) a proposition assumed as an argument's premise; a supposition made on the basis of limited evidence as a starting point for further investigation. *A study of more than 30,000 galaxies has found evidence to support a controversial new hypothesis suggesting that gravity might behave and arise differently than predicted by Albert Einstein.*

24. **Infer**: (verb, with object) derive from reasoning; conclude from evidence and reasoning rather than from explicit statements. *When we infer, we listen closely to someone and guess at things they mean but haven't actually stated.*

25. **Implement**: (verb, with object) fulfill, carry out; put in effect a decision, plan, agreement, etc.. (noun) an article used in some activity, such as a tool. *Once a change in an organization is planned, it is important to have good communication about the implementation of the change.*

26. **Implicit**: (adjective) implied but not plainly expressed; essentially or very closely connected with; always to be found in; potentially contained (usually followed by "in".) *Her comments were seen as implicit criticism of the new policies.*

27. **Interpret**: (verb, with object) to explain the meaning of information, words, or actions; understand an action, mood, or type of behavior as having a particular meaning. *Knowing how to recognize and interpret microexpressions is an essential part of understanding nonverbal behavior.*

28. **Intrinsic**: (adjective) belonging by nature to a thing; essential. *Intrinsic motivation refers to behavior that comes from within the individual out interest for an activity at hand; no external rewards are required to encourage an intrinsically motivated person into action. Extrinsic motivation involves engaging in behavior in order to earn external rewards or to avoid punishment.*

29. **Liberal**: (adjective) favorable to progress or reform; favorable to individual freedoms and rights; of education, concerned primarily with broadening a person's general knowledge and experience, rather than with purely professional or technical training. *The purpose of the Bachelor of Liberal Studies degree is to provide students with a multidisciplinary preparation in social sciences, natural sciences, the humanities, and the arts, allowing them to pursue careers in education, government, arts, business, and other such fields.*

30. **Mechanism**: (noun) natural or established process by which something is brought about; a system of parts working in a machine. *The immune system's mechanism for detecting pathogens attacks microorganisms that attempt to invade and cause diseases to the host.*

31. **Media**: (noun, plural) primary means of mass communication, such as in broadcasting, publishing, and the Internet, regarded collectively. The singular form is "medium." *News media are important in order to receive information on various subjects, most importantly current affairs, but we should seek information from a wide variety of media, or we may develop an incomplete or distorted picture.*

32. **Protocol**: (noun) the official system of rules governing affairs of state or diplomatic occasions; the accepted or established code of procedure for an organization, group, or situation; official record of scientific experimental observations. *Long-established protocol indicates how presidents are expected to behave when meeting with foreign heads of state.*

33. **Qualitative**: (adjective) relating to, measuring, or measured by the something's quality instead of its quantity. *We call data quantitative when in numerical form and qualitative when not; qualitative research is multimethod in focus, involving an interpretive, naturalistic approach.*

34. **Revise**: (verb with object) alter something in the light of new evidence; re-examine and alter written or printed work to improve it. *The professor gave the class the opportunity to revise their research papers for higher grades, warning them that revision meant more than simply correcting spelling, grammar, and format errors; they needed to look at their presentation of logic and evidence.*

35. **Significant**: (adjective) sufficiently important to be worthy of attention; noteworthy; in science, relating to or having statistical significance, which is the extent to which a result deviates from that expected to arise simply from mere chance or errors in sampling. *In principle, a statistically significant result, usually a difference), is a result that is not attributed to chance.*

4. Terms That Are Commonly Confused

It is also important to know what a word doesn't mean and how it isn't used. There are many words that are commonly misunderstood, misused, and misspelled. Following is a list of some of the most commonly confused ones.

1. **accept, except**. "Accept" is a verb that means "to receive willingly." "Except" is a preposition meaning "but, not including."

2. **adapt, adopt, adept**. "Adapt" is a verb that means to "make suitable for a new purpose"; to "become accustomed to," or to "alter a text into another form, such as a film or play." "Adopt" is a verb that means to "take on or assume as one's own. "Adept" is an adjective meaning "very skilled at something."

3. **adolescents, adolescence**. "Adolescence" is a noun referring to the teenage years. "Adolescents" is the plural of "adolescent," which means "a person in his or her adolescence."

4. **affect, effect**. Each word can be a verb or a noun, but only "effect," when it means "a result or consequence of an action or other cause," is common as a noun. "Effect" as a verb means "to bring about." "Affect" as a verb usually means "to produce an effect on, to influence." It can also mean "to pretend to feel an emotional state or to have a particular trait."

5. **allude, elude**. "Allude" is a verb that means "to suggest or call attention to something indirectly or in a disguised way." A related word is "allusion," a noun meaning "an expression designed to call something to mind without mentioning it explicitly." "Elude" is a verb that means "to escape from something," or, referring to ideas or achievements, "to fail to be attained."

6. **among, between**. "Among" is a preposition meaning "surrounded by; in the company of; being a member or members of a group; involving the members of a group," and it is used with more than two people or things. "Between" is a preposition indicating a "separating interval or a relationship between people or things," and it is generally used with only two only things.

7. **assure, ensure, insure**. "Assure" means "to make someone confident of something." "Ensure" means "to make certain that something will happen." "Insure" means "to issue an insurance policy."

8. **book, novel**. A book is any full-length prose (non-verse) work. A novel, however, is a book-length work of prose fiction. Any is a book, but most books aren't novels.

9. **cannot, can not**. Technically, both "cannot" and "can not" are acceptable, but "cannot" is the safest choice in most instances because it is far more common, and "can not" is treated in some style manuals as an error—unless the word "not" is supposed to be emphasized.

10. **censor, censure**. "Censor" means "to examine a work, like a book, film, or song, and suppress any parts deemed unacceptable." The noun "censor" refers to a person doing the censoring. To "censure" something means "to express severe disapproval" of it, typically in a formal statement.

11. **cite, site**. To "cite" is "to give credit to a source used in research." A "site" is the location on which something is constructed or where human activities occurred and left material evidence.

12. **complement, compliment**. "Complement" means "to make complete." A "compliment" is an expression in praise of something."

13. **decent, descent, dissent**. "Decent" means "morally respectable," "appropriate," or "of an acceptable standard." "Descent" refers to the "action of moving downward." "Dissent" as a verb means "to hold or express opinions that are at variance with those previously, commonly, or officially expressed." As a noun it means "the expression or holding of opinions at variance with those previously, commonly, or officially held."

14. **elicit, illicit**. "Elicit" is an adjective meaning "to draw out information or a reaction by one's questions or actions." "Illicit" is an adjective that means "prohibited by law, moral standards, rules, or customs."

15. **emigrate, immigrate**. To "emigrate" means "to leave one country to settle in another." To "immigrate" means "to come to live in a new country."

16. **enervate, energize**. The "ener" of "enervate" causes many people to assume that it means the same thing as "energize," but the words are actually opposites. The verb "enervate" means to "cause someone to feel weakened or drained of energy," and the adjective means "lacking energy or vitality." "Energize" means "give vitality and enthusiasm to" someone.

17. **explicit, implicit**. "Explicit" means "expressly and clearly stated." "Implicit" means "implied but only indirectly expressed." It can also mean with no qualification or question."

18. **fewer, less**. "Few" means "a small number of." Use "fewer" with things that can be individually counted. "Less" means "a smaller amount of; not as much." Use "less" with abstract qualities or quantities that cannot be individually counted.

19. **immanent, imminent, eminent**. "Immanent" means "existing or operating within; inherent." "Imminent" means "about to happen." "Eminent" means "famous and respected."

20. **later, latter**. "Later" is the comparative form of "late," which means "taking place near the end of a particular time or taking place after the usual or expected time." "Latter" means "indicating the second or second mentioned of two people or things."

21. **lay, lie**. "Lie" is an intransitive verb, which means that it doesn't take a direct object. "Lay" is a transitive verb, which means it needs a direct object; it means to "put down, especially carefully."

22. **literally, figuratively**. "Literally" means "exactly"; use it only for something that is actually true. "Figuratively" is the term to use when an expression is metaphorical, "departing from a literal use of words."

23. **precede, proceed**. To "precede" is to "come before." To "proceed" is to "begin or continue a course of action; to move forward."

24. **simple, simplistic**. "Simple" means "uncomplicated; not complex" or "easily understood or accomplished." It can be either positive or negative, depending on context. "Simplistic" means "treating complex issues as if they were much simpler than they really are." It is always used negatively.

25. **which, that**. Most grammar experts advise using "which" to introduce nonrestrictive information and "that" to set off restrictive information. Nonrestrictive information refers to terms or phrases that can be removed from a sentence without changing its basic meaning, as opposed to restrictive information, which would change a sentence's meaning if removed.

Name: _____ Section: _____ Date: _____

Part Two

Chapter 7 Workshop

The following section contains a series of ten tasks that, if completed, will help you gain mastery over the content in this chapter. Your instructor will assign some (or all) of them to you as a way to practice the material presented here. Notice that some of them are global and focus on the entirety of the skills laid out in this chapter, while others are more focused and explore only one or two sections of the chapter. Also notice that some are shorter; some are longer; all are designed to flip the classroom and put the power of learning directly into your hands.

Workshop One.

Overview: Summarize all of the major sections and/or bullet points that you find in this chapter.

Each major section or heading should be clearly labeled and should have at least a one-sentence discussion. You might have a dozen or more headings and sentences here. Be thorough and accurate to show that you have read and comprehended this chapter's contents. Avoid the temptation to judge or add anything new (even critical discussion of the content); this is an act of pure summary. Tell your instructor exactly what came in this chapter and in what order.

Workshop Two.

Overview: This workshop has you examine all of the wrong answers from your chapter diagnostic and respond to them.
1. Make a list of each question from the chapter diagnostic that you got wrong.
2. For every question you got wrong, do the following:

a. Identify the page number where the correct vocabulary definition was found.

b. Supply the correct definition.

c. Create your own sentence using the word.

Workshop Three.

Overview: Write a short, personal essay explaining the content of this chapter. The point of this essay is to directly address what you have learned from the chapter and how it will impact your future academic writing. Consider some or all of the following:

A. How do you feel about your own vocabulary? Is it ready for college, or do you feel you need to expand it? Why?

B. How can you implement the six tips for expanding your vocabulary? Be specific with how this can benefit you in the future.

C. What words from the vocabulary lists here were new to you?

D. Refer to the section on terms that are commonly confused. Which of these are you guilty of, and how can you make sure you correct this in the future?

E. Your instructor will provide you with more details such as the length of the piece, if you should use quotation from the chapter, if personal anecdotes and casual language are allowed, etc.

Workshop Four.

Overview: Write a series of short answers (several sentences per answer) to the following questions below in order to critically examine the content of this chapter. Note: This workshop can be completed only after you have made the effort to practice all seven of the tips for improving your vocabulary listed in this chapter.

1. Which of these are you finding to be most effective, and why?

2. Describe each of the seven tips in your own words, and follow with a discussion of how effective each is for you.

3. Which of these are you finding to be most effective, and why?

4. Which ones are you finding less effective, and why?

5. Indicate what words that you have learned that you think will be most valuable in college writing, and define them.

Workshop Five.

<u>Overview</u>: Create a PowerPoint presentation or website that cover the basic elements of this chapter that you would share with your peers and professor.

     A. Your PowerPoint or website must cover the seven ways to improve your vocabulary.

     B. Your PowerPoint or website must discuss and define several of the words on the Academic Word List, and you must explain why you selected these words out of the long list provided in the chapter.

     C. Your PowerPoint or website must discuss the terms that are commonly confused.

Workshop Six.

<u>Overview</u>: Often, teaching something can be the best way to learn it yourself on a deeper level. Therefore, write a quiz for future students that covers the basics of *how to expand your vocabulary.*

This quiz should include various styles of questions, including multiple choice, short answer, and true/false. Check with your instructor on specifics.

     A. This quiz should be designed to show mastery of the skills from another student at your own level.

     B. You must write an answer key starting on a new page after the quiz. This answer key must include the page numbers from *Flipping English* where students can find the answer. It must also include a complete sentence for each quiz question you generated to explain to the instructor why you thought this question targeted a critical skill discussed in this chapter.

Workshop Seven.

Overview: Often, bettering the vocabulary found in a piece of writing comes later in the writing process and is part of revision, not the first draft. To practice this, take an older piece of your writing, and expand the vocabulary by doing the following things. Note: Ask your instructor if you should use a piece of writing from your current class or if you can use an older piece of writing from a previous class.

    A. Revise your paper to improve your use of vocabulary. To do so, find at least five words that you could improve upon and use newer, more collegiate vocabulary instead.

    B. Revise your paper to include at least five of the vocabulary terms found in this chapter.

    C. Print your paper, and take a highlighter to all the changes you made, so your instructor can easily see the new improvements.

    D. Write a one page response to this exercise. How difficult was it to expand the vocabulary of your paper? How big of an impact do you think it had? Does your paper sound more scholarly and collegiate with these changes? Will you continue to practice this in the future—why or why not?

Workshop Eight.

Overview: This workshop will get you to familiarize yourself with the use of a thesaurus or a thesaurus website or app.

    A. Write a paragraph on a topic given to you by your instructor take a paragraph from a previous piece of writing. This paragraph should be at least eight sentences long, so feel free to expand it or include part of the next paragraph to get that length.

    B. Using a thesaurus, look up alternative words for things you said in each sentence. For each sentence you have written, you must replace TWO of the words with new synonyms found in the thesaurus.

    C. Next, reflect on these changes. In a short paragraph discuss which of these words felt like they made your writing better, and which (if any) felt out of place or a bit odd compared to the rest of your writing style? What was your favorite change, and what felt the most forced.

D. Finally, print this entire workshop out and use a highlighter to show the instructor which two words you changed in each sentence.

Workshop Nine.

Overview: One good way to expand your vocabulary is to look at lists of words that many people don't know and then look them up and use them in a sentence.

A. Find two terms from each of the tables (Tables 7.1 through 7.10). For each of these terms, write out a dictionary definition as well as another similar word that you could use instead of this one in your writing.

B. Next, for each of these twenty terms, write your own sentence (don't use one you find in your dictionary) that uses the word properly.

C. Provide a works cited page for the dictionary you used to find your definitions.

Workshop Ten.

Overview: What is your take away from this chapter? What did you learn and what questions do you still have?

1. Write a short response of several sentences that covers the three main things that you learned from this chapter.

2. Write out at least five questions you still have about the chapter. What things would you want to communicate to your instructor? What would you like to see discussed in class or handled with more depth to help you master this chapter's content.

3. What is one thing that you have taken away from this chapter and will use on your next writing task? Why is this thing important, and how do you plan to implement it?

CHAPTER 8

How to Write Grammatical and Properly Punctuated Sentences

In this chapter, you will learn about the following:

While we recommend that you read the whole chapter through once, we also suggest that you use this chapter outline as a quick reference to the rules and definitions you will need in the future.

Part One

Punctuation and Grammar Basics

It is day one of the semester, and Dwayne is excited about his English composition class. He has done fairly well in his high school writing courses, but he has heard that a college English class is a different beast. The professor comes into the room, goes over her syllabus, and then hands out a sheet listing all the writing skills she thinks Dwayne and the other students should already know.

Dwayne's confidence in his writing is seriously shaken. The jargon and terms that are on the list start to make him freak out: subjects, predicates, indirect objects, dependent clauses, nonrestrictive elements, colons, and semicolons. (He didn't know there were two types of colon!) If Dwayne is like you, then once your instructor starts to throw around punctuation and grammar terms, you get a bad feeling in the pit of your stomach.

How is anyone supposed to keep all of this straight, and when, exactly, did most people learn it? Every writer has strengths and weaknesses when it comes to grammar and punctuation. This chapter is designed to help you brush up on (or learn for the first time) the skills, terms, and concepts you'll need to succeed in any college classroom. We promise that we'll throw relatively little jargon at you—just the bare minimum needed to understand the basic concepts for writing grammatical and correctly punctuated sentences. You know what punctuation marks are, but what, exactly, is grammar? The term refers to the set of structural rules that govern how we put together clauses and phrases to form sentences. So we'll start with some basic definitions and then connect everything together. Punctuation and grammar can seem tricky, but remember: this is punctuation and grammar made easy.

1. Understanding Subjects, Verbs, and Predicates

The **subject** in a simple English sentence is the person, animal, idea, or thing that the sentence is about—it is *doing* or *being* something. It can be a single word, usually a noun or a pronoun, or a phrase. You can find the subject of a sentence if you can find the **verb** because all verbs have a subject. The subject is the word or phrase that controls the verb. A verb is the part of speech that conveys an action (*read, run, act*), an occurrence (*happen, become*), or a state of being (*be, exist, is*). A **predicate** is the part of a sentence that contains the verb controlled by the subject. The purpose of the predicate is to complete an idea about the subject, such as what it does or what it is like.

2. Understanding Direct and Indirect Objects

Some verbs have an object as well as a subject. The object is what is being affected by the verb, and there are two kinds: direct objects, the nouns or pronouns directly affected by the action of the main verb (they receive the action), and indirect objects, which indentify to or for whom or what the action of the verb is performed. Indirect objects are the recipients of the direct objects. Sentences must have subjects and verbs, but they do not always have direct objects. Indirect objects are relatively rare.

TABLE 8.1. Showing the Complete Predicate

Subject	Complete Predicate		
	Verb	Direct Object	Indirect Object
Birds	have	feathers.	
Birds	chirp.		
Birds	feed	their babies	worms.
Many varieties of birds	migrate.		

Note: Subjects, verbs, and objects do not have to be in the order presented above. In the following sentences, for example, the subject is *the professor*, the indirect object is *students*, and the direct object is *assignments*. The *assignments* received the action of being given by the professor (the subject), and the students were the ones affected by the action.

The professor gave her students assignments.

Assignments were given by the professor to her students.

The second sentence provides an example of what we call *passive voice*—that happens when you make the object of an action into the subject of a sentence. In other words, whoever or whatever is performing the action is not the grammatical subject of the sentence. Many professors frown on this, but some others, such as those in the sciences, encourage its use because they believe it sounds more objective. It is always a good idea to find out what a professor prefers. And it may change from course to course.

3. Understanding Clauses and Phrases

Independent clauses (also called main clauses) have subjects and verbs and can stand alone as complete sentences. **Dependent clauses** (also called subordinate clauses) have subjects and verbs but cannot stand alone as sentences because they begin with subordinating words, such as subordinating conjunctions. **Phrases** lack a subject or a verb or both.

TABLE 8.2. Examples of Clauses and Phrases

Independent Clause	Dependent Clause	Phrase
I love pizza	when I make pizza	make it often
I went to the store	after I got back from the store	bought groceries
Jo washed the dishes	since I cooked dinner	

Independent clauses can be sentences, but in order to form complete sentences, dependent clauses and phrases must be connected to independent clauses.

> I love pizza.
> I love pizza and make it often.
> I went to the store and bought groceries.
> Jamal washed the dishes since I cooked the dinner.
> Since I cooked the dinner, Jamal washed the dishes

4. Using Independent Clauses

We usually punctuate consecutive main (independent) clauses in four ways:

1. We can use a comma before a coordinating conjunction (for, and, or, nor, or, yet, so).

Astronaut André Kuipers was trying to phone a Houston space station, and he dialed 911 instead.

The sixty-year-old astronaut hung up promptly, but his call triggered an alert some 200 miles below at Mission Control.

2. We can use a period (or other terminal punctuation mark, like a question mark or exclamation point).

Kuipers wouldn't have minded a visit—he joked that he was a little disappointed that they did not come up.

How often do astronauts accidentally call 911? You would be surprised.

3. We can use a semicolon.

The International Space Station's phone system uses voice over Internet protocol; this is the same technology that lets Earthbound people place Internet calls over Skype.

4. Dashes and colons can also occasionally be used between independent clauses.

- Dashes indicate shifts in tone and can sometimes replace commas, periods, and semicolons.

Kuipers wouldn't have minded a visit—he joked that he was a little disappointed that they did not come up.

- Colons can be used after independent clauses to introduce other independent clauses.

Kuipers made the following joke: "I was a little disappointed that they had not come up."

5. Using Dependent Clauses

How we use punctuation when we add dependent clauses to independent clauses depends on the order they are in.

When a dependent clause comes before an independent clause, we use a comma to signal the beginning of the independent clause.

> While trying to contact NASA's Johnson Space Center in Houston, Kuipers missed an all-important number.

We do not need any punctuation mark when the dependent clause follows the main clause because the subordinating word signals the end of the independence clause and the beginning of the dependent clause.

> Kuipers missed an all-important number while trying to contract NASA's Johnson Space Center in Houston.

To help you recognize dependent clauses, look at Table 8.5 under "Understanding Subordinating Conjunctions" later in this chapter for a list of some common subordinating words.

6. Using Phrases

Phrases, like dependent clauses, cannot stand alone as sentences, so we treat them the way we treat dependent clauses. Whether we use commas depends on whether they precede or follow a main clause. When a phrase comes before an independent clause, we use a comma to signal the beginning of the independent clause.

> Joking about accidentally calling 911, British astronaut Tim Peake posted on Twitter.

We do not need any punctuation mark when the phrase follows the main clause.

British astronaut Tim Peake posted on Twitter and joked about accidentally calling 911.

7. Using Restrictive and Nonrestrictive Elements

Other information can be added to clauses and phrases. Restrictive material is grammatically and logically essential to the sentence it is within. If you remove the material, you change the meaning of the sentence. You do not alter the meaning of a sentence by removing nonrestrictive material. This material may contain important ideas that a writer wishes to convey—the point to remember is that nonrestrictive information is not unimportant information; it is simply information that would not alter the sentence it is in if it wasn't there.

Here is an example (underlined) of a restrictive element in a sentence:

> Canada repealed all laws <u>that were found to be unconstitutional, redundant, or just too old and weird.</u>

If we removed the restrictive element, it would sound like Canada repealed all of its laws.

> Canada repealed all laws.

The meaning has clearly changed—the altered sentence does not convey the actual intent of the original sentence.

Here is an example (underlined) of a nonrestrictive element in a sentence:

> Canada repealed a number of so-called "zombie laws," <u>which were laws that were found to be unconstitutional, redundant, or just too old and "weird."</u>

If we take the nonrestrictive element out, we have the following, which does not change the sentence's essential meaning:

Canada repealed a number of so-called "zombie laws."

We do not set restrictive elements off with any punctuation marks. If you look at the following example, you'll see that the restrictive element, which is underlined, is crucial to the meaning of the sentence.

The teenager in Utah <u>who wore a blindfold while driving</u> crashed into another car.

If we removed the restrictive element, the sentence would not make much sense since people know that there is more than one teenager in Utah.

The teenager in Utah crashed into another car.

We set nonrestrictive elements off with commas. If you look at the following examples, you'll see that the nonrestrictive elements, which are underlined, are not crucial to the basic meaning of the sentences even though they add interesting information.

The teenager in Utah who wore a blindfold while driving, <u>which he did as part of the so-called *Bird Box* challenge</u>, crashed into another car.

The movie *Bird Box*, <u>which stars Sandra Bullock</u>, is about people having to move about the outside world wearing blindfolds to avoid seeing a monster.

If we removed the nonrestrictive elements, we would not be changing the essential meaning of the sentences:

The teenager in Utah who wore a blindfold while driving crashed into another car.

The movie *Bird Box* is about people having to move about the outside world wearing blindfolds to avoid seeing a monster.

Part Two

Parts of Speech

The English language has eight major parts of speech: noun, pronoun, verb, adverb, adjective, conjunction, preposition, and interjection. Why do you need to know this? Because if you can't recognize and distinguish between these, you are likely to make a number of common punctuation mistakes, and you won't know which letters at the beginnings of words in titles and subtitles to capitalize and which not to.

1. Understanding Nouns

Nouns name persons, animals, places, ideas, objects, and events. Proper nouns refer to specific entities and need to be capitalized, for example, "Beyoncé," "California," and "Bill of Rights." Common nouns are the generic names of things, such as "singer," "state," and "document."

2. Understanding Pronouns

Pronouns function as replacements for nouns. There are several types of pronouns, and some words can be different types, depending on context.

    A. Personal pronouns stand in for people or things, such as "she," "he," "you," "your," and "it." These have three "cases": subjective, objective, and possessive, which we discuss later.

    B. Demonstrative pronouns stand in for specific people or things that have been previously mentioned or are understood from context. There are four demonstrative pronouns: "this," "that," "these," and "those."

    c. Reciprocal pronouns express a mutual action or relationship. English has two: "each other" and "one another."

    d. Indefinite pronouns stand in for non-specific people or things. The most common ones are "all," "any," "anyone," "anything," "each," "everybody," "everyone," "everything," "few," "many," "nobody," "none," "one," "several," "some," "somebody," and "someone." To avoid problems with subject-verb agreement, it is important to note that the pronouns "anybody," "anyone," "nobody," "somebody," "someone," "no one," "each one," "everyone," and "everybody" are singular, as are the words "each," "either," and "neither."

e. **Relative pronouns** introduce adjective clauses, which follow a noun to identify it or tell us something about it. They are "that," "which," "who," "whom," and "whose."

f. **Interrogative pronouns** are used to ask questions; the interrogative pronoun represents the thing that the question is about. The four most common interrogative pronouns are "who," "whom," "whose," "which," and "what." "Whoever," "whomever," "whichever, and "whatever" can also be interrogative pronouns.

g. **Reflexive pronouns** are used with nouns or other pronouns when something does something to itself. The reflexive pronouns are "myself," "yourself," "herself," "himself," "itself," "ourselves," "yourselves," and "themselves."

h. **Intensive pronouns** refer back to nouns or other pronouns in sentences in order to emphasize them. They are the same words as the reflexive pronouns—it's just that their purpose is different: "myself," "yourself," "herself," "himself," "itself," "ourselves," "yourselves," and "themselves."

3. Understanding Verbs

Verbs show physical or mental actions, such as "think," "run," "vote," and "play," or states of being, such as "am," "is," "are, "was," and "were." Sometimes a word can be more than one part of speech, depending on context. In "I voted," "vote" is a verb; in "I want your vote," "vote" is a noun. An important part of writing grammatical sentences is making sure that you don't separate a subject from its verb with a comma or other punctuation mark, which is a common mistake when the subject is composed of several words. The same verb, "is," is used in the following two sentences:

TABLE 8.3. Understanding Verbs	
Incorrect	Separating the subject of a sentence with a comma or other punctuation mark, is just fine.
Correct	Separating the subject of a sentence with a comma or other punctuation mark is a grammatical error.

You might want to know why the sentence "The same verb, 'is,' is used in the following two sentences" is grammatical since we have a comma after the first "is." That is because the first "is" is a nonrestrictive element—one that can be removed from the sentence without changing meaning—so it must be set off with commas. We could also have written, "The same verb is used in the following two sentences." In this case, we should not have a comma.

You also need to make sure that subjects and verbs agree in number. Plural nouns need plural verbs, and singular nouns need singular verbs. See examples below.

> My cat loves catnip.
> Her cat<u>s</u> love catnip, too.

4. Understanding Adjectives

Adjectives are the words that describe nouns and pronouns. Separate multiple adjectives from each other with commas, but do not separate an adjective from the word that it is modifying with a comma. Examples of adjectives include "purple," "interesting," and "bad." There are also possessive adjectives, which look like (and are often confused with) possessive pronouns. Here is the list: "my," "your," "her," "its," "our," "their," and "whose."

5. Understanding Adverbs

Like adjectives, adverbs also describe words, but adverbs describe adjectives, verbs, or other adverbs, for example, "swiftly," "happily," and "badly." Sometimes a word can be both an adjective and an adverb, depending on context. In "most difficult," "most" is an adverb because "difficult" is an adjective, as in "difficult problem." In "most students," "most" is an adjective because "students" is a noun." Separate multiple adverbs from each other with commas, but do not separate an adverb from the word that it is modifying with a comma.

6. Understanding Conjunctive Adverbs

Conjunctive adverbs are a particularly important type of adverb to recognize. They can connect clauses, providing useful transitions. They show relationships, such as contrast, sequence, and cause and effect. They may be moved around in the clause in which they appear. They can also begin or end a sentence. Here is a list of common conjunctive adverbs:

TABLE 8.4. Examples of Common Conjunctive Adverbs			
accordingly*	furthermore	moreover	so*
also	hence*	namely	still
anyway	however	nevertheless	then
besides	incidentally	next	thereafter
certainly	indeed	nonetheless	therefore*
consequently*	instead	now	thus*
finally	likewise	otherwise	undoubtedly
further	meanwhile	similarly	wherefore*

* For words with an asterisk, see chapter 5 to understand how these adverbs can also act as conclusion indicator words in arguments.

Note: Don't be confused by the inclusion of "so" in this table. "So," like several other words, can also act as a coordinating conjunction or an adverb, depending on context.

7. Understanding Coordinating Conjunctions

Coordinating conjunctions are used to join individual words, phrases, and independent clauses—units of equal "rank." You need to recognize them because their uses include connecting independent clauses, in which case they require a comma in front of them, and because they are words that we don't capitalize in titles or subtitles unless they begin or end titles and subtitles. The seven coordinating conjunctions are "for," "and," "nor," "but," "or," "yet," and "so." You can use the mnemonic (memory tool, pronounced "nə'mänik") "FANBOYS" to remember all seven. When connecting two independent clauses, always have a comma after the first clause and before the coordinating conjunction.

8. Understanding Subordinating Conjunctions

A subordinating conjunction joins a dependent clause (also called a subordinate clause) to an independent clause (also called a main clause). You need to recognize them because whether or not you use a comma with a dependent clause depends on whether it follows an independent clause (no comma) or precedes it (use a comma between them). Some subordinating conjunctions are formed of two or three words. Following are some common subordinating conjunctions:

TABLE 8.5. Examples of Common Subordinating Conjunctions

after	as though	in order that	that
although	because*	lest (that)	though
as*	before	now that	unless
as if	even if	provided*	until
as long as	even though	since*	when
as much as	if	so that*	where
as soon as	inasmuch*	than	wherever

* For words with an asterisk, see chapter 5 to understand how these conjunctions can also act as premise indicator words in arguments.

9. Understanding Prepositions

Prepositions are words that express the relationship between two other nouns or pronouns. You need to recognize them because, among other things, they are words that we don't capitalize in titles or subtitles unless they begin or end titles and subtitles. Following are some common prepositions:

TABLE 8.6. Examples of Common Prepositions			
about	behind	down	into
above	below	during	of
after	beneath	except	off
against	between	for	on
at	beyond	from	with
among	by	in	within
around	close to	inside	without

10. Understanding Articles

English has three parts of speech called articles: "a," "an," and "the." Why are they called "articles," which seems like a confusing term? They get their name from a Latin word, *articulus,* which means "small connecting part." It is important to recognize articles because we don't capitalize them in titles or subtitles unless they begin or end titles and subtitles. Also, if we have authorless works on a works cited page, we have to begin the entries with the works' titles. If a work begins with "a," "an," or "the," we leave the word at the beginning of the title, but we do not use it to alphabetize the entry. For example, "The Earthquake Preparedness

Guide" would come before "How to Prepare for the Next Earthquake" because "e" precedes "h" alphabetically.

If entries have authors but you have two or more works by the same author, you also put them in order according to the first important word in the title after alphabetizing by he author's last name. For example, if your works cited page had Madeleine L'Engle's books *A Wrinkle in Time* and *The Arm of the Starfish*, *The Arm of the Starfish* would precede *A Wrinkle in Time*. Also, we would not spell L'Engle's name after the first entry; we would just use three hyphens instead.

11. Understanding Interjections

Interjections are words used to express feelings, for example, "ugh," "oops," and "uh oh." They are also sometimes referred to as exclamations. "Well" is also such a word when it is not being used as an adjective or an adverb. When writing, don't begin sentences with useless exclamations like "well."

Part Three
Pronoun Use Made Easy

1. Understanding Subjective, Objective, and Possessive Cases

To understand how to use the right pronouns in sentences, you need to understand pronoun case. Pronoun case expresses the relationship of a pronoun to other words in the sentence. There are only three pronoun cases.

1.	**Subjective Case**	The case of pronouns used as subjects.
2.	**Objective Case**	The case of pronouns used as direct or indirect objects of verbs or prepositions.
3.	**Possessive Case**	The case of pronouns used to express ownership.

TABLE 8.7. Examples of Three Pronoun Cases		
Singular Case	**Objective Case**	**Possessive Case**
I	me	mine
you	you	yours
she, he, it	her, him, it	his, hers, its
we	us	ours
they	them	theirs
who	whom	whose

2. Problems with Compound Subjects and Objects

Compound subjects and objects make pronoun choice confusing, especially since many of us were brought up to believe that "I" is a more "polite" or formal pronoun that "me." Pronoun case has to do with a word's function in the sentence—it has nothing to do with courtesy or formality. Sometimes the simplest way to figure out what form to use it to drop one of the words from the compound to see how the sentence sounds without it.

TABLE 8.8. Issues with Compound Subjects and Objects	
You <u>would not</u> write or say:	"The new rules benefit I."
You <u>should not</u> write or say:	"The new rules benefit my team and I."
You <u>should</u> write or say:	"The new rules benefit my team and me."
You <u>would not</u> write or say:	"Me went to the concert."
You <u>should not</u> write or say:	"Fatima and me went to the concert."
You <u>should</u> write or say:	"Fatima and I went to the concert."

TABLE 8.8. (*continued*)	
You <u>would not</u> write or say:	"Carmen tutors I."
You <u>should not</u> write or say:	"Carmen tutors both Isaiah and I."
You <u>should</u> write or say:	"Carmen tutors both Isaiah and me."

Sometimes a descriptive noun phrase follows a personal pronoun.

You <u>would not</u> write or say:	"Us want lower book prices."
You <u>should not</u> write or say:	"We want lower book prices."
You <u>should</u> write or say:	"We students want book prices."

3. Problems with "Who" and "Whom"

"Who" and "whom" correspond to "they" and "them" and so on. "Who" is the subjective form, and we use it when an action is being performed. "Whom" is the objective form, and we use it when a person is the recipient of an action or if the action is being performed for him or her. It is helpful to remember that while not all pronouns in the objective case end with the letter "m," the only pronouns that end with "m" are in objective case. A quick and easy way to figure out whether you should use "whom" in your writing (it has fallen into disuse in most spoken English) instead of "who" is to see if "them" or "him" would work in its place if you reworded the sentence to answer a question.

Whom did you invite?	You invited them.
Who helps you?	They help you.
To whom should I give the form?	Give the form to him.

4. Problems with Pronouns Used in Comparisons

Pronouns used in comparisons can also be tricky. Comparisons usually follow "than," "as," or "like." Comparisons usually omit words since they are clearly implied, and we don't really need them. If you complete the comparisons in your head, you can choose the correct case for the pronouns. You can also think about how the pronouns would sound if you were not making comparisons. If the technically correct way sounds awkward to you, you can rephrase the sentence.

TABLE 8.9. Issues with Pronouns Used in Comparisons

If you wrote or said, you are really saying:	"Tiana is faster than me," "Tiana is faster than me [am fast]."
You could write or say:	"Tiana is faster than I."
You could also write or say:	"Tiana is faster than I am."
If you wrote or said, you are really saying:	"Jake is taller than him," "Jake is taller than him [is tall]."
You could write or say:	"Jake is taller than he."
You could also write or say:	"Jake is taller than he is."
If you wrote or said, you are really saying:	"The talk offended her more than I," "The talk offended her more than [it offended] I."
You could write or say:	"The talk offended her more than me."
You could also write or say:	"The talk offended her more than it did me."
If you wrote or said, you are really saying:	"I sound just like him when I laugh," "I sound just like him [sounds] when I laugh."
You could write or say:	"I sound just like he when I laugh."
You could also write or say:	"I sound just like he does when I laugh."

5. Problems with Noun and Pronoun Agreement

Pronoun agreement is important in writing. Pronouns should clearly agree with specific antecedents (the nouns that they stand in for) and with each other (when referring to the same antecedents) in number (plural or singular), gender (male or female), and person (first, second, or third.)

6. Agreement in Number and Gender

As we mentioned earlier, the pronouns "anybody," "anyone," "nobody," "somebody," "someone," "no one," "each one," "everyone," and "everybody" are singular, as are the words "each," "either," and "neither." Gender disagreement issues can pop up when you refer to everyone in a group as either male or female (unless you happen to know for sure that only one gender is represented in the specific group). "He and she" can sound awkward when repeated over and over, so a simple solution is to make both the nouns and pronouns plural. The MLA does not recommend the plural pronouns "they," "their," "them," and "themselves" to refer to singular nouns. The singular "they," while common in spoken English and in some informal writing contexts, should be avoided in formal writing. it is best to reword for agreement in number.

TABLE 8.10. Rewording for Agreement in Number	
Incorrect	"When a person speeds, they can get pulled over by the police."
Incorrect	"When a person speeds, he can get pulled over by the police."
Correct	"When a person speeds, he or she can get pulled over by the police."
Correct	"When people speed, they can get pulled over by the police."
Incorrect	"Everyone should turn their essay in on time."
Incorrect	"Everyone should turn his essay in on time."
Correct	"Everyone should turn his or her essay in on time."
Correct	"Students should turn their essays in on time."

TABLE 8.10. (*continued*)	
Incorrect	"Neither of the woman gave up her position."
Incorrect	"Neither women gave up her position."
Correct	"Neither of the women gave up her position."
Correct	"Neither woman gave up her position."

The MLA does allow for exceptions to use of a singular "they," as it supports the choice of individuals to choose their own descriptors. People who prefer to use non-gender-specific pronouns to refer to themselves can use "they," "their," and so on. The MLA also advises that writers follow the personal pronoun choices of individuals they write about when these people's preferences are known.

7. Agreement in Person

We use the terms first, second, and third person to describe points of view. When we talk about ourselves and groups we are belong to, we generally speak in the first person, using first-person pronouns. "I," "me," "my," "mine" and "myself" are first-person singular pronouns. "We," "us," our," and "ourselves" are first-person plural pronouns. The second-person point of view belongs to people that are being addressed. This is the "you" perspective. "You," "your," "yours," "yourself," and "yourselves." Many college professors prefer that students avoid second person in their writing, finding it too informal and imprecise. The third-person point of view belongs to the people being talked about. Third-person singular pronouns include "she," "her," "hers," "herself," "he," "him," "his," "himself," "it," "its," and "itself," and third-person plural pronouns include "they," "them," "their," "theirs," and "themselves."

TABLE 8.11. Rewording for Agreement in Person	
Incorrect	If we manage our time, you will do better in your classes
Correct	If you manage your time, you will do better in your classes. If we manage our time, we will do better in our classes.

Sometimes using a noun again instead of a pronoun is the best solution if a sentence doesn't make totally clear what noun a pronoun refers to.

TABLE 8.12. Using a Noun Instead of a Pronoun for Clarity	
Confusing	The cases have sturdy lids, but they may still need to be replaced eventually.
Clear	The cases have sturdy lids, but the lids may still need to be replaced eventually.
Clear	The cases have sturdy lids, but the cases may still need to be replaced eventually.

Part Four

Punctuation Marks Made Easy

1. Commas Made Easy

When we have consecutive independent clauses that are joined by a coordinating conjunction, we use a comma before the conjunction (for, and, or, nor, or, yet, so).

That's my story, and I'm sticking to it.

I studied a lot, so I did well on the last exam.

When an independent clause or a phrase precedes an independent clause, separate them with a comma.

Because I studied a lot, I did well on the last exam.

Feeling anxious about my math class, I went to the tutoring center four times this week.

When the phrase is very short, and there is no possibility of confusion, the comma is optional.

> Every summer, we go to the beach.

> Every summer we go to the beach.

Use commas to separate three or more items in a series (as long as the items themselves don't have commas—see the section on semicolons), including a comma before the word "and" joining the last item to the list. You may have been told by some people to leave the comma before "and" out; however, the MLA, the most common style arbiter, requires this comma. Other styles, such as journalistic style, do not include it.

> I'm taking psychology, English, logic, and communications this semester.

This comma actually has its own name: the Oxford comma. People who support the use of the Oxford comma have pointed out that it doesn't hurt anything—and in many cases, it corrects potential ambiguities. Consider the following two sentences from a humorous example that has been circulating the Internet for years.

> We invited the strippers, JFK, and Stalin.

In this statement, albeit an impossible claim, the unidentified "We" invited strippers *and* JFK *and* Stalin to something.

> We invited the strippers, JFK and Stalin.

In this statement, the strippers' names are JFK and Stalin. There have actually been court cases that were won or lost based on the absence of an Oxford comma (we are serious—Google it.)

Use commas to separate two or more words that are the same parts of speech in a series, like adjectives or adverbs.

> The sky was a deep, clear, beautiful blue. (Three adjectives modifying a noun.)

The documentary provided a deeply moving, intellectually challenging experience. (Two adverbs modifying two adjectives).

Use commas after introductory words—like "stated," "said," "says," "asserts," "suggests," and "writes" —when they come before direct quotations.

Karl Marx said, "History repeats itself, first as tragedy, second as farce."

Note: If you follow words like "said" and "stated" with the relative pronoun "that," you should not use a comma before the quotation.

Picasso said that "Every child is an artist. The problem is how to remain an artist once we grow up."

Use commas before quoted material that you interrupt with a phrase of your own.

The unexamined life," according to Socrates, "is not worth living."

Use commas before quotations preceded by introductory phrases.

To quote Bertrand Russell, "This is patently absurd, but whoever wishes to become a philosopher must learn not to be frightened by absurdities."

Use commas before contrasting elements.

I said I read a story by Roald Dahl, not "rolled doll."

Use commas to set off "or" and a word or phrase when they are being offered as a synonym or definition of a word preceding these.

She said they were *meshuggeneh*, or crazy.

Note: *meshuggeneh* is Yiddish, and the MLA recommends italicizing foreign words except when they have become "normalized" into the English language, such as more common Latin terms and abbreviations, like "pro bono," "e.g.," and "i.e" and words like "raison d'être" and "hacienda."

2. Semicolons Made Easy

Use semicolons to set off two closely related independent clauses when they don't have a coordinating conjunction between them.

> Isabel Allende's first novel is *La casa de los espíritus;* the English title is *The House of the Spirits.*

> The film version of *The House of the Spirits* won many awards; however, it did not earn a lot of money.

Use semicolons to set off items in a series of three or more when one or more of those items has a comma.

The following series names three cities and the states they are in:

> Last summer she visited Seattle, Washington; San Diego, California; and Chicago, Illinois.

Sometimes people get confused and reverse the semicolons and commas. Remember that in sentences like the one above, the commas are serving as connectors—they connect an explanation, description, or some other piece of information about an item to that item—and the semicolons are functioning as separators between the different items. Ask yourself this question: "Which looks bigger and stronger, the comma [,] or the semicolon [;]?" Make sure that you understand where each item begins and leaves off, and put the semicolons where you are separating these items.

> Last summer she visited [1] **Seattle**, Washington; [2] **San Diego**, California; and [3] **Chicago**, Illinois.

Remember—in MLA format, we put a comma in front of "and" when it sets off the last item in a series of three or more. When the items themselves have commas, turn all the commas that we would ordinarily have in a series into semicolons, including the one preceding "and."

3. Colons Made Easy

Use colons to introduce sentence elements, but *only* after independent clauses. Use them when an independent clause is designed to create a feeling of anticipation for the information that is to follow. They can introduce a series, direct quotations, or even other independent clauses if the second clause interprets, explains, or amplifies the first.

> Modern Library's list of 100 best novels includes the following: *To Kill a Mockingbird, Catch-22,* and *The Grapes of Wrath.*

> George Santayana is credited for this aphorism: "Those who cannot remember the past are condemned to repeat it."

Do not use a colon if the element being introduced does not follow an independent clause. (Hint: you won't have a colon after a verb.)

> Modern Library's list of 100 best novels includes *To Kill a Mockingbird, Catch-22,* and *The Grapes of Wrath.*

Use colons between titles and subtitles.

> *Roots: The Saga of an American Family.*

Note: An exception occurs when a title is followed by another punctuation mark before the subtitle, as in the following example:

> *Trust Us, We're Experts! How Industry Manipulates Science and Gambles with Your Future.*

4. Apostrophes Made Easy

The apostrophe has two primary uses: forming contractions and making nouns possessive. In the past, it was commonly used to make numerals denoting decades and years plural, but MLA style no longer recommends this: you should write "the 1990s," not "the 1990's," though you would write "the '90s" since that is a contraction.

Use apostrophes to form contractions by inserting them in place of missing letters or numbers.

"It's" is the contraction of "it is" (it is not the possessive form of "it").

Use apostrophes to make nouns—not pronouns—possessive. Where or whether an "s" is added depends on whether a word is singular or plural and on its spelling.

When words do not end with an "s," make them possessive by adding an apostrophe and then an "s."

one <u>dog</u>'s chew toys	the <u>children</u>'s school	the <u>women</u>'s soccer team

When words end with an "s," add only an apostrophe when no extra "s" sound is pronounced.

two <u>dogs</u>' toys	both <u>houses</u>' roofs	all the <u>bosses</u>' offices

When words end with an "s" or an "s" sound, and an extra "s" sound is added when the word is made possessive, add an apostrophe and an "s" after it.

her <u>house</u>'s roof	his <u>boss</u>'s office	the <u>fox</u>'s lair

Subjects in sentences may share possession of something or have separate possession of different things.

With shared possession—when the subjects are functioning as a single unit—add the apostrophe and, if necessary, an additional "s" after the last name or item in the series.

Hiro and Riku's home is just a few blocks from the campus.

If the subjects do not share possession, make each name or item in the series possessive.

Ari's and Daniella's classes are on different days.

5. Quotation Marks Made Easy

Use quotation marks when you reproduce someone else's exact phrasing (unless the quotation is over four lines in your paper, in which case you indent two tabs (one inch) from the left margin instead).

Rani said, "I love director Mira Nair's movies."

Use quotation marks around the titles of works like poems, short stories, essays, and articles (works that are contained in periodicals and books).

Vladimir Nabokov's short story "That in Aleppo Once . . ." takes its title from a line in *Othello.*

For quotations or titles of such works inside a quotation, use single quotation marks (also called "inverted commas") inside the quotation. Use the apostrophe key on your keyboard.

Christina said, "My favorite short story is Tim O'Brien's 'The Things They Carried.'"

Putting periods and commas outside of closing quotation marks is not correct in MLA, APA, or other standard American formats. The only time you should have a sentence's period outside a closing quotation mark is when the sentence is followed by a parenthetical in-text citation. The period follows the citation unless you have an indented quotation. If you need a colon or a semicolon after material in quotation marks, the colon or semicolon should follow the closing quotation mark.

Adiva's essay analyzed a theme in James Joyce's story "Araby": the loss of innocence.

Alejandro wrote about "A Little Cloud"; it is also a story in Joyce's collection *Dubliners*.

If you directly quote a question or if a question mark is part of a title, the question mark goes inside the closing quotation mark. Also, only one terminal punctuation mark is used with quotation marks, so you don't follow a quotation with a period if you have a quotation mark inside.

"She asked, "What was the name of that short story we read by Joyce Carol Oates?"

The name of the story is "Where Are You Going, Where Have You Been?"

If you ask a question about material enclosed within quotation marks, the question mark goes outside the closing quotation mark.

Did you know that the movie *A.I. Artificial Intelligence* was based on the Brian Aldiss story "Supertoys Last All Summer Long"?

6. Question Marks Made Easy

Use question marks at the end of sentences that ask questions, including rhetorical questions and requests made in the form of questions. A rhetorical question is a question asked with no expectation of an answer. The question might be one that has an obvious answer, but it has been asked to make a point, to persuade, or for literary effect (thus the term "rhetorical question").

What topic did you choose for your research paper?
Are you nuts?

Remember that placement of question marks in relation to quotation marks is important. If you are quoting a question, put the closing quotation mark after the question mark.

The professor asked, "Does anyone have any questions?"

If you are asking a question about a quotation, place the question mark after the closing quotation mark.

> Did you really mean it when you said, "That's the best cake I've ever tasted"?

7. Periods Made Easy

Use a period at the end of a complete sentence that is a statement, not a question. If the last item in the sentence is an abbreviation that ends in a period, do not follow it with another period.

> Air travelers should not pack liquids in their carry-on bags, such as shampoo, lotion, water, etc.

Another thing to remember is that periods go inside closing quotation marks unless you have parenthetical in-text citations.

> In our literature class, we just read Poe's "The Cask of Amontillado."

> "The thousand injuries of Fortunato I had borne as I best could, but when he ventured upon insult I vowed revenge" (Poe 207).

8. Exclamation Marks Made Easy

Exclamation marks, also called exclamation points, are used to express excitement, astonishment, or other strong emotions. Beginning writers often use them in papers in an attempt to emphasize a point they are making. However, they come across as rather amateurish. If your point is strong, that will be conveyed by the content. Our advice is to avoid exclamation points in college papers. To quote F. Scott Fitzgerald, "Cut out all those exclamation points. An exclamation point is like laughing at your own jokes."

9. Ellipsis Marks Made Easy

Ellipsis marks (a set is called an ellipses) are indicated by three periods. An ellipsis can appear next to other punctuation, including a sentence's period (resulting in four periods). Use four only when the words on both sides of the ellipsis make full sentences. The MLA recommends that you have spaces before and after each ellipsis mark.

Use ellipses to indicate the omission of quoted material. The current convention is to put brackets around ellipses that you insert into direct quotations to make it clear that the ellipses aren't part of the original passage.

> William James wrote, "There is only one thing a philosopher can be relied upon to do [. . .] contradict other philosophers."

The use of brackets around ellipses within quoted material is a relatively recent practice, so you have probably seen more examples of ellipses without brackets than with them. The brackets indicate that the writer quoting William James added the ellipses, not James.

Use ellipses to indicate a sentence or clause that is allowed to deliberately trail off, suggesting a pause or unfinished comment or idea.

> There is something I've been meaning to tell you . . . .

In the example above, a period follows the three ellipses marks because the sentence ends.

10. Parentheses Made Easy

Use parentheses to enclose in-text citations.

The period follows the citation, not the quotation, summary, or paraphrase (unless you have indented direct quotations).

"The test of learning psychology is whether your understanding of situations you encounter has changed, not whether you have earned a new fact" (Kahneman 174).

Use parentheses to enclose clarifying information or information that is used as an aside.

Do not have spaces before the first word or after the last word in a parenthetical element. Unless you have a complete sentence within parentheses that is not enclosed inside another sentence, do not use a period in a parentheses. You may, however, add a question mark or exclamation point if called for.

The Bridezilla made everyone's life miserable (as usual).

Elizabeth Bishop's poem "One Art" contains parenthetical elements:

—Even losing you (the joking voice, a gesture
I love) I shan't have lied. It's evident
the art of losing's not too hard to master
though it may look (*Write* it!) like disaster.

Use parentheses to enclose abbreviations or acronyms after the first use of something's full name.

In 1925, the American Civil Liberties Union (ACLU) partnered with attorney Clarence Darrow to defend substitute biology teacher John T. Scopes, who was prosecuted by the state of Tennessee for daring to teach about evolution in a high school class. Darrow and the ACLU lost the case, but the guilty verdict was later overturned on a technicality.

11. Brackets Made Easy

We use square brackets when we insert material into, delete, or change material within quotations in order to make our additions or changes clearly distinct from the actual quoted material.

Use brackets to add explanatory information to a direct quotation.

> W. Somerset Maugham once said, "Only a mediocre [not first rate] person is always at his best."

Use brackets when you change an upper-case letter to a lower-case letter or a lower-case letter to an upper-case letter in a direct quotation.

Here are the first four lines from William Shakespeare's Sonnet 116:

> Let me not to the marriage of true minds
> Admit impediments. Love is not love
> Which alters when it alteration finds,
> Or bends with the remover to remove.

If you wished to incorporate these lines into a sentence of your own and still follow conventional capitalization guidelines for sentences, you could write the following:

> I feel, like Shakespeare, that "Love is not love // [which] alters when it alteration finds // [or] bends with the remover to remove."

Note: A forward slash is used to indicate a division between lines of poetry in the original version, but it does not need to be enclosed in brackets. If a stanza break occurs, indicate that with two forward slashes.

Use brackets when you change a word in a quotation.

Take, for example, the following sentence from an article on the History Channel website:

> "He was the driving force behind watershed events such as the Montgomery Bus Boycott and the 1963 March on Washington, which helped bring about such landmark legislation as the Civil Rights Act and the Voting Rights Act."

Out of context, this could be confusing, so it could be altered to the following:

> "[Martin Luther King, Jr.] was the driving force behind watershed events such as the Montgomery Bus Boycott and the 1963 March on Washington, which helped bring about such landmark legislation as the Civil Rights Act and the Voting Rights Act."

Use brackets around the term *sic* (Latin for "thus") to indicate errors or unusual spelling variations that are "thus in the original."

> Jonson told Drummond that "Shakespeare [*sic*] wanted art."

Use brackets around ellipses [. . .] to indicate that material has been deleted. Only delete words if you are in not any way altering the meaning of the original passage.

Here is an original quotation:

> "An award-winning and prolific writer, Steinem has authored several books, including a biography on Marilyn Monroe, and the best-selling *My Life on the Road*. Her work has also been published and reprinted in numerous anthologies and textbooks."

Leaving out the information on the two books would not alter the basic meaning of the sentence:

> "An award-winning and prolific writer, Steinem has authored several books . . . . Her work has also published and reprinted in numerous anthologies and textbooks."

In the example above, the entire end of the opening sentence was cut, so a period is added after the three ellipsis marks. If words within a single sentence were cut, there would be only three ellipses and the word following the bracket would not be capitalized unless it was a proper noun.

Name: _____ Section: _____ Date: _____

Part Five

Chapter 8 Workshop

The following section contains a series of ten tasks that, if completed, will help you gain mastery over the content in this chapter. Your instructor will assign some (or all) of them to you as a way to practice the material presented here. Notice that some of them are global and focus on the entirety of the skills laid out in this chapter, while others are more focused and explore only one or two sections of the chapter. Also notice that some are shorter; some are longer; all are designed to flip the classroom and put the power of learning directly into your hands.

Workshop One.

<u>Overview</u>: Summarize all of the major sections and/or bullet points that you find in this chapter.

Each major section or heading should be clearly labeled and should have at least a one-sentence discussion. You might have a dozen or more headings and sentences here. Be thorough and accurate to show that you have read and comprehended this chapter's contents. Avoid the temptation to judge or add anything new (even critical discussion of the content); this is an act of pure summary. Tell your instructor exactly what came in this chapter and in what order.

Workshop Two.

<u>Overview</u>: This workshop has you examine all of the wrong answers from your chapter diagnostic and respond to them.

1. Make a list of each question from the chapter diagnostic that you got wrong.

2. Go through the chapter to look up the rules on each question. For every question you got wrong, do the following:
   A. Identify the page number where the rule was found.
   B. Discuss what the right answer should have been on the diagnostic test.
   C. Discuss how you can avoid this error in future writing and/or tests.

Workshop Three.

Overview: Write a short, personal essay explaining the content of this chapter. The point of this essay is to directly address what you have learned from the chapter and how it will impact your future academic writing. Consider some or all of the following:

   A. What is your biggest weakness when it comes to punctuation and grammar? What did the chapter discuss to help you fix this weakness?
   B. What is your biggest strength when it comes to punctuation and grammar? What did the chapter say to help you polish those skills even more?
   C. Commas tend to be the most common trouble area for students. What are some of the comma rules that were new to you?
   D. What other elements covered in the chapter were helpful, and how do you think you will be able to use your new mastery of these rules in your college essays?

Workshop Four.

Overview: Create a PowerPoint presentation or website that can be shared with your colleagues and professor that cover the basic elements of the portion of the chapter called "Punctuation and Grammar Basics."

   A. Your PowerPoint or website must cover the basics of subjects, verbs, and predicates.
   B. Your PowerPoint or website must explain the difference between independent and dependent clauses.

C. Your PowerPoint or website must explain the differences between restrictive and non-restrictive elements.

D. Your PowerPoint or website should cover any other details from the chapter that you feel would be helpful in a presentation.

Workshop Five.

Overview: Create a PowerPoint presentation or website that can be shared with your colleagues and professor that cover the basic elements of the portion of the chapter called Punctuation "Marks Made Easy".

A. Your PowerPoint or website must cover the most common rules of comma usage.

B. Your PowerPoint or website must cover the most common rules of semicolon usage.

C. Your PowerPoint or website must cover the basics of using apostrophes.

D. Your PowerPoint or website must cover the use of quotation marks.

E. Your PowerPoint or website should cover any other details from the chapter that you feel would be helpful in a presentation.

Workshop Six.

Overview: Often, teaching something can be the best way to learn it yourself on a deeper level. Therefore, write a quiz for future students that covers the basics of Parts of Speech.

A. This quiz should include various styles of questions, including multiple choice, short answer, and true/false. Check with your instructor on specifics.

B. This quiz should be designed to show mastery of the skills from another student at your own level.

C. You must write an answer key starting on a new page after the quiz. This answer key must include the page numbers from *Flipping English* where students can find the answer. It must also include a complete sentence for each quiz question you generated to explain to the instructor why you thought this question targeted a critical skill in writing properly punctuated sentences.

Workshop Seven.

<u>Overview</u>: Often, teaching something can be the best way to learn it yourself on a deeper level. Therefore, write a quiz for future students that covers the various rules associated with the use of commas.

     A. This quiz should include various styles of questions, including multiple choice, short answer, and true/false. Check with your instructor on specifics.

     B. This quiz should be designed to show mastery of the skills from another student at your own level.

     C. You must write an answer key starting on a new page after the quiz. This answer key must include the page numbers from *Flipping English* where students can find the answer. It must also include a complete sentence for each quiz question you generated to explain to the instructor why you thought this question targeted a critical skill in writing properly punctuated sentences.

Workshop Eight.

<u>Overview</u>: Often, teaching something can be the best way to learn it yourself on a deeper level. Therefore, write a quiz for future students that covers the various rules associated with the use of pronouns.

     1. This quiz should include various styles of questions, including multiple choice, short answer, and true/false. Check with your instructor on specifics.

     2. This quiz should be designed to show mastery of the skills from another student at your own level.

     3. You must write an answer key starting on a new page after the quiz. This answer key must include the page numbers from *Flipping English* where students can find the answer. It must also include a complete sentence for each quiz question you generated to explain to the

instructor why you thought this question targeted a critical skill in writing properly punctuated sentences.

Workshop Nine.

Overview: One way that a lot of writers complete the editing process is by marking up an older draft to look for particular weaknesses and errors. Practice doing this on an older paper of yours.

1. Take a piece of writing you have done already (for this class or for another if you haven't written one yet). If you have an electronic copy, print out a fresh one. If not, work with the one that your previous instructor returned to you.
   a. Work on commas. Take a highlighter and highlight every single comma in the paper.
   b. Then, look up the rules associate with each comma. When you are done, go through and look at each one. If each comma is correct, simply write "correct" above it. If you found an error, then you will correct it with a pencil and write the rule that shows it is wrong.
2. Work on a weakness. Identify a weakness in your own grammar and punctuation (work with your professor if you're not sure). Mark it up with a highlighter and complete the process described above with commas.
3. Write a paragraph that reflects on this process. Did you find fewer or more mistakes than you anticipated? Were there rules you were unaware of? Will these rules be easy to remember while writing your rough draft, or will a process like this be the best way to find those errors as they creep in to future writing projects?

Workshop Ten.

Overview: What is your take away from this chapter? What did you learn and what questions do you still have?

1. Write a short response of several sentences that covers the three main things that you learned from this chapter.
2. Write out at least five questions you still have about the chapter. What things would you want to communicate to your instructor? What would you like to see discussed in class or handled with more depth to help you master this chapter's content.
3. What is one thing that you have taken away from this chapter and will use on your next writig task? Why is this thing important, and how do you plan to implement it?

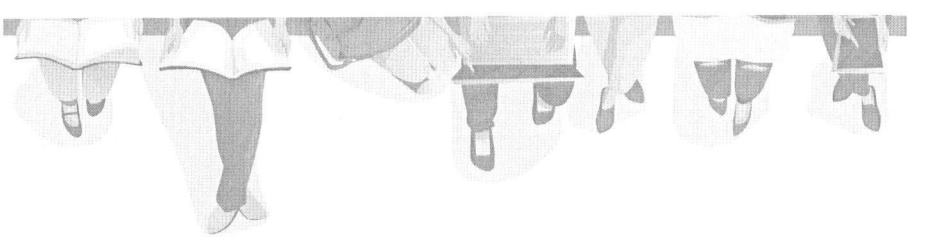

CHAPTER 9

How to Use the Basics of MLA Format

In this chapter, you will learn about the following:

Part One: Formatting Documents in MLA Style

Part Two: Creating In-Text Citations in MLA Format

11. Citations for Films and Television Programs
12. Speeches and Lectures
13. Interviews

Part Three: Creating Works Cited in MLA Format

1. Types of Works Cited Entries
2. Basic Rules for MLA Works Cited Pages
3. Books and Plays
4. A Single Article, Essay, or Other Work in a Collection of Anthology
5. Multiple Selections from a Collection or Anthology (Cross-References)
6. Periodicals: Scholarly Journals, Magazines, and Newspapers
7. Websites
8. Speeches and Lectures
9. Interviews

Part Four: Workshop

Part One

Formatting Documents in MLA Style

The following is a list of the elements in this section governing the basic format for the documents that you submit to your professors: General Appearance of Papers, Personal and Class Identification Headings, Titles, Sample First Page, Italics and Quotation Marks, Numbers, Dates, and Potential Problems in Word Processing Programs.

1. General Appearance of Papers

- **Margins and Printing**: Your paper should have one-inch margins on all sides. Paper documents should be printed on one side of the paper only and fastened with a single staple in the upper-left corner.

- **Justification**: Except for titles and works cited headings, justify the paper at the left margin. Center the title and the heading for the list of works cited using "Center," not the space bar. Do not full-justify a paper; it can create odd spacing between words.

- **Preferred Font**: MLA recommends that you choose a simple, legible font like Times New Roman, 12 point, and that you use the same font for the entire paper. With a basic font like Times New Roman, the regular and italics type styles contrast enough to be easily distinguished.

- **Sentence, Line, and Paragraph Spacing**: In the past, two spaces after terminal punctuation marks (periods, question marks, and exclamation points) was recommended. Current MLA style recommends using only one space. The entire paper should be double-spaced. Don't add extra spaces between paragraphs or above or below titles, headings, or in between works cited entries. Indent the first line of each paragraph one-half inch from the left margin. Use the Tab key instead of hitting the space bar.

- **Header**: The header goes in the upper-right corner of each page of your paper and includes your last name, a space, and page number (just the number—don't use pg. or p.) Use "Header" in Word or Pages in the "Insert" menu to put it in the correct place in your paper in the upper right margin, one half inch from the top and flush with the right margin.

2. Personal and Class Identification Headings

The following information should be in four lines in the upper-left corner of the first page of a paper. Just like the rest of the document, it should be entirely double-spaced. (Do not put this information in the "header" in your word-processing program.)

1. **Your full name**. Put the components in the typical format, with your first name first, middle initial (if you use one), and your last name.

2. **Your professor's name**. Only use your professor's last name, preceded by the title "Professor" unless he or she prefers "Doctor."

3. **The name of the course**. Do not abbreviate the course discipline. Instructors with multiple sections of the same class may want students to follow the class name with a colon and the starting time and days abbreviated to the days' first letters, such as English 1A: 1:00 MW for a

class that starts at 1:00 on Mondays and Wednesdays. Online classes can use course reference numbers (CRNs), for example, English 1A: 31402.

4. **The date the paper is turned in**. The day and month should precede the year. Do not abbreviate the month or use commas.

3. Titles

The title of your paper should be interesting and informative. Avoid titles like Essay One or Research Paper. Center it over the body of your paper.

Capitalize the first letters of all words in your titles except the following (unless they are the first or last words of a title or subtitle): articles ("a," "an," and "the"), prepositions ("above," "at," "before," "in," "of," "with," etc.), coordinating conjunctions ("for," "and," "nor," "but," "or," "yet," "so"), and the "to" in infinitives. You should also capitalize the words that follow hyphens in compound words. If you have a subtitle, use a colon after the title (unless the first part of your title is a question).

Do not put your own titles in italics or quotation marks or follow them with periods. You may, however, use a question mark if your title asks a rhetorical question. Avoid exclamation points—they come across as rather juvenile. However, if you come up with a funny title and an exclamation point seems appropriate, that is an exception. Check with your professor, though, just to be safe. If your title refers to a work that should be italicized or enclosed in quotation marks, retain that format.

If your title is very long and fills all or most of an entire line or even goes into a second line, create an inverted pyramid shape, as in the following example:

The Retreat of Democracy and the Rise of Authoritarianism: The

Worldwide Resurgence of "Strongmen"

4. Sample First Page

Following is a sample first page of an essay in MLA format. Technically, there should be a header in the upper right corner, Ruiz 1, but that is hidden by the table heading.

TABLE 9.1. Sample First Page of An Essay in MLA Format

Amelia Ruiz

Professor Abadi

English 1A

15 April 2019

Gender Roles in the Classic Fairy Tales:

How they Affect Young Girls

Children are more affected by the messages they receive through stories, television, and other forms of media than many people think. While some argue that children are capable of critical thinking when it comes to ideas they are exposed to, studies show that young children are vulnerable to adopting the ideas they are exposed to in the media they are shown. Specifically, it seems as though children are influenced by patriarchal messages regarding stereotypical gender roles. When young girls are presented with sexist messages in the media they consume, they are set up to develop negative views of both themselves and the adult women around them. Popular classic fairy tales like "Cinderella," "Sleeping Beauty," and "Snow White" that portray their heroines as passive and helpless victims in need of rescue by men negatively impact the development of self-image in female children. Furthermore, the portrayal of older female characters in fairy tales primarily as old hags, witches, and greedy and unscrupulous old women has a detrimental effect on children's views of women and aging. Educators should be wary of relying on them for use in the classroom, and parents should be wary of relying on them for a staple of entertainment during children's most formative years.

TABLE 9.1 (*continued*)

Young girls who only see women in fairy tales as either pretty princesses or ugly and wicked old hags are at risk for thinking there aren't any other options for growing up female. Diversity in children's media is incredibly important because children need to see examples of people reflective of themselves living healthy, average lives. For young girls, this means seeing positive examples of strong, independent women in the television shows and movies they watch.

---

5. Italics and Quotation Marks

Typically, "big" sources—those that are independent—get italicized, but "little" ones—the ones that are contained inside the bigger ones—are enclosed in quotation marks. This is a generalized guideline, but a good one to remember in most cases. You might get confused when you look at how some sources, such as newspapers, treat titles. They are not using MLA format. Newspapers never italicize text, so they put books, films, periodicals, and other sources that we italicize into quotation marks instead. This does not mean that you should do so in your college papers.

Sometimes titles of works contain the titles of other works. As noted earlier, if a title that you put inside quotation marks includes the title of something that should be italicized, it is simple: just make sure that works that should be italicized are italicized. If a title that you put inside quotation marks includes the title of something that should also be enclosed within quotation marks, use single quotation marks (the apostrophe key) for the work inside. If a title on a works cited page or that you refer to in the body of your essay that is in italics includes the title of something that should also be italicized, then put the internal title into regular, non-italic font so that it clearly stands out as a title.

TABLE 9.2. Using Italics and Quotation Marks	
Using Italics	**Using Quotation Marks**
Book or play	**Essay, short story, poem, titled book chapter, or titled act from a play**
Othello: *The State of Play* (book)	"Politics and the English Language" (essay)
Churchill and Orwell: The Fight for Freedom (book)	"The Tiger's Bride" (short story)
Othello, the Moor of Venice (play)	"Dream Deferred" (poem)
	"Orwell Becomes 'Orwell'" (titled book chapter)
Note: In the first book's title, we do not italicize *Othello* because it is the name of the play that the book is about. Not italicizing it sets it off.	Note: In the book chapter's title, we use single quotation marks around the second use of Orwell's name because there were quotation marks around it in the title.
Periodicals	**Articles in periodicals**
The Midwest Quarterly (scholarly journal)	"A Tradition of Male Poetics: Mary Shelly's *Frankenstein* as an Allegory of Art" (journal article)
New Yorker (magazine)	
The Washington Post (newspaper)	
Website	**Posting or article on website**
Humanesociety.org (organization's site)	"American Wolves Need To Be Protected, Not Hunted" (blog post)
SurLaLune Fairy Tales (individual's site)	"Children and Fairy Tales" (article)
The Huffington Post (Internet newspaper)	
Feature film or documentary	**The specific scene of a movie, often called "chapters" in the feature of a DVD**
The Fellowship of the Ring (feature film)	"Farewell, Dear Bilbo"
The Central Park Five (documentary)	

TABLE 9.2. (*Continued*)

Encyclopedia or dictionary *Encyclopedia Britannica* *Oxford Dictionary of English*	**Article from an encyclopedia or dictionary** "Swashbuckling Sisters: Six Lady Pirates" (from an encyclopedia) "Post-Truth" (from a dictionary)
Television series *Game of Thrones*	**Specific episode of a television series** "The Long Night"
Radio series or podcast *All Things Considered*	**Specific episode of a radio series or podcast** "College Board to Give Students 'Adversity Score' Based on Social and Economic Factors"

6. Numbers

In the bodies of essays, you should typically write numbers in full up through ninety-nine. For 100 and up, use numerals. There are exceptions. Use numerals for more complicated, lengthy numbers: *4 1/2* instead *of four and a half*, and so on. Large numbers may be written in a combination of numerals and words, such as *12.5 million*. However, if a number starts a sentence, write out the number or re-word the sentence so that you can use a numeral inside it. In citations and works-cited entries, use numerals. In ranges of numbers give all numbers in full up through 99. For numbers over 99, drop the first numeral of the last page number if the page numbers are in the same range of a hundred or a thousand.

7. Dates

Do not abbreviate dates in the bodies of essays—only abbreviate them in your list of works cited. You may use either the day-month-year style or the month-day-year style in the body (remember the identification information in the upper-left corner of the first page must use the day-month-year format). Just be consistent with the style you choose to use in the body.

Bodies of Papers	Works Cited	First Page, Upper Left
17 September 2019	17 Sept. 2019	17 September 2019
September 17, 2019		

Always use standard abbreviations when you abbreviate months. For example, you may find an article in a database where the database abbreviates September to Sep. Databases do not use MLA format, so you should use Sept, not Sep.

8. Potential Problems in Word Processing Programs

MLA paper layout is the part of MLA format that is perhaps the easiest to master, but word processing programs can cause problems. The default settings of Microsoft Word, for example, automatically make changes that violate MLA format.

Extra Line Spacing Between Paragraphs

By default, Word adds an extra space between paragraphs, which is improper for MLA format. Go to the Home Tab and hit the Paragraph settings. When the dialog box opens, click the box that says something like "Don't add space between paragraphs of the same style." Do this before you type anything or after you do a "Select All," or the change will only be applied to the line the cursor is on.

Bottom Margins

In spite of your setting the bottom margin to the proper single inch, Word often pushes lines of text to the next page, making the printed margin larger than an inch. You have to modify your margins as you type to make sure that the bottom margin comes as close to an inch as possible when the document is printed. Getting into the paragraph settings and working with what is called "Widow/Orphan" controls will sometimes help, but not always.

Font Changes

The default font in Word is Calibri 11 point, but MLA recommends Times New Roman 12, but changing the font for the body of the paper does not change the font in the header. Access the page's header to change the font there, as well.

Spelling and Grammar Checking

This not only helps you to catch and correct typos and misspellings, it will tell you to add missing accent marks where needed (all you have to do is accept the suggested change), it will tell you if you have accidentally typed extra spaces between words, and so on. However, sometimes this feature will suggest that a phrase is ungrammatical when it isn't. It may suggest an incorrect word when it finds a misspelling or a name. If you automatically accept all suggestions, you can create errors.

URLs and Hyperlinks

When you create works cited entries for sources you find online, you will have to copy and paste URLs into your paper. Word will often make these hyperlinks "live," which will add underlining and changes the color to blue. Make your cursor hover over the hyperlink, select "edit hyperlink," and remove the hyperlink.

Google Docs

Google Docs is a useful tool for student collaborations on projects, but it lacks the robust formatting options of Microsoft Word, Pages, and other programs. We recommend avoiding Google Docs when you write your essays.

Part Two

Creating In-Text Citations in MLA Format

1. Why We Need Parenthetical In-Text Citations?

In MLA format, we use in-text parenthetical citations every time we directly quote, summarize, or paraphrase any information we take from a source unless it is considered common knowledge. Common knowledge refers to generally known facts that the average reader knows, such as widely known dates and facts. Determining whether something should be considered common knowledge can be tricky, so cite a source if you're not sure.

The following is a list of the elements in this chapter governing the format in-text citations: Basic Guidelines, One Author, Two Authors, Three or More Authors, No Author Provided, Same Source Used More Than Once in One Paragraph, Sources Quoting Other Works, More Than One Work by the Same Author, Two or More Authors with the Same Last Name, Information from More Than One Source, Citations for Films and Television Programs, Speeches and Lectures, Interviews.

2. Basic Guidelines

The information beginning your in-text citations must correspond to the beginning of the entries on your works cited page so that readers can easily locate the full publication information for each source that you use in your paper. Typically, an in-text citation will use the author's last name. In this section, we will tell you what to do when you have multiple authors or unknown authors.

Follow authors or title words with page numbers, if provided by the source, with no commas or abbreviations before the numbers. Do not use the abbreviations "p.," "pp." "pg." or the word "page" before page numbers; simply provide the page number. If you have used the name of the author (or title if there is no author) in your text, you may supply just the page number in the in-text citation. If the material spans two pages, hyphenate the two numbers.

When a work does not have page numbers, simply use the author's last name or the first important words of the title if no author is provided. For sources with no page numbers, provide an in-text citation with the author or first noun phrase of the title even if you have used the name of the source in your text. An in-text citation makes it clear what information you have taken from the source so that you may avoid accusations of plagiarism. The citation is also helpful because it indicates where the information from the source ends if you are paraphrasing or summarizing rather than directly quoting. That way, your readers won't be confused about where the source material ends and your own interpretations or explanations begin.

Some sources provide paragraph numbers instead of page numbers, especially online sources. Provide the relevant numbers, preceded by "par." Add a comma after the author's name (or first important word of the title). Do not provide paragraph numbers unless your source provides them—do not count them on your own.

Most electronic readers (such as a Kindle) include a numbering system that tells users their location in the work. Do not cite this numbering because it may differ for other users. If the work is divided into consistent numbered sections, such as chapters, the numbers of those sections may be cited, with a label identifying the nature of the number, as in this example: (ch. 3).

3. One Author

With one author, provide the author's last name and the page number(s) for paginated works. Do not use a comma. In the following example, the material spanned two pages. When this happens, we drop the first numeral of the last page number if both are in the same range of a hundred or a thousand.

> "The figure of 6 million is usually assigned to the Nazi genocide against Jews. Then came the killings in Cambodia, in Rwanda, and as the century neared its end, in Bosnia, Kosovo, and East Timor" (Singer 111-12).

If you indicate the author in your text, you can simply provide the page numbers.

4. Two Authors

If there are two authors, provide both last names separated by "and." Do not use commas or change the order of authors as presented in the work. The following information is not enclosed in quotation marks because it is a paraphrase.

In this century, international spread of communication over computer networks has opened up growing and diverse chances for economic growth, but it has also caused growing and diverse threats to countries' safety and human rights (Poblet and Kolieb 259).

5. Three or More Authors

If there are three or more, MLA recommends using just the first author's last name followed by the Latin "et al.," which means, roughly, "and others"; do not use a comma:

> "According to the first research on the topic, authoritarianism should be regarded as the consequence of the entwinement of individual characteristics and social dynamics" (Roccato et al. 14).

6. No Author Provided

If no author is named, use the first important words of the title (omit "a," "an," or "the," but keep these words in the work cited entry). Make sure that you have enough words to distinguish between titles that begin the same. Follow this with a page number if one is provided. Format the words you take from the title as formatted in the works cited entry, using quotation marks for articles, essays, short stories, and encyclopedia entries, etc., and italics for books, plays, and websites, etc.

> According to the California Department of Forestry and Fire Protection, twelve of the wildfires in California in 2017 were probably caused by reckless and illegal actions on the part of the Pacific gas and Electric Co. ("PG&E" 9).

> "You can protect your child against measles with a combination vaccine that provides protection against three diseases: measles, mumps, and rubella (MMR). The MMR vaccine is proven to be very safe and effective" ("Measles").

7. Same Source Used More Than Once in One Paragraph

You may quote the same source more than once in a single paragraph. As long as you do not include any quotations from other sources or any information that you have thought of on your own in between, you can use one parenthetical citation after the last quotation.

> Thomas E. Ricks points out that "Only a few writers took much note of Orwell during his life," but now, decades later, "In opinions issues by members of the U.S. Supreme Court, Orwell was the third most cited author, coming after Shakespeare and Lewis Carroll (247, 249).

In this example, note that a comma is used between the different page numbers, not a hyphen, because the student writing the paper is taking different quotations from nonconsecutive pages, not presenting a single quotation, summary, or paraphrase that spans the pages.

8. Sources Quoting Other Works

You will often find writers who quote other people. Introduce the person being quoted before the quotation, but refer to the author of your source in your citation—that is what leads your readers to the correct work cited entry. Put your source's name inside the citation preceded by the abbreviation for "quoted in." Do not use "qtd. in" if you are quoting your source's own words; use it only when your source is using someone else's words.

> Critic Philip French referred to Orwell as "possibly the greatest writer of the twentieth century" (qtd. in Ricks 249).

9. More Than One Work by the Same Author

If you are citing more than one work by an author, include the first important word of the title of the work you are citing in addition to the author's name and relevant page number(s). Separate the author's name (if you need it in the citation) and the title with a comma. If you have named the author before the information you used, just give the first important word of the title and the page number.

Stephen Jay Gould states, "Nature is not an intrinsic harmony of clearly defined units. Nature exists in multiple levels, interacting with fuzziness at their borders" ("Humongous" 343).

"It would be an impoverished and bleak world indeed if we encountered nothing but humans and a rat or cockroach now and then" (Gould, "Continuity" 429).

Note: When you have more than one work by the same author, arrange the works cited entries alphabetically by the first important word of the title, and use three hyphens for the author's name for every entry after the first one.

10. Two or More Authors with the Same Last Name

If your paper uses sources by different authors with the same last name, include each author's first initial in the in-text citations (use the whole first name if the initials are the same), as in the examples below of a direct quotation and a paraphrased section.

"Advocates of cross-cultural competence emphasize the need to understand one's own worldview, but most training or efforts to provide training associated with 'minority' clients tend to focus on the cultural experience of the 'minority' person'" (R. Carter 20).

When Eunice Hunton volunteered with other women to go to Europe during WWI to help the troops' morale in a program arranged by the YMCA, she also ended up helping to document the poor treatment of soldiers of color by their own army (S. Carter 32.)

11. Information from More Than One Source

If you have information that comes from different sources, indicate them all, separated by semicolons to indicate that the authors represent different, not coauthored, sources. The following is a paraphrase:

Throughout the history of the folktale, no matter what their respective classes or status, women across the social spectrum shared and modified fairy tales (Smith 172; Warner 316-17).

12. Citations for Films and Television Programs

In your entries for films and similar works, you have choices about how to begin an entry. You can begin with the tile of the work followed by contributors, or you can begin with primary contributors. What goes inside your citation is what you use at the beginning of the work-cited entry. If you have used a director's name as the first word in an entry about a film, that name is what you should use, as in the second example, which is from the same film.

> The destruction over a decade ago of thousands of brand new, extremely efficient prototype electric cars suggests that the auto industry's aversion to change and its reliance on oil have seriously delayed its ability to implement available solutions (*Who*).

> The destruction over a decade ago of thousands of brand new, extremely efficient prototype electric cars suggests that the auto industry's aversion to change and its reliance on oil have seriously delayed its ability to implement available solutions (*Paine*).

13. Speeches and Lectures

If you have taken information from a speech or lecture, use the last name of the lecturer or speaker for the in-text citation, as with the following paraphrase. Instead of giving your references list the heading Works Cited, you should use Sources Cited since people are not "works").

> Most people have heard of King Arthur and the Round Table, but they may not know the symbolism of the famous Round Table. When Arthur became king, he built the Round Table to show that everyone was equal (Kumelos).

14. Interviews

In-text citations for interviews should contain the interviewed person's last name and page numbers when present.

> "There has been a tremendous amount of change in public attitude and there has been a change in the information we have about sexual harassment. Even a few years ago, people were ambivalent about what the consequences should be concerning behaving incredibly badly in the workplace" (Hill).

Part Three
Creating Works Cited Pages in MLA Format

The Works Cited section is the final page (or pages) of your paper, containing all the information a reader needs to find the sources you have used. You may find yourself using a speech, lecture, or interview in your paper. If you do, use the heading Sources Cited instead of Works Cited.

1. Types of Works Cited Entries

The following is a list of the elements in this chapter governing the format for the entries that go on the page or pages listing all of the works used in a paper: Basic Rules for MLA Works Cited Pages; Basic Forms for Books and Plays; Book or Play with One Author; Book or Play with Two Authors; Book or Play with Three or More Authors; Book or Play with No Author Given; eBooks; A Single Article, Essay, or Other Work in a Collection or Anthology; Multiple Selections from a Collection or Anthology (Cross-References); Basic Forms for Works from Periodicals; Scholarly Journal Article in Print, in Databases, and Online; Magazine Articles in Print and Online; Newspapers Article in Print and Online; Websites; Speeches, Lectures, and Interviews.

2. Basic Rules for MLA Works Cited Pages

- The Modern Language Association (MLA) made major changes in format in 2016. Make sure that you use current, not obsolete, format. Many examples that you find on the web and in older publications will give you examples of outdated format.

- The Works Cited page always begins at the top of a new page; use "page break" to set it off from the body of your paper.

- Center the heading Works Cited (or Sources Cited if you include interviews, etc.) at the top.

- Everything on the page should simply be double spaced, so don't add an extra space under the heading or between the entries.

- The first line of each entry should be flush with the left margin—and remember that the margins of your documents should only be one inch. Each line of an entry after the first should be indented one-half inch from the left. Set up a "Hanging Indent" in your word processor.

- All entries must go in alphabetical order using individuals' last names (such as authors, editors, or whomever else comes at the beginning of the entry) or by the first words of titles when they begin an entry; with titles, ignore the parts of speech called articles ("a," "an," and "the") if they begin titles, but do not delete them or move them to the end of the title.

- If the work was originally published in another language, add "Translated by" followed by the translator's or translators' names, a comma, the publisher, a comma, the year, and a period.

- When there is more than one creator of a work, reverse the first and last names only of the first person at the beginning of an entry, and don't change the order of the contributors.

- Capitalize the first letter of each word in titles except for articles, prepositions, coordinating conjunctions, and the "to" in infinitives (unless any of these is the first or last word of a title or subtitle). Capitalize the words following hyphens in compound words.

- Use quotation marks around the titles of articles, short stories, poems, TV and radio episodes, and other works located in books, periodicals, websites, and so on (unless they are plays or books).

- Italicize titles of books, journals, magazines, newspapers, plays, databases, websites, TV and radio series, and movies.

- When titles of books or plays are parts of the title of a book, do not italicize these; this makes it easier for readers to identify these as distinctive parts of the overall title.

- Works cited entries typically begin with the authors (or other creators) and followed by titles of works, and we normally follow these titles with periods. However, if titles include another punctuation mark at the end as part of the title, such as a quotation mark or exclamation point, use these instead of adding a period. If no author is given, we begin with the titles.

- If titles have subtitles, you must set the subtitles off with **colons** unless the part of the title before the subtitle is followed by another punctuation mark, such as a quotation mark or exclamation point. (To determine if a book has a subtitle, look at the title page and publication data; sometimes the spines or covers of books omit subtitles or add blurbs that look like subtitles but aren't.)

- Abbreviate all months except for May, June, and July; days should come before the months and years in dates, and no commas are used. For works that span two months, hyphenate the months, for example, Sept.-Oct. If you are getting an article from a database, keep in mind that databases do not follow MLA format, and may use abbreviations like "Sep." instead of "Sept." Don't copy what the database does; use standard abbreviations.

- Only a single space should follow a period. (This is true for sentences; too, not just works cited entries).

- Spaces should follow periods and commas after the individual components in entries, such as authors, titles, publishers, etc.; however, spaces do not follow periods inside most abbreviations made of lowercase letters, such as a.m. and p.m. in entries that involve time-based media.

- The date of access is no longer required for works accessed electronically. However, if your instructor requires the date of access, it should be the last item in the entry, preceded by a period and "Accessed" before the date. End the entry, as always, with a period.

- The city of publication is no longer required for most works cited entries. Exceptions are made for books published before 1900 when no publisher is given and for books published in different countries where changes have been made to the original versions. Provide the city before the publishing company, followed by a comma (not a colon, as in previous versions of MLA format).

- Sources may have other types of contributor. You may provide optional listings of other people involved with the creation of a work. Provide their names the way the example of the translators shows, preceded by the descriptive term, such as "illustrated by," "introduction by," and "edited by."

Following are common descriptors:

> adapted by
> directed by
> edited by
> epilogue by
> illustrated by
> introduction by
> narrated by
> performance by

3. Books and Plays

While this first section focuses on books and plays, it covers format issues that are relevant to other sources, as well, such as what to when there are one, two, or three or more authors given, no authors given, translators, multiple works by single authors, and so on.

Identifying and Naming Book Publishers

When providing publishers' names, omit "business" words and their abbreviations, such as "Company," "Ltd.," and "Inc." With University Presses, replace University with U and Press with P, without periods. Leave the U and the P where the words University Press are in the name. For example, University Press of Colorado should be UP of Colorado, University of California Press should be U of California P, and Columbia University Press should be Columbia UP. For all other publishers, give the names in full except for the business terms, keeping word like "Publishers," "Press," "Books," and so on.

Basic Forms for Books and Plays

Print Versions
Begin with authors and a period, followed by the title of the book or play in italics, a period, the publisher, a comma, and the year.

Author(s). *Title*. Publisher, year of publication.

Book or Play with One Author
Dreisinger, Baz. *Incarceration Nations: A Journey to Justice in Prisons around the World*. Other Press, 2017.

Albee, Edward. 1962. *Who's Afraid of Virginia Woolf?* Scribner, 2003.

Note: If a title ends with a question mark or an exclamation point, do not follow it with a period. If a book or play was originally published significantly earlier than the copy that you have, you may include the original publication date, followed by a period, after the book's title

Book or Play with Two Authors

Separate the authors with a comma preceding "and." Do not change the order of the authors, and do not reverse the first and last names of any author but the first.

Shermer, Michael, and Stephen Jay Gould. *Why People Believe Weird Things: Pseudoscience, Superstition, and Other Confusions of Our Time.* Holt, 2002.

Book or Play with Three or More Authors

When you have three or more authors, MLA suggests that you provide only the first author's name, followed by "et al." (You will use this author's last name in the in-text citations, also followed by "et al.")

Wilson, James Q., et al. *American Government: Institutions and Policies.* Cengage Learning, 2015.

If you have a reason to include all of the authors' names, you may do so, despite the MLA's current preferences. Options are allowed. You may wish to discuss the background of each author if your instructor asks you to do so. Remember—always ask your professor's preferences about optional elements.

Wilson, James Q., John J. Dilulio, Jr., and Meena Bose. *American Government: Institutions and Policies.* Cengage Learning, 2015.

Book or Play with No Author Given

If no author is provided, begin with title.

Hazards of Primary Care in Aging Populations. J.B. Lippincott, 1978.

eBook from an Internet provider, Non-Subscription Service

Author(s). *Title.* Publisher, year of publication. *Provider*, URL (unless a professor's preference is to skip this and use *web* instead; MLA advises the URL).

When you provide the URL, drop the *http//* or *https//* from the beginning, and "break" the URL if needed to move part of it up. You do not want to leave blank spaces.

Hosokawa, Bill. *Colorado's Japanese Americans:* From 1886 to the Present. UP of Colorado, 2005. *Project MUSE*, muse.jhu.edu/book/3803.

Richards, John F. *The Unending Frontier: An Environmental History of the Early Modern World.* U of California P, 2003. *ACLS Humanities E-book,* hdl.handle .net/2027/fulcrum.g158bh96t.

eBook from a library subscription collection
Author(s). *Title.* Publisher, date. *Provider*, URL.

Fredrickson, George M. *Black Liberation: A Comparative History of Black Ideologies in the United States and South Africa.* Oxford UP, 1996. *eBook Academic Collection*, web.b.ebscohost.com/ ehost/detail/detail?vid=3&sid= b48e0ca5-7987-486c-9180-87cf5682598d% 40sessionmgr 106 &hid=115&bdata=JnNpdGU9ZWhvc3QtbGl2ZSZzY29wZT1zaXRl #AN= 143953&db =e000 xna.

More Than One Work by The Same Individuals
When you are using more than one work by the same authors or editors, organize these works alphabetically using the last name of the first author and then the first important word of the title (ignore *a, an,* and *the*). For every entry for these people after the first entry, use three hyphens instead of their names if the names are exactly the same and in the same order. In the following examples, we do not use three hyphens for the third use of Gaiman's name because he co-authored that book with Terry Prachett.

Gaiman, Neil. American Gods. Morrow, 2001.

---. Anansi Boys. Headline Review, 2006.

Gaiman, Neil, and Terry Pratchett. *Good Omens: The Nice and Accurate Prophecies of Agnes Nutter.* Morrow, 2011.

Cities of Publication

MLA has dropped the city of publication from most works cited entries. Exceptions are made for books published before 1900 when no publisher is given and for books published in different countries where changes have been made to the original versions. Provide the city before the publishing company, followed by a comma (not a colon, as in previous versions of MLA format).

Burgess, Anthony. *A Clockwork Orange.* New York, W. W. Norton, 1962.

Stoker, Bram. *Dracula.* London, 1897.

4. A Single Article, Essay, or Other Work in a Collection or Anthology

We usually refer to a book containing multiple works by a single author as a collection, while the term anthology refers to a published collection of works by a variety of people.

Author(s) of work. "Title of Work." *Title of Anthology,* edited by editors' names, not reversed (give them in the order that they are provided when there is more than one), publisher, year, pp. first page-last page.

Bambara, Toni Cade. "The Lesson." *The Norton Introduction to Literature,* edited by Kelly J. Mays, W. W. Norton, 2019, pp. 146-51.

5. Multiple Selections from a Collection or Anthology (Cross-References)

Note: To avoid unnecessary repetition of publishing information, when you have more than one work from an anthology, provide one entry just for the anthology and provide separate cross-references for each of the works that you take from it.

The anthology has all the regular components of a book, with the addition of the abbreviation for "editors" after the editors' names.

A cross-reference typically has only four elements: (1) the author of the work, (2) the title of the work, (3) the editors' last names, and (4) the page numbers of the work. You would only have three components if no author was provided. you would have a fifth component if you provided a translator.

> Author(s) of work. "Title of Work." Editors' last names, pp. first page-last page.

Note: Sometimes anthologies (for example, textbooks for introductory literature courses) contain not just essays, short stories, and poems, but also plays, novellas, and even entire novels. In these cases, these works' titles are italicized, just as they would be if they were published alone.

> Editor(s) of anthology, editors. *Title of Anthology*. Publisher, year.

Remember—all works on a works cited page should be in alphabetical order. Don't automatically group cross-references under their anthologies. They will follow them only if alphabetical order determines it.

Bambara, Toni Cade. "The Lesson." Hays, pp. 146-51.

Mays, Kelly, editor. *The Norton Introduction to Literature*. W. W. Norton, 2019.

Paley, Grace. "A Conversation with My Father." Mays, pp. 50-54.

6. Periodicals: Scholarly Journals, Magazines, and Newspapers

Periodical is the term for publications providing collections of articles and other works published at regular intervals.

Scholarly journals are also referred to as academic journals and peer-reviewed journals because for most journals, panels of experts reviw articles before they are published. A large number of periodicals and articles can be accessed electronically through databases that institutions subscribe to, such as Academic Search Premier, Business Source Elite, and the Psychology and Behavioral Sciences Collection.

Magazines can have useful information, but scholarly journals are preferable. Magazines usually contain secondary or tertiary information when discussing research (readers are getting the information second-hand or third-hand). Some magazines are aimed at particular ideological groups and will be more biased than more neutral periodicals, both in terms of how articles are slanted and the issues they cover.

Newspapers report news on a daily or weekly basis. As with magazines, they provide only secondary or tertiary information when discussing research. Some newspapers are also aimed at particular groups, and their treatment of news stories and what they cover will be more biased than more neutral periodicals.

In databases, different icons are used to distinguish between different types of periodical. Somewhat confusingly, magazines are represented with an icon saying "Periodical" even though all of these are periodicals. Also, something identified as a review can be from any type of periodical; you will have to look at the name of the periodical and look it up to see if it is from a journal, a magazine, or a newspaper. Following are screenshots of the icons:

Scholarly Journal	Magazine	Newspaper	Review (any medium)
Academic Journal	Periodical	News	Review

Basic Forms for Works from Periodicals

Author(s). "Title of Article: Complete with Subtitle." *Title of Periodical*, (volume
      number and issue number for scholarly journals only), day (if provided)
      month (if provided), season (if provided; don't add a comma after the
      season) year of publication, pp. first page-last page.

Note that the authors and the title of the work are followed by periods. Commas
separate the other elements, and a period follows the page numbers. With a print
source, that period ends the entry. If a work is in an issue that spans two months,
hyphenate the two months (Jan.-Feb.). When works are not on consecutive pages,
provide the first page and a plus sign. Sometimes journals have volumes and not
issues, and vice versa. Provide what is given.

For electronic versions, the following would be provided after the pages (or year
if there are no pages):

Database or provider (if applicable) and DOI or URL for online sources.

URL stands for "uniform resource locator," and DOI stands for "digital object identifier." Use DOIs instead of URLs if they are provided, as with some journals. Cite
the DOI number preceded by "doi," for example, doi.10.1353/pmc.20000.0021.
The URL or DOI follows the database when provided or the year if there is no
database. Drop "http//" and "https//" in URLs and DOIs, and note that we put
the term "DOI" in lower-case letters: "doi."

The *MLA Handbook*, eighth edition, states that URLs and DOIs can be eliminated
from entries if instructors prefer students not to include them. In these cases, entries
would end with the provider, the word "web," or terms like "Kindle edition" in
order to make it clear that students are not consulting the print versions of these
works. It makes sense to provide clarification that the source was found online.
If your professor asks you not to use URLs, ending the entry with *web* makes it
clear how the information can be located. Since a comma and the URL would

otherwise follow the year, follow the year with a comma and *web*, not capitalized, italicized, or enclosed in quotation marks. If there is a DOI, MLA recommends using that because DOIs enable the work to be accessed easily and they are short. Also, while MLA now suggests that we should no longer end Internet accessed works with the dates of access, it concedes that online works can be changed and that in some cases, your date of access should end the entry for an online source. Precede dates with "Accessed," for example, "Accessed 25 Dec. 2019."

Scholarly Journals
A Scholarly Journal Article in Print.

Author(s). "Title of Article: Subtitle." *Title of Journal*, volume number, issue
number [day, month and season if provided; don't follow with a comma],
year of publication, pp. first page-last page.

Journals use the word *Issue* for issue numbers. In MLA format, we use "vol." for volume and "no." for issue number. Neither print versions nor online versions of periodicals put information in MLA format for you.

Barzilay, Arianne Renan. "Power in the Age of In/Equality: Economic Abuse,
Masculinities, and the Long Road to Marriage Equality." *Akron Law Review*,
vol. 51, no. 2, Feb. 2018, pp. 323-66.

A Scholarly Journal Article From a Library's Database.
The journals found in college and university subscription databases usually have print counterparts—though the libraries may have only the electronic versions.

Author(s). "Title of Article: Complete with Subtitle." *Title of Journal*, volume
number, issue number, month and season (if provided; don't follow
with a comma) year of publication, pp. first page-last page. *Database*,
DOI or URL. [Some professors may prefer the database followed by
the name of the company, not a URL if there is no DOI and the URL
is very long. Ask.]

Remember to put databases in italics. The service supplying the database (for example, EBSCOhost) is optional. If you use it, do not italicize it since it is a service, not a database itself.

Igenoza, Mary. "Race, Femininity and Food: Femininity and the Racialization of
     Health and Dieting." *International Review of Social Research*, vol. 7, no. 2, Nov.
     2017, pp. 109-18. *Academic Search Complete*, doi: 10.1515/irsr-2017-0013

Following is what the article looked like when located in the database *Academic Search Complete* using the subject search term "femininity." Note the differences between the way the database presents the information and the way MLA requires it. We don't recommend using online citation services—they often present the information incorrectly, too, and may even be using outmoded (pre-2016) MLA format.

4. Race, **Femininity** and Food: **Femininity** and the Racialization of
Health and Dieting.

Academic
Journal

By: Igenoza, Mary. International Review of Social Research. Nov2017, Vol. 7 Issue 2, p109-118. 10p.
DOI: 10.1515/irsr-2017-0013.

Subjects: FEMININITY; FOOD habits; BLACK women; WHITE women; DIET

PDF Full Text (1.8MB)

A Scholarly Journal Article from an Online-Only Scholarly Journal.

Author(s). "Title of Article: Complete with Subtitle." *Title of Journal*, volume
     number, issue number, month and season (if provided; don't follow
     with a comma) year of publication, pp. first page-last-page. *Provider*,
     DOI or URL (unless your instructor prefers that you not add either and
     use "web" instead).

Kennedy, Gwynne, and Jennifer Dworschack-Kinter. "'Once More, with
     Feeling': Emotional Self-Discipline in *Buffy the Vampire Slayer." Slayage:
     The Journal of Whedon Studies*, vol. 16, no 2, Summer-Fall 2018,
     www.whedonstudies.tv/uploads/2/6/2/8/26288593/7._kennedy.dwo

rschack-kinter_-_slayage_16.2.pdf.

Note: Since this journal does not use page numbers, the URL is the "location," which is why it follows the year and comma, not a period.

Magazines and Newspapers

You should format the entries for works in magazines and newspapers almost exactly the same way that you format entries for works in journals, but without volume and issue numbers. Also, newspapers and weekly and biweekly magazines provide days, which should precede the months.

A Magazine Article in Print.

Author(s). "Title of Article: Complete with Subtitle." *Title of Magazine*, date
(day-month-year format unless there is no day), pp. first page-last-page. (If
an article is on only one page, precede it with p. If it is on discontinuous
pages, use pp. and follow the first page number with a plus sign.)

Heller, Nathan. "The Structure of Equality." *New Yorker,* 7 Jan. 2019,
pp. 46-55.

A Newspaper Article in Print.

Author(s). "Title of Article." *Title of newspaper* [city added in angle brackets if not
in title unless it is a national paper], date (day month year format), pp.
first page-last-page. (If an article is on only one page, precede it with p.
If it is on discontinuous pages, use pp. and follow the first page number
with a plus sign.)

If a city of publication is not part of the title of a locally published paper, add it in brackets after the name of the paper. You do not need to add cities for nationally published newspapers, such as *The Guardian* and the *Wall Street Journal*.

Bergman, Joe. "Kit-fox Probe Begins." *The Renegade Rip* [Bakersfield], 3 May
2016, pp. 1+.

"PG&E Could Face Charges in Wildfires." *The Bakersfield Californian*, 31 Dec.
2018.

Note: The first article began on page 1 and was continued on page 4.

A Magazine Article Published Online.
The format is the same as for a print article, but end with the URL in place of page
numbers. Remember to drop *http//* from the beginning of the URL.

Sedaris, David. "Father Time." *New Yorker*, 7. Jan. 2019, www.newyorker.com/
magazine/2019/01/07/father-time.

7. Websites

Following is the basic format for sources from the Internet.

Author(s). "Title of Article: Complete with Subtitle." *Site*, date, DOI or URL
(unless your instructor prefers you to omit the DOI or URL and use the
word "web").

Article on a Collaborative Project's Website

Morton, Ella. "How England's First Feline Show Countered Victorian Snobbery
about Cats." *Atlas Obscura*, 13 May 2016, www.atlasobsucra.com/
articles/how-englands-first-cat-show-countered-victorian-snobbery-
about-cats.

Authorless Article on an Organization's Website

"Philippines: New President Should Break Cycle of Human Rights Violations, Not Compound Them." *Amnesty International*, 10 May 2016, www.amnesty.org/en/latest/news/2016/05/philippines-new-president-should-break-cycle-of-human-rights-violations/.

Web Project as a Whole

Many projects on the Web were developed over a span of time. In these cases, cite the entire range of dates provided.

Creator(s) or editor(s), descriptive term. *Site*. Dates provided, URL.

Jokinen, Anniina, editor. *Luminarium*. 1996-2014, www.luminarium.org.

8. Speeches and Lectures

Sometimes your sources are people you interview or hear in public settings. For lectures and other public addresses, give the name of the speaker, followed by the title of the lecture or address. Follow with the sponsor of the talk, the date, and the city. If the city is included in the name of the venue, you do not need to repeat it.

Speaker. "Title." Sponsor, date, Venue [include city unless the name of the venue includes it].

Kumelos, Rae Ann. "Got Myth: A Discussion on How Myths Still Have an Impact on Today's World." The Norman Levan Center, 10 Oct. 2018, Bakersfield College, Lecture.

When you are citing a class lecture, if the class lecture does not have a title (they usually don't), provide the course name and course number after the professor's name and write "Class lecture" after the location for the sources-cited entry,

Dunlop, Robbie. The Health Effects of Climate Change. 11 Apr. 2018, Bernard

Evans Universitau. Class lecture.

9. Interviews

Works-cited entries for interviews should begin with the interviewed person's last name. Cite published interviews you find in print or broadcasts with the interviewed person's name, the title of the interview or a description if there is no title, the publication or program name, the date, page numbers if applicable, and the medium.

Use titles for works-cited entries for interviews when they are provided.

Blackmun, Harry. "Vice Traces Dick Cheney's Ascent from Yale Dropout to

Political Power Player." Fresh Air, NPR, 3 Jan. 2019.

Hill, Anita. Interview with John Oliver. *Last Week Tonight*, 29 July 2018.

Broadcast.

In work-cited entries for any sources that are untitled, provide the term for the type of source, neither italicized nor enclosed in quotation marks. When you conduct the interview, you do not need to include your own name.

Dyson, Michael Eric. Personal interview. 8 Feb. 2018.

Cite online interviews the same way as other published interviews. Include the name of the website and the access date.

Yolen, Jane. Interview with Harold Underdown. *The Purple Crayon*, 2001,

www.under down.org/yolen.htm.

Name: _____ Section: _____ Date: _____

Part Four

Chapter 9 Workshop

The following section contains a series of ten tasks that if completed will help you gain mastery over the content in this chapter. Your instructor will assign some (or all) of them to you as a way to practice the material presented here. Notice that some of them are global and focus on the entirety of the skills laid out in this chapter, while others are more focused and explore only one or two sections of the chapter. Also notice that some are shorter; some are longer; all are designed to flip the classroom and put the power of learning directly in your hands.

Workshop One.

<u>Overview</u>: Summarize all of the major sections and/or bullet points that you find in this chapter.

Each major section or heading should be clearly labeled and should have at least a one-sentence discussion. You might have a dozen or more headings and sentences here. Be thorough and accurate to show that you have read and comprehended this chapter's contents. Avoid the temptation to judge or add anything new (even critical discussion of the content); this is an act of pure summary. Tell your instructor exactly what came in this chapter and in what order.

Workshop Two.

<u>Overview</u>: This workshop has you examine all of the wrong answers from your chapter diagnostic and respond to them.
1. Make a list of each question from the chapter diagnostic that you got wrong.
2. Go through the chapter to look up the rules on each question. For every question you got wrong, do the following:

A. Identify the page number where the rule was found.

B. Discuss what the right answer should have been on the diagnostic test.

C. Discuss how you can avoid this error in future writing and/or tests.

Workshop Three.

<u>Overview</u>: Write a short, personal essay explaining the content of this chapter. The point of this essay is to directly address what you have learned from the chapter and how it will impact your future academic writing. Consider some or all of the following:

A. How will MLA format help you streamline the paper writing process?

B. How is a universal format for everyone to use while writing a paper helpful? How is this helpful for you?

C. What MLA element(s) did you already know about?

D. How will proper use of MLA format help you avoid accidental plagiarism in the future?

E. If appropriate, use some of the techniques and language from the actual chapter in your paper to help illustrate mastery.

F. Your instructor will provide you with more details such as the length of the piece, if you should use quotation from the chapter, if personal anecdotes and casual language are allowed, etc.

Workshop Four.

<u>Overview</u>: Create a PowerPoint presentation that can be shared with your colleagues and professor that cover the basic elements of MLA format.

1. Your PowerPoint must cover the basics of MLA document layout, header, margins, etc.

2. Your PowerPoint must explain the basics of how a parenthetical citation works as well as give examples of some common variations in citations from different types of sources.

3. Your PowerPoint must explain the basics of how a Works Cited Page function as well as give examples of some common variations in works cited entries from varied sources such as print books, e-books, scholarly journals, and websites.

Workshop Five.

Overview: Often, teaching something can be the best way to learn it yourself on a deeper level. Therefore, write a quiz for future students that covers the basics of MLA document format and layout.

1. This quiz should include various styles of questions, including multiple choice, short answer, and true/false. Check with your instructor on specifics.
2. This quiz should be designed to show mastery of the skills from another student at your own level.
3. You must write an answer key starting on a new page after the quiz. This answer key must include the page numbers from *Flipping English* where students can find the answer. It must also include a complete sentence for each quiz question you generated to explain to the instructor why you thought this question targeted a critical skill in MLA format.

Workshop Six.

Overview: Often, teaching something can be the best way to learn it yourself on a deeper level. Therefore, write a quiz for future students that covers the basics of MLA Style Parenthetical Citations.

1. This quiz should include various styles of questions, including multiple choice, short answer, and true/false. Check with your instructor on specifics.
2. This quiz should be designed to show mastery of the skills from another student at your own level.
3. You must write an answer key starting on a new page after the quiz. This answer key must include the page numbers from *Flipping English* where students can find the answer. It must also include a complete sentence

for each quiz question you generated to explain to the instructor why you thought this question targeted a critical skill in MLA format.

Workshop Seven.

<u>Overview</u>: Often, teaching something can be the best way to learn it yourself on a deeper level. Therefore, write a quiz for future students that covers the basics of MLA Works Cited Pages.

1. This quiz should include various styles of questions, including multiple choice, short answer, and true/false. Check with your instructor on specifics.
2. This quiz should be designed to show mastery of the skills from another student at your own level.
3. You must write an answer key starting on a new page after the quiz. This answer key must include the page numbers from *Flipping English* where students can find the answer. It must also include a complete sentence for each quiz question you generated to explain to the instructor why you thought this question targeted a critical skill in MLA format.

Workshop Eight.

<u>Overview</u>: Take a previous paper you have written and put it in proper MLA format. This could be a paper that wasn't required to be in MLA format to begin with, or you can edit and revise a paper to correct errors in MLA format that you previously wrote before you mastered MLA format.

1. Take a piece of writing you have done already (for this class or for another if you haven't written one yet) and put it in proper MLA format.
2. Make sure the header, class identification heading, margins, and all the basics of document format are correct.
3. Make sure your parenthetical citations are correct.
4. Make sure your works cited page is correct.

Workshop Nine.

<u>Overview</u>: Creating a real Works Cited page is the often the best way to learn the format. Thus, for this workshop, you will find sources and create a real Works Cited page.

1. Find a total of four books, two scholarly journal articles, and two reputable websites. If you have not covered research yet, feel free to talk to your instructor about this or to use sources you have already used in this class or another.
2. Create an accurate, MLA style Works Cited Page for these eight sources.

Workshop Ten.

<u>Overview</u>: What is your take away from this chapter? What did you learn and what questions do you still have?

1. Write a short response of several sentences that covers the three main things that you learned from this chapter.
2. Write out at least five questions you still have about the chapter. What things would you want to communicate to your instructor? What would you like to see discussed in class or handled with more depth to help you master this chapter's content.
3. What is one thing that you have taken away from this chapter and will use on your next writing task? Why is this thing important, and how do you plan to implement it?

CHAPTER 10

How to Identify and Avoid Plagiarism

In this chapter, you will learn about the following:

Part One: On Plagiarism
   1. How to Identify Plagiarism
   2. Types of Plagiarism
   3. Learn How to Avoid Plagiarism

Part Two: Workshop

Part One

On Plagiarism

Lita spent an entire weekend in the library working on her research paper. It was a six-page essay on news media ownership, and she found a lot of good sources in support of her arguments, just as she was taught. She spent a lot longer than she anticipated going over MLA rules to make sure she cited her quotations and had everything just as her professor wanted it. Two weeks later, her professor returned Lita's paper along with everyone else's in class. Lita took it and walked outside to see the grade (she hated doing it around other people). She was hoping for at least a grade of a B as she flipped to the last page to find out it got a...zero.

A zero! She immediately read the comments. The professor accused Lita of plagiarizing and referred to a passage on page three. Lita flipped to the page and saw
the section in question. There was a parenthetical citation there, so she couldn't
have plagiarized, could she?

The answer is yes. Even when students create parenthetical citations, the type
of material they include in their papers and the ways they treat direct quotations
could lead them to plagiarizing. In fact, you might plagiarize without using an
outside source at all. Having a tutor or a friend do too much of your revision for
you or even submitting a paper you turned in to a different professor in an earlier
semester can all count as plagiarism. So how do you avoid getting a shock like
Lita did when you get your paper back? Helping you avoid that kind of shock is
why this chapter is here.

1. How to Identify Plagiarism

Often students don't know exactly what plagiarism is—only that it is bad. They
know it is a form of cheating or academic dishonesty, but they may not know
much more than that. In writing, plagiarism can be defined as the unattributed
use of other people's ideas or words. In other fields, such as music or graphic arts,
phrases or sentences may not be what are stolen, but melodies or designs. In any
case, theft is wrong, including intellectual theft. It is also lazy scholarship, and it
will get you into trouble—often big trouble.

While some students don't know what plagiarism is and do it by accident, others
know exactly what it is. They do it willfully, often paying money to get someone
else to write their work or to download a paper from a paper mill and submit it
as their own.

Why Avoid It

First, you want to avoid plagiarism because there are serious academic consequences
that can hurt your entire college career. At the least serious end, the penalty may be
a score of zero only on the assignment in question. However, depending on campus

policy and the nature of the professor, it could also lead to an F in the course, removal from an academic department, and even loss of scholarships or financial aid. At its very worst, plagiarism can get you kicked out of a college or university and have legal consequences, such as a lawsuit about theft of intellectual property.

Second, you should avoid plagiarism because it is unethical. It is a type of cheating, and that isn't something that should mar your college career, even if you don't get caught. It is a form of theft. You may not be stealing something physical, but you are stealing the ideas, hard work, writing, language, and expertise of another author. Someone else spent weeks (or months or years) working on a piece of writing, and by plagiarizing, you are stealing their work and passing it off as your own. Again, this can have legal consequences depending on the seriousness of the offense. Don't steal. It's sleazy.

Finally, plagiarism robs not only the original author; it robs you. The whole point of college is for you to learn, expand your boundaries, leave your comfort zone, and master new skills. By taking someone else's writing or thinking and passing it off as your own, you have done none of these things. The act of researching and writing a research paper changes you; it makes you internalize information in a way that no other project can. (That is why we assign them.) By cheating, you are robbing yourself of a very serious chance for growth, and that is just a shame.

2. Types of Plagiarism

There are several types of plagiarism, ranging from intentional to accidental. Find them listed below. Note that at the beginning of each definition, we identify each type as "Intentional," "Accidental," or "Intentional/Accidental" (a combination of both). Professors and school administrators are most likely to punish students for the intentional types. However, the others represent types of academic dishonesty, too, and can land you in trouble, even if you were unaware of them.

TABLE 10.1. Types of Plagiarism	
Type	**Description**
Buddy or Tutor Plagiarism *Intentional/Accidental*	Submitting someone else's paper as your own. (E.g., buying from a paper mill website, sharing among friends,. paying someone to write a paper for you.) This is the worst kind.
Substantial Plagiarism *Intentional*	Copying passages or pages from sources and claiming them as your own. (E.g., copying from articles in scholarly databases or websites like Wikipedia.)
Occasional/Mosaic Plagiarism *Intentional/Accidental*	Borrowing facts, phrases, or ideas from sources and claiming them as your own. (E.g., not giving credit to a source, "thesaurus bombing," using too may direct quotations without providing credit.)
Self-Plagiarism *Intentional*	Using a paper you wrote for one class and submitting the same paper for another class without getting permission.
Total/Complete Plagiarism *Intentional*	Accepting any substantial changes made by other people without crediting them as co-authors. (E.g., taking significant revisions made by a tutor, writing specialist, roommate, or another professor or working with a classmate on the same essay prompt and cutting and pasting collaborated on work without writing it on your own.)

Total/Complete Plagiarism
Type: Intentional

This is the most egregious form of plagiarism—the one that can get deans and department chairs involved because of the violation of college policies regarding academic dishonesty. In this case, a student knowingly uses someone else's paper and submits it as his or her own writing. Students might download a paper from the Internet or copy paragraphs from a newspaper or magazine posted online, someone's personal webpage, or a social media post. Someone might purchase a paper from a paper mill website that stores thousands of essays, or they might know of a campus stash (sometimes rumored to be part of fraternities, sororities, campus clubs, or organizations) where they can swipe an older paper and recycle it as their own. A student might also pay a more competent writer to write the paper for them so that it directly answers the prompt. All of these are examples of the worst, most unscrupulous form of plagiarism, and they are likely to get you expelled from a class or even the entire school.

Substantial Plagiarism
Type: Intentional

Substantial plagiarism is not quite as egregious as the type above, but it is still willful and intentional. In this case, students will steal entire passages or pages from somewhere and put it in their papers, trying to pass it off as their own writing. Students will find articles in scholarly databases or on the Web and cut and paste entire sections into their essays. Again, this type of plagiarism is intentional and can carry with it the steepest of punishments.

Occasional/Mosaic Plagiarism
Type: Intentional/Accidental

The occasional or mosaic pattern of plagiarism is committed when a student uses facts, phrases, or ideas from other people that are discovered in a copyrighted context but placed in the student's paper without providing a reference. If there is a particularly catchy sentence, mosaic plagiarists may steal it for their own papers to make their writing style seem more polished. There may also be ideas or conclusions that a source comes to that students borrow for their papers without using exact quotations. It can also be an instance of putting a couple of direct quotations from other sources into their papers but not giving any credit to the original authors. Another technique that some dishonest students use is the "thesaurus bomb." They take an original passage and then find a thesaurus to change specific words and alter the vocabulary but not the sentence pattern or substance. This changes the surface of the sentence, but not the core of the thing. In this case, students steal the idea of the original author and plagiarize by not citing the source.

Alternatively, you might find that while paraphrasing someone else's words, you accidentally borrow too many direct phrases and pass them off as your own. This may not seem like much, but it is still dishonest. It wasn't your phrase; it was someone else's. So trying to act as if you thought it or said it in exactly that manner is not true. In this case, you can plagiarize even if you provide a parenthetical citation. This form of plagiarism can be done accidentally although it is also often done intentionally.

Self-Plagiarism
Type: Intentional

Self-plagiarism seems like an odd notion to some students: "How can I be guilty of stealing ideas from myself?" The answer is simple. You commit academic dishonesty when you write a paper or complete an assignment for a different professor but pawn the same paper off on another professor as though you did the paper for that professor's class. Here is why: professors expect you to complete the work they assigned to you because the act of completing it is teaching you something crucial for their class. If you simply recycle a paper from an earlier semester, you are not doing the work you were asked to do, and you are being dishonest about it.

You might find that a paper from a previous class fits in nicely with what you are doing in a current semester. It is fine to revisit it and remind yourself of what you did. Indeed, professional writers and scholars do this all the time and actually quote and cite themselves and their earlier work so that nobody can accuse them of reusing older ideas of theirs. Our advice is simple: talk to your professor. If you have an earlier paper you want to use, some instructors will allow it since it is your work. Others will allow you to quote it as a source in your new paper, and others will allow you use parts of it but ask you to modify it to fit the current term and essay prompt. Many professors, however, will give you a hard "no." Never assume it is okay to recycle all or part of an earlier paper. Always ask your professor before you try any of the options listed here.

Buddy or Tutor Plagiarism
Type: Intentional/Accidental

This type of plagiarism occurs during the editing and revising stage of the writing process. A student may have written a complete rough draft of an essay and then taken it to a tutor, a writing specialist, a roommate, or even another professor for feedback on it. What happens is the tutor or proofreader makes substantial changes using their own language and ideas to the point where the original author can no longer claim the work as entirely his or her own. At a certain point, the tutor would need to be credited as a co-author, which a professor probably won't allow. Another variation of this may be if you and a friend take a class together. You might meet up to help each other out with the assignment. In doing so, you may write one master assignment together and then cut and paste it to submit it separately. In doing so, you have both plagiarized since neither of you did the work by yourself. Again, by talking to the professor in advance, you might get permission to work in teams and turn in the same work. However, never assume this to be the case.

3. How to Avoid Plagiarism

Now that you know the different types of plagiarism, it should be rather easy to avoid them. Total plagiarism and substantial plagiarism are the easiest to avoid. Just don't cheat intentionally, and you'll be good. Avoiding the others may take a bit more finesse and planning to make sure you are on the right side of the law. Below are some tips on how to make sure you avoid accidental plagiarism.

4. Tips to Avoid Accidental Plagiarism

1. Be Honest.

Always be honest when you write a paper. If an idea, phrase, date, statistic, or concept didn't come from your brain, then it obviously came from somewhere else. As long as you are cognizant of that and make it known, you will not plagiarize. If you use other people's thoughts, but you give them credit, introduce your sources in your paper's body, and then give parenthetical citations with works cited entries to match, you are moving in the right direction in a major way. Also, practice paraphrasing. Be sure you know how to restate an author's original passage in different enough language that you are avoiding occasional/mosaic plagiarism.

2. Use Accurate MLA Format Citations.

As long as you accurately cite using MLA format, you are probably fine and didn't accidentally plagiarize unless you borrowed too many phrases from the original and didn't use quotations marks around those phrases. Giving sources credit through proper MLA format in-text citations and works cited entries is crucial.

3. Use Direct Quotations.

If you are worried about accidentally using too much of your sources' original wording in your summaries or paraphrases (even when you did use a parenthetical citation), the best method may be to rely on direct quotations instead. If you use a direct quotation, proper quotation mrks (or indent quotations over four lines long in your essay), and MLA format citations, you won't be accused of using too much of the original wording; indeed, you are using the original wording in its entirety, and you're citing it, so you have nothing to worry about.

4. Use I.C.E.

One way to smoothly incorporate outside sources into your own work is to use a system called I.C.E. The key to the I.C.E. technique is in the words that create the acronym: Introduce, Cite, Explain. If you get in the habit of **introducing** where your material came from, then **citing** it, and then **explaining** exactly what it does to prove your points, you will be clearly showing your audience that these ideas are not your own. You will have told the audience where your outside information came from before introducing your own critical thoughts about this information.

Name: _____ Section: _____ Date: _____

Part Two

Chapter 10 Workshop

The following section contains a series of ten tasks that, if completed, will help you gain mastery over the content in this chapter. Your instructor will assign some (or all) of them to you as a way to practice the material presented here. Notice that some of them are global and focus on the entirety of the skills laid out in this chapter, while others are more focused and explore only one or two sections of the chapter. Also notice that some are shorter, some are longer, but all of them are designed to flip the classroom and put the power of learning directly into your hands.

Workshop One.

Overview: Summarize all of the major sections and/or bullet points that you find in this chapter.

Each major section or heading should be clearly labeled and should have at least a one sentence discussion. You might have a dozen or more headings and sentences here. Be thorough and accurate to show that you have read and comprehended this chapter's contents. Avoid the temptation to judge or add anything new (even critical discussion of the content); this is an act of pure summary. Tell your instructor exactly what came in this chapter and in what order.

Workshop Two.

Overview: This workshop has you examine all of the wrong answers from your chapter diagnostic and respond to them.

1. Make a list of each question from the chapter diagnostic that you got wrong.

2. Go through the chapter to look up the rules on each question. For every question you got wrong, do the following:
   A. Identify the page number where the rule was found.
   B. Discuss what the right answer should have been on the diagnostic test.
   C. Discuss how you can avoid this error in future writing and/or tests.

Workshop Three.

<u>Overview</u>: Write a short, personal essay explaining the content of this chapter. The point of this essay is to directly address what you have learned from the chapter and how it will impact your future academic writing. Consider some or all of the following:
   A. What types of plagiarism were new to you?
   B. What fail safes can you put in place to make sure you don't plagiarize in the future?
   C. What writing element(s) did you already know about? Did you already use them in your writing, or did you ignore them for some reason? If so, what was the reason?
   D. If appropriate, use some of the techniques and language from the actual chapter in your paper to help illustrate mastery.
   E. Your instructor will provide you with more details, such as the length of the piece, if you should use quotation from the chapter, if personal anecdotes and casual language are allowed, etc.

Workshop Four.

<u>Overview</u>: Practice paraphrasing to make sure you aren't accidentally plagiarizing.
   1. Find an article online or one you used in class. Take a section of one or two paragraphs and reword it in your own words.
   2. Make sure you include a proper MLA style parenthetical citation.
   3. Print out your work. Now, do a sentence-by-sentence exploration of the original piece and the new version you have written. If you find any phrases or wordings that are identical, use colored highlighter

to highlight the phrase or word. (Alternatively, your instructor may allow you to swap with a peer and do this comparison for each other.)

4. If you have any identical phrases, cross them out and write new wording above them to make a final correction that your instructor can see.

Workshop Five.

Overview: Take the online plagiarism quiz from Cornell University and reflect on your results.

1. Visit website: https://plagiarism.arts.cornell.edu/tutorial/exercises.cfm and take the quiz on plagiarism. Click the "I am a guest" button to start (unless you are a Cornell student.) Before you begin the quiz, read the other questions below.

2. As you complete each question, the website tells you if you got the answer wrong or right. You need to reflect one each answer you provided as you go along on an assignment you will submit to your instructor.

3. For each correct answer, reflect on it. How did you know it was correct? What rules from this chapter may have helped you make that determination? What was it about the language that set itself off from the original passage?

4. For each incorrect answer, discuss. What was it about this rephrasing that made you think it was not plagiarism? Did you learn any techniques to help you in the future? How could the example have been done differently to avoid plagiarism?

Workshop Six.

Overview: Using the anti-plagiarism service Turnitin.com, submit an essay and reflect on the results. This one will only work if your class and your institution has a subscription to the Turnitin.com service.

1. Submit your essay to your class Turnitin.com account.

2. Look over your "Originality Report." It will highlight every passage that it has found in other college papers, books, articles, etc. This does not

mean that everything highlighted is plagiarized. For example, it will highlight many direct quotations that you have enclosed in quotation marks and cited or, if over four lines in your paper, indented one inch from the left margin and cited. This is why it is called your "Originality Report," not a plagiarism report. It will also recognize works cited entries when other students have used your sources for their papers.

3. Go over every single match that the service highlights on your paper. Look to make sure there is no plagiarism by commenting on the following elements. A) Did I have a parenthetical citation in proper MLA format? B) Was all or part of the wording an exact match with another source even though I thought it was a paraphrase and therefore wouldn't have verbatim language? C) Did any direct quotations fail to get a citation? If you found instances of plagiarism, comment on that, as well, and correct them.

4. Write a response to what you've found here. Did you have more or fewer matches in the Originality Report than you thought? Do you think you need more or fewer direct quotations on your next paper? Do you think you need more or fewer paraphrases and summaries in your next paper? What did you learn from Turnitin.com that will help you avoid plagiarism and be a better writer in the future?

Workshop Seven.

Overview: Find out about a famous plagiarist and think about what he or she did, why he or she did it, and what the consequences were.

1. Do some research online to find a list of famous plagiarists. These could be authors, politicians, spouses of politicians, musicians, or even film makers. They don't need to be academics, since intellectual theft can happen in art, song, and film as well as in papers or books.

2. Select one plagiarist and write a one-paragraph summary of what he or she plagiarized and how the person got caught. Why do you think the writer plagiarized, and do you think it was accidental or on purpose? Be sure you use parenthetical citations on any information you find, so you don't plagiarize.

3. Write another paragraph that discusses the consequences of the plagiarist's action, if any. Was there legal action taken? Did the writer get fired or asked to resign a position? Was it just a black eye on the author's reputation?

Workshop Eight.

Overview: Create a PowerPoint presentation or website that can be shared with your colleagues and professor that cover the major concepts about plagiarism as found in this chapter.

       A. Your PowerPoint or website must cover how to identify plagiarism.

       B. Your PowerPoint or website must cover the different types of plagiarism.

       C. Your PowerPoint or website must cover how to avoid plagiarism in your own writing.

       D. Your PowerPoint or website should cover any other details from the chapter that you feel would be helpful in a presentation.

Workshop Nine

Overview: Often, teaching something can be the best way to learn it yourself on a deeper level. Therefore, write a quiz for future students that covers the basics of plagiarism.

1. This quiz should include various styles of questions, including multiple choice, short answer, and true/false. Check with your instructor on specifics.

2. This quiz should be designed to show mastery of the information presented in this chapter from another student at your own level.

3. You must write an answer key starting on a new page after the quiz. This answer key must include the page numbers from *Flipping English* where students can find the answer. It must also include a complete sentence for each quiz question you generated to explain to the instructor why you thought this question targeted a critical skill in writing properly punctuated sentences.

Workshop Ten.

<u>Overview</u>: What is your take away from this chapter? What did you learn and what questions do you still have?

1. Write a short response of several sentences that covers the three main things that you learned from this chapter.

2. Write out at least five questions you still have about the chapter. What things would you want to communicate to your instructor? What would you like to see discussed in class or handled with more depth to help you master this chapter's content?

3. What is one thing that you have taken away from this chapter and will use on your next writing task? Why is this thing important, and how do you plan to implement it?

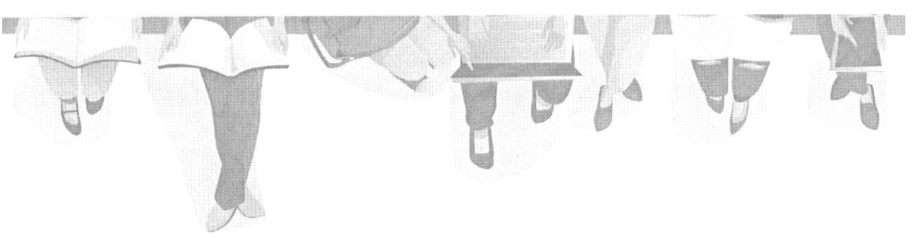

APPENDIX I

Global Pretest Diagnostic

Chapter 1. Global Diagnostic

1. Students should take notes during lectures but not when reading texts because the texts themselves can take the place of notes.

    A. True   B. False

2. Social media are reliable news sources.

    A. True   B. False

3. The best way to get accurate news about the country and the world is to find a news source that you feel comfortable with and stick to it.

    A. True   B. False

4. When you feel strongly about an issue, you should search for evidence that your beliefs might be wrong.

    A. True   B. False

5. It is important to take a strong "yes" or "no" stand on important issues; anything else is just wishy-washy.

    A. True   B. False

6. Knowing whether a media outlet is considered either left-wing or right-wing is enough to determine whether it neglects factual reporting in favor of producing "fake news."

    A. True   B. False

7. All that most people really need to do to get to the truth of issues is to use common sense.

    A. True   B. False

8. Magazines are among the best sources for college research papers.

    A. True   B. False

9. A peer-reviewed periodical is one where the articles in it are evaluated before publication by others working in the same field as the articles' authors.

    A. True   B. False

10. Primary sources are first-hand accounts of a topic from people who had a direct connection with it, such as original research.

    A. True   B. False

Chapter 2. Global Diagnostic

Note #1. The formal writing process is made up of the following steps (but not necessarily in this order): Researching (if required), revising, prewriting, drafting, proofreading, editing, oulining, thesis generation, and publication of the final draft.

11. Which of these tasks should come first for a college writer?

    A. Proofreading
    B. Editing
    C. Outlining
    D. Prewriting
    E. Thesis generation

12. Which of these two should you complete first: drafting or thesis generation?

    A. Drafting
    B. Thesis generation

13. Which of these two should come first, outlining or revising?

    A. Outlining
    B. Revising

14. Which of the following steps of the writing process is best defined by the following: "an informal act of pure creation and imagination that will help you develop the topics you will pursue in your paper"?

    A. Drafting
    B. Outlining

    C. Prewriting

    D. Editing

    E. Thesis generation

15. Which of the following steps of the writing process is best defined by the following: "a formal way to map out your paper, so it is easier and more logically written"?

    A. Drafting

    B. Outlining

    C. Prewriting

    D. Editing

    E. Thesis generation

16. Which of the following steps of the process is best defined by the following: "the act of writing a single sentence that is the controlling idea of your entire paper"?

    A. Drafting

    B. Outlining

    C. Prewriting

    D. Editing

    E. Thesis generation

17. Which of the following steps of the writing process is best defined by the following: "the act of reading over your completed paper to look for errors"?

    A. Drafting

    B. Outlining

    C. Prewriting

    D. Editing

    E. Thesis generation

18. Read this excerpt from a sample outline and answer the question below.

Sample Outline

I. Health epidemic

    1. Impact on youth

        A. Define youth

        B. Stats on rise in problems

    2. Premature high blood pressure

    3. Obesity

    4. Diabetes

The labels on this outline are correct (the letters and numbers such as I, 1, A)

    A. True   B. False

19. Read this excerpt from a sample outline and answer the question below.

    <u>Sample Outline</u>

    I. *Health epidemic*

        A. *Impact on youth*

            1. *Define youth*

            2. *Stats on rise in problems*

        A. *Premature high blood pressure*

        B. *Obesity*

        C. *Diabetes*

The labels on this outline are correct (the letters and numbers such as III, A, 1)

    A. True   B. False

20. In a formal outline, how much should you indent each level of the outline?

    A. One inch indent for each level

    B. Half an inch for each level

    C. You don't need to indent

    D. All levels will be at a 1 inch indent, so it is even down the page

    E. All levels will be at a 1/2 inch indent, so it is even down the page

Chapter 3. Global Diagnostic

21. Every essay that you write, including research papers, should have a main idea.

    A. True   B. False

22. Declarative sentences end with _____.

    A. Question marks

    B. Exclamation points

    C. Periods

    D. Any of the above

23. The best place for a thesis statement in a college essay is _____.

    A. At the beginning of the introductory paragraph

    B. At the end of the introductory paragraph

    C. At the beginning of the concluding paragraph

    D. At the end of the concluding paragraph

24. A thesis statement can be phrased as a question.

    A. True   B. False

25. A thesis statement can be any number of sentences.

    A. True   B. False

26. A thesis statement for an expository essay

    A. Should not express an opinion or take a position on a topic

    B. Should take a stand on an issue and be debatable

    C. Should be answering a "how" or "why" question

    D. All of the above

27. A thesis statement for an analytical essay

    A. Should not express an opinion or take a position on a topic

    B. Should take a stand on an issue and be debatable

    C. Should be answering a "how" or "why" question

    D. All of the above

28. A thesis statement for an argumentative essay

    A. Should not express an opinion or take a position on a topic

    B. Should take a stand on an issue and be debatable

    C. Should be answering a "how" or "why" question

    D. All of the above

29. Generally speaking, the _____ your thesis is, the more effective your argument will be.

    A. Narrower

    B. Broader

30. You need to be sure that you write a thesis statement for an essay that won't change as you write your paper.

    A. True   B. False

Chapter 4. Global Diagnostic

31. Which of the following are types of opening hooks you can use to grab your reader's attention in a paper's introduction?

    A. Quotation

    B. Personal anecdote

    C. Background information

    D. Rhetorical question

    E. All of the above

32. In your paper's body paragraphs, which one of these should come first?

    A. Thesis reminder

    B. Topic sentence

33. A thesis sentence and topic sentence are the same exact thing.

    A. True   B. False

34. Which of the following parts of the body paragraph can be defined as "a sentence that comes ate the start of the paragraph to tell your reader the exact content that is to come in the paragraph"?

    A. Critical discussion

    B. Topic sentence

    C. Transition

    D. Primary content

    E. Thesis reminder

35. When writing a paper for the humanities, you should start your paper with your thesis sentence.

    A. True   B. False

36. Which of the following parts of the body paragraph can be defined as "the portion of the paragraph that lets your reader know you are done with one point or argument and are moving on to another"?

    A. Critical discussion

    B. Topic sentence

    C. Transition

    D. Primary content

    E. Thesis reminder

37. Which of the following elements is not part of a typical college essay's introduction?

    A. Opening hook

    B. Topic sentence

    C. Gradual build up

    D. Thesis sentence

    E. None of the above

Read the following paragraph. Then, answer the questions below in reference to its content.

Paragraph #1

[1] When I was a junior in high school, I was thrilled one day when I got a phone call from a manager at a local restaurant called Poppy Burger. [2] He asked my name and then simply said, "you got the job." [3] I suddenly felt very adult

and responsible and was ready to prove my worth and earn a living. [4] However, within weeks I realized the sad truth. It was job where I was exploited for my labor. [5] I was asked to work after I had clocked off; I regularly had my schedule changed for the worst, and I was reminded regularly how replaceable I was. [6] This is not an uncommon experience for many teenaged fast food workers. [7] Managers commonly have empolyees clock off and then ask them to do simple tasks, which are now free labor for the company. [8] Also, the jobs can be dangerous since the cash registers are often robbed, especially late at night at a drive-thru window. [9] One other negative element of the fast food industry is sexual abuse that can be leveled at underaged and inexperienced employees. [10] These three negative elements plague the fast food industry for teenagers, and since the big fast food chains continue to make money off of these tactics, the best solution will be for the rise of strong restaurant unions which will regulate these workspaces.

38. Refer to Paragraph #1: Sentences [1] through [5] provide an example of what formal element from an introduction paragraph?
    A. Topic sentence
    B. Gradual build up
    C. Opening hook
    D. Thesis sentence
    E. Rhetorical mode

39. Refer to Paragraph #1: Sentences [6] through [9] provide an example of what formal element from an introduction paragraph?
    A. Topic sentence
    B. Gradual build up
    C. Opening hook
    D. Thesis sentence
    E. Rhetorical mode

40. Refer to Paragraph #1: Sentences [10] is an example of what formal element from an introduction paragraph?
    A. Topic sentence
    B. Gradual build up
    C. Opening hook
    D. Thesis sentence
    E. Rhetorical mode

Chapter 5. Global Diagnostic

41. What is the least number of statements that can make up an argument?
     A. One
     B. Two
     C. Three
     D. Four
     E. Five or more

42. Arguments may use questions as evidence.
     A. True   B. False

Read the following argument. Then, answer the questions below in reference to its content.

Argument #1

[1] Anything that is learned is not spontaneous in our human nature and [2] anything that is spontaneous in our human nature is good. [3] Human nature is intrinsically bad, as [4] goodness is not spontaneous. [5] People must learn how to be good.

43. Refer to Argument #1: Which statement in the argument represents the conclusion?
     A. Statement [1]
     B. Statement [2]
     C. Statement [3]
     D. Statement [4]
     E. Statement [5]

44. Refer to Argument #1: Which statements in the argument represent the premises or evidence?
     A. Statements [3], [4], and [5]
     B. Statements [1], [2], [4], and [5]
     C. Statements [2], [3], [4], and [5]
     D. Statements [1], [2], [3], and [4]
     E. Statements [1], [2], [3], and [5]

45. Refer to Argument #1: Are there are indicator words in the argument?
     A. Yes   B. No

46. Which set of words <u>all</u> represent indicators that an argument is likely to be being made by someone?
    A. Therefore, since, as such, if,
    B. Thus, because, but, we may conclude
    C. It follows that, inasmuch as, thus, then
    D. Hence, as a result, we may infer, entails that

47. Does an argument have to actually prove something or can it just attempt to prove something?
    A. Prove   B. Attempt to prove

48. Is an explanation of something also an argument?
    A. True   B. False

49. What type of sentences do arguments use?
    A. Interrogative
    B. Imperative
    C. Declarative

50. An argument has to have true premises in order to have good reasoning.
    A. True   B. False

Chapter 6. Global Diagnostic

51. Which of these is not a rhetorical strategy you can use to write a paper?
    A. Description
    B. Process analysis
    C. Narration
    D. Note taking
    E. Definition

52. Which rhetorical mode can be defined as "a mode that uses engages the senses in order to explain the details of an object, event, place, etc"?
    A. Definition
    B. Process analysis
    C. Argument/persuasion
    D. Description
    E. Division/classification

53. Which rhetorical mode can be defined as "a discussion of how one event leads to another and consequences that go along with that chain of events"?
    A. Division/classification
    B. Cause/effect

    C. Comparison/contrast

    D. Example/illustration

    E. Argument/persuasion

54. Which rhetorical mode can be defined as "using formal outside evidence such as a quote from an expert"?

    A. Problem/solution

    B. Process analysis

    C. Example/illustration

    D. Comparison/contrast

    E. Definition

55. Which rhetorical mode can be defined as "a discussion of the steps one needs to follow in order to achieve or complete some task"?

    A. Narration

    B. Example/illustration

    C. Problem/solution

    D. Comparison/contrast

    E. Process analysis

56. Which rhetorical mode can be defined as "discussing the similarities and/or differences between two things to help make a point in an essay"?

    A. Problem/solution

    B. Comparison/contrast

    C. Process analysis

    D. Example/illustration

    E. Division/classification

57. It is appropriate to tell a story using a narrative rhetorical mode in a college essay.

    A. True   B. False

Read the following paragraph. Then, answer the questions below in reference to its content.

Paragraph #2

[1] There are two camps of thought when it comes to video games. [2] Many people might say that video game addiction is when someone plays so many video games that it harms their outside life. [3] This harm could be physical neglect of one's own body, damage to relationships, and even loss of money due to difficulties

at work. [4] These facts might make someone want to ban the Xbox from their living rooms. [5] One scholar, however, argues that "video games help to expand people's imagination, especially young children who play age-appropriate games. [6] Gaming has even been shown to lead to better social skills if gamers play collaborative games online" (Boxy 77). [7] This quotation shows a stark difference between the two ideas. [8] Video games are seen by some as being negative, but others focus on the positive outcomes that come from gaming. [9] Perhaps the truth is really somewhere in the middle of these two extremes.

58.   Sentences 2 through 4 are an example of what type of rhetorical mode?
    A.   Description
    B.   Definition
    C.   Narration
    D.   Example/illustration
    E.   Comparison/contrast

59.   Sentences 5 and 6 are an example of what type of rhetorical mode?
    A.   Description
    B.   Definition
    C.   Narration
    D.   Example/illustration
    E.   Comparison/contrast

60.   Sentences 7 through 9 are an example of what type of rhetorical mode?
    A.   Description
    B.   Definition
    C.   Narration
    D.   Example/illustration
    E.   Comparison/contrast

Chapter 7. Global Diagnostic

For each of the following, choose the term that most closely fits the definition provided.

61.   The official system of rules governing affairs of state or diplomatic occasions; the accepted or established code of procedure for an organization, group, or situation.
    A.   Criterion
    B.   Protocol

    C. Constitution

    D. Template

62. Favorable to progress or reform; favorable to individual freedoms and rights.

    A. Civil

    B. Hierarchal

    C. Liberal

    D. Conservative

63. Indicated but not plainly expressed; essentially or very closely connected with; always to be found in; potentially contained.

    A. Discreet

    B. Explicit

    C. Implicit

    D. Coherent

64. A proposition assumed as an argument's premise; a supposition made on the basis of limited evidence as a starting point for further investigation.

    A. Data

    B. Guess

    C. Hypothesis

    D. Significance

65. Open to two or more interpretations; equivocal; unclear because a choice between alternatives has not been offered.

    A. Ambidextrous

    B. Ambivalent

    C. Indecisive

    D. Quandary

66. Originating, based on, concerned with, or verifiable by observation or experience rather than theory or speculation.

    A. Empirical

    B. Pragmatic

    C. Practical

    D. Experimental

67. A standard or principle by which a decision or judgment is made.

    A. Archetype

    B. Exemplar

    C. Prototype

    D. Criterion

68. Factual information, such as statistics and results of scientific research, used for calculation and reasoning; in computing, information in digital form.
    A. Lore
    B. Data
    C. Dossier
    D. Results
69. Consist of; be made up of; constitute.
    A. Comprise
    B. Compass
    C. Contain
    D. Comprehend
70. Individually distinct; constituting a separate entry.
    A. Discreet
    B. Discrete
    C. Empirical
    D. Demonstrable

Chapter 8. Global Diagnostic

71. Which of the following sentences has no punctuation or grammar errors?
    A. David Robert Jones, known professionally as David Bowie, was a leading figure in the music industry and is considered one of the most influential musicians of the 20th century.
    B. David Robert Jones, known professionally as David Bowie was a leading figure in the music industry, and is considered one of the most influential musicians of the 20th century
    C. David Robert Jones, known professionally as David Bowie was a leading figure in the music industry and is considered one of the most influential musicians of the 20th century
    D. David Robert Jones, known professionally as David Bowie, was a leading figure in the music industry, and is considered one of the most influential musicians of the 20th century.
72. Which of the following sentences has no punctuation or grammar errors?
    A. Bowie's early albums include *The Man Who Sold the World*, which was released in 1970; *The Rise and Fall of Ziggy Stardust and the Spiders from Mars*, which was released in 1972; and *Aladdin Sane*, which was released in 1973.

B. Bowie's early albums include: *The Man Who Sold the World*, which was released in 1970; *The Rise and Fall of Ziggy Stardust and the Spiders from Mars*, which was released in 1972; and *Aladdin Sane*, which was released in 1973.

C. Bowie's early albums include *The Man Who Sold the World*; which was released in 1970, *The Rise and Fall of Ziggy Stardust and the Spiders from Mars*; which was released in 1972, and *Aladdin Sane*; which was released in 1973.

D. Bowie's early albums include: *The Man Who Sold the World*; which was released in 1970, *The Rise and Fall of Ziggy Stardust and the Spiders from Mars*; which was released in 1972, and *Aladdin Sane*; which was released in 1973.

73. Which of the following sentences has no punctuation or grammar errors?

A. Bowie's early albums include the following *The Man Who Sold the World*, *The Rise and Fall of Ziggy Stardust and the Spiders from Mars*, and *Aladdin Sane*.

B. Bowie's early albums include the following: *The Man Who Sold the World*; *The Rise and Fall of Ziggy Stardust and the Spiders from Mars*; and *Aladdin Sane*.

C. Bowie's early albums include the following: *The Man Who Sold the World*, *The Rise and Fall of Ziggy Stardust and the Spiders from Mars*, and *Aladdin Sane*.

D. Bowie's, early albums include, the following: *The Man Who Sold the World*, *The Rise and Fall of Ziggy Stardust and the Spiders from Mars*, and *Aladdin Sane*.

74. Which of the following sentences has no punctuation or grammar errors?

A. Because Bowie was such a talented writer and performer he had a large cult following for decades.

B. Because Bowie, was such a talented writer and performer, he had a large cult following for decades.

C. Because Bowie was such a talented writer and performer, he had a large cult following for decades.

D. Because Bowie was such a talented writer and performer; he had a large cult following for decades.

75. Which of the following sentences has no punctuation or grammar errors?

    A. Since automobiles were first marketed to consumers, there have been many safety scandals, including ones associated with the following companies: Ford, Takata, and Volkswagen.

    B. Since automobiles were first marketed to consumers, there have been many safety scandals, including ones associated with the following companies; Ford, Takata, and Volkswagen.

    C. Since automobiles were first marketed to consumers, there have been many safety scandals including ones associated with the following companies: Ford, Takata, and Volkswagen.

    D. Since automobiles were first marketed to consumers, there have been many safety scandals, including, ones associated with the following companies; Ford, Takata, and Volkswagen.

76. Which of the following sentences has no punctuation or grammar errors?

    A. *The Ballad of Buster Scruggs* is a 2018 American western anthology film written, directed, and produced by the Coen brothers; Tom Waits has a small role as a gold prospector.

    B. *The Ballad of Buster Scruggs*, is a 2018 American western anthology film written; directed; and produced by the Coen brothers. Tom Waits has a small role as a gold prospector.

    C. *The Ballad of Buster Scruggs*, is a 2018 American western anthology film written, directed, and produced by the Coen brothers; Tom Waits has a small role as a gold prospector.

    D. *The Ballad of Buster Scruggs*, is a 2018 American western anthology film, written, directed and produced by the Coen brothers; Tom Waits has a small role as a gold prospector.

77. Which of the following sentences has no punctuation or grammar errors?

    A. Tom Waits' and Patrick Fugit's 2007 black comedy is called *Wristcutters: A Love Story*.

    B. Tom Waits' and Patrick Fugit's 2007 black comedy, is called *Wristcutters: A Love Story*.

    C. Tom Waits and Patrick Fugit's 2007 black comedy, is called *Wristcutters: A Love Story*.

    D. Tom Waits and Patrick Fugit's 2007 black comedy is called *Wristcutters: A Love Story*.

78. Which of the following sentences has no punctuation or grammar errors?
    A. It's based on a story by Etgar Keret called "Kneller's Happy Campers," and its premise is set in an afterlife way-station.
    B. It's based on a story by Etgar Keret called "Kneller's Happy Campers," and it's premise is set in an afterlife way-station.
    C. Its based on a story by Etgar Keret called "Kneller's Happy Campers," and its premise is set in an afterlife way-station.
    D. Its based on a story by Etgar Keret called "Kneller's Happy Campers," and it's premise is set in an afterlife way-station.

79. Which of the following sentences has no punctuation or grammar errors?
    A. The U.S. womens' soccer teams victory over the Netherlands in the finals of the World Cup made world headlines.
    B. The U.S. women's soccer teams' victory over the Netherlands in the finals of the World Cup made world headlines.
    C. The U.S. women's soccer team's victory over the Netherlands in the finals of the World Cup made world headlines.
    D. The U.S. women's soccer team's victory over the Netherlands in the final's of the World Cup made world headlines.

80. Which of the following sentences has no punctuation or grammar errors?
    A. Lee's and Ann's voices are very good; between you and I, I think they are the best in the choir.
    B. Lee and Ann's voices are very good; between you and I, I think they are the best in the choir.
    C. Lee's and Ann's voices are very good; between you and me, I think they are the best in the choir.
    D. Lee's and Ann's voice's are very good; between you and me, I think they are the best in the choir.

Chapter 9. Global Diagnostic

81. For titles and subtitles, the first letter of every single word should be capitalized
    A. True   B. False

82. Books, periodicals, websites, and plays should be
    A. Italicized
    B. Enclosed in quotation marks
    C. Both italicized and enclosed in quotation marks
    D. In bold font

83. Essays, articles, poems, and short stories should be
    A. Italicized
    B. Enclosed in quotation marks
    C. Both italicized and enclosed in quotation marks
    D. In bold font

84. Only direct quotations need parenthetical in-text citations.
    A. True   B. False

85. MLA format in-text citations should include the author's last name and the year of publication.
    A. True   B. False

86. The first line of a works cited entry should be flush with the left margin, and every line after that in the entry should be indented one-half inch.
    A. True   B. False

87. On a works cited page, all the sources should be listed
    A. In the order they are used in the paper
    B. By date of publication
    C. In alphabetical order by authors' last names when authors are provided
    D. In alphabetical order by titles for works with and without authors

88. If you have a paper with one entry from an anthology and two or more entries from another anthology, all of the work cited entries should be done in the same format.
    A. True   B. False

89. When an author is not provided, begin the work-cited entry with
    A. The publisher
    B. The date of publication
    C. The title of the work
    D. The city the work was published in

90. The title of your paper should include a phrase such as "Essay One" or "Research Paper" to indicate the type of paper you are writing.
    A. True   B. False

Chapter 10. Global Diagnostic

91. As long as you change a few words here and there in sentences that you take from sources, you don't need quotation marks.
    A. True   B. False

92. You need in-text citations for all material that you take from a source, whether directly quoted, summarized, or paraphrased, unless it is considered "common knowledge."

    A. True   B. False

93. All you need for direct quotations under four lines long are in-text citations, not quotation marks.

    A. True   B. False

94. Instructors use plagiarism detection services like Turnitin, so it is easy for them to see if you've copied and pasted other people's work or bought papers from websites.

    A. True   B. False

95. If detection services like Turnitin don't catch plagiarized sentences and passages in your papers, professors won't realize that the material has been plagiarized.

    A. True   B. False

96. You cannot plagiarize from yourself.

    A. True   B. False

97. When you quote a source, you can set up the quotation using the word "quoted," as in "Smith quoted that" followed by Smith's words.

    A. True   B. False

98. "Common knowledge" refers to facts that are widely known.

    A. True   B. False

99. You can have too many citations in a paper.

    A. True   B. False

100. An academic integrity violation can become part of your permanent record. You can also be suspended from school for a period of time. At its worst, it can get you kicked out of a college or university.

    A. True   B. False

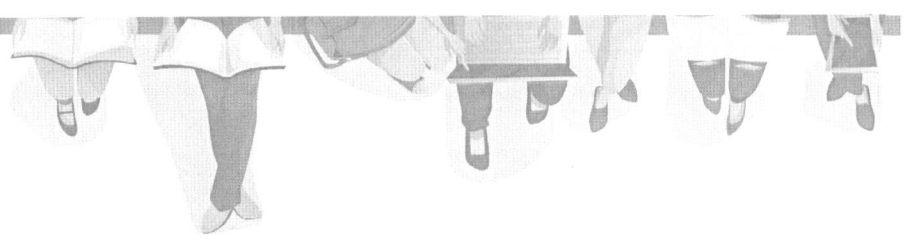

APPENDIX II

Pretests for Chapters 1-10

Chapter 1. Chapter Pretest

1. Primary sources are usually the best sources for research papers.
   A. True   B. False

2. Peer-reviewed journals are among the best sources for research papers.
   A. True   B. False

3. "Context" refers to circumstances that form the setting, background, and roots for something, such as a statement, idea, or argument.
   A. True   B. False

4. "Annotation" refers to a note, explanation, or other comment that you add to a text.
   A. True   B. False

5. Magazines usually provide primary sources.
   A. True   B. False

6. Falsehoods spread extremely rapidly on social media, outdistancing genuine information.
   A. True   B. False

7. Some people create websites promoting fake news in order to make a profit.
   A. True   B. False

8. Tabloids are reliable news sources for information about celebrities because it is easy for celebrities to sue them and win in court if they publish lies.
   A. True   B. False

9. A rhetorical précis is a very specific type of summary.
    A. True   B. False
10. "Critical reading" refers to being able to criticize what you read.
    A. True   B. False

Chapter 2. Chapter Pretest

Note #1: The formal writing process is made up of the following steps (but not necessarily in this order): Researching (if required), revising, prewriting, drafting, proofreading, editing, outlining, thesis generation, and publication of the final draft.

1. Which of the following two should you complete first: thesis generation and revising?
    A. Thesis generation
    B. Revising
2. Which of the following two should you complete first: researching and prewriting?
    A. Researching
    B. Prewriting
3. Which of the following two should come first: outlining or editing
    A. Outlining
    B. Editing
4. Which of the following steps of the writing process is best defined by the following: "the act of writing the entire first version of your paper before you check it for errors of any type."
    A. Drafting
    B. Revising
    C. Proofreading
    D. Prewriting
    E. Thesis generation
5. Which of the following steps of the writing process is best defined by the following: "looking a paper over to find out what needs to be fixed in the next stage"?
    A. Drafting
    B. Revising
    C. Proofreading

    D. Prewriting

    E. Thesis generation

6. Which of these steps of the writing process is best defined by the following: "the act of reading the entire paper over and making changes to the content and flow of the essay"?

    A. Drafting

    B. Revising

    C. Proofreading

    D. Prewriting

    E. Thesis generation

7. Which of these steps of the writing process is best defined by the following: "the act of formalizing and writing out the controlling idea of your entire essay in one single sentence"?

    A. Drafting

    B. Revising

    C. Proofreading

    D. Prewriting

    E. Thesis generation

Read this excerpt from a sample outline and answer the question below.

<u>Sample Outline.</u>

I. Health epidemic

a. Impact on youth

    1. Define youth

    2. Stats on rise in problems

b. Premature high blood pressure

c. Obesity

d. Diabetes

8. True or False. The labels on this outline are correct (the letters and numbers such as I, a, 1).

    A. True   B. False

Read this excerpt from a sample outline and answer the question below.

<u>Sample Outline.</u>

1. Health epidemic

I. Impact on youth

A. *Define youth*

B. *Stats on rise in problems*

  II. *Premature high blood pressure*

  III. *Obesity*

  IV. *Diabetes*

9. True or False. The labels on this outline are correct (the letters and numbers such as 1, I, A).

    A. True   B. False

Read this excerpt from a sample outline and answer the question below.

  <u>Sample Outline.</u>

  III. *Health epidemic*

  A. *Impact on youth*

    1. *Define youth*

    2. *Stats on rise in problems*

  B. *Premature high blood pressure*

  C. *Obesity*

  D. *Diabetes*

10. True or False. The labels on this outline are correct (the letters and numbers such as III, A, 1).

    A. True   B. False

Chapter 3. Chapter Pretest

1. The main purpose of an expository essay is to

    A. Focus on examining and interpreting something

    B. Explain or describe something using factual information

    C. Convince readers that a theory, opinion, or assertion of policy or action is superior to other alternatives

    D. All of the above

2. The main purpose of an analytical essay is to

    A. Focus on examining and interpreting something

    B. Explain or describe something using factual information

    C. Convince readers that a theory, opinion, or assertion of policy or action is superior to other alternatives

    D. All of the above

3. The main purpose of an argumentative essay is to
    A. Focus on examining and interpreting something
    B. Explain or describe something using factual information
    C. Convince readers that a theory, opinion, or assertion of policy or action is superior to other alternatives
    D. All of the above

4. A thesis statement must be a declarative sentence.
    A. True   B. False

5. Generally speaking, the broader your thesis is, the more effective will be.
    A. True   B. False

6. The best place for a thesis statement for a college essay is at the beginning of the introductory paragraph.
    A. True   B. False

7. When you write an essay, the only audience you should imagine is your professor.
    A. True   B. False

8. In an expository essay, you should be dealing just with facts, not your own beliefs.
    A. True   B. False

9. An argumentative essay should not explore potential solutions to a problem the paper explores.
    A. True   B. False

10. Which of the following is the most sophisticated and demanding type of college paper?
    A. The expository essay
    B. The analytical essay
    C. The argumentative essay
    D. They are all equally sophisticated

Chapter 4. Chapter Pretest

1. One good way to structure a paper's conclusion is to roughly model it as the reverse order of your paper's introduction.
    A. True   B. False

2. You should never use a direct quotation in your paper's introduction. The intro should be 100% your own ideas and words.
    A. True   B. False

3. You shouldn't try to include every major argument/point from your paper into your introduction. It will be too much information; feel free to leave some out until it is revealed in the body.
    A. True   B. False

4. Which of the following parts of the body paragraph can be defined as "the portion of your paragraph that shows your audience that one idea is now finished and another one is about to begin"?
    A. Thesis reminder
    B. Primary content
    C. Topic sentence
    D. Critical discussion
    E. Transition

5. True or false: A thesis sentence and topic sentence are the same exact thing.
    A. True   B. False

6. The thesis statement should come where in your paper if writing in the humanities?
    A. The very first sentence of your introduction
    B. The middle of the introduction after your hook
    C. The very first sentence of your paper's body
    D. There is no preference where the thesis appears as long as it is well written
    E. None of the above

Read the following paragraph. Then, answer the questions below in reference to its content.

Paragraph #1

[1] *Pokemon* is an intellectual property that spans films, video games, books, and other types of media; in spite of its age, it is just as popular now as was it when it first released. [2] In 1996, the first *Pokemon* game video game came out. [3] In a matter of years, there were multiple sequels, a highly lucrative card game, and a television series which spread the franchise's popularity. [4] As many adults who were too old to play the game dismissed this franchise as losing its impact, the mobile phone game *Pokemon Go* came out in 2016. [5] According to Anita Bennett, head editor for news website *Deadline*, in the first twenty-four hours, 7.5 million people downloaded the game in the US (Bennett, par. 4). [6] This ongoing popularity of the game shows that over twenty years

later, *Pokemon* is still as successful as it ever was, thanks to one-time children coming of age and continuing to play (and getting their own children to play as well). [7] However, *Pokemon* is not the only tame that has lasted for decades. Another is *Magic: The Gathering.*

7. Sentence 1 is an example of what formal element from a body paragraph?
    A. Thesis reminder
    B. Primary content
    C. Transition
    D. Topic sentence
    E. Critical discussion

8. Sentences 2 through 5 are an example of what formal element from a body paragraph?
    A. Thesis reminder
    B. Primary content
    C. Transition
    D. Topic sentence
    E. Critical discussion

9. Sentence 6 is an example of what formal element from a body paragraph?
    A. Thesis reminder
    B. Primary content
    C. Transition
    D. Topic sentence
    E. Critical discussion

10. Sentence 7 is an example of what formal element from a body paragraph?
    A. Thesis reminder
    B. Primary content
    C. Transition
    D. Topic sentence
    E. Critical discussion

Chapter 5 Pretest

1. Which of the following *best* represents the top three critical elements to any argument?
    A. A relationship of support, premises, and conclusion
    B. Declarative sentences, explanations, and evidence

      C. Conclusion, indicator words, and a relationship of support

      D. Expositions, declarative sentences, and premises

2. What is an *explanandum*?

      A. A previously known factual statement that is being explained by a previously unknown set of fact(s)

      B. A set of statements that prove the evidence true

      C. A previously unknown factual statement explaining a previously known fact

3. Which words represent premise indicators in a given argument?

      A. Provided that, as such, if, owing to

      B. Seeing that, since, in that, for

      C. Because, hence, to infer, given that

      D. Given that, provided that, implies that, as such

4. Which the following choices *best* represents the logical structure of an argument?

      A. Known fact X because of unknown fact Y

      B. Unknown debatable statement C because of known fact X

      C. Known fact X because of debatable fact Y

      D. Unknown debatable statement C because of debatable known fact

Read the following passage and answer the following questions.

Passage #1

    [1]St. Helm is a town of about 2,000 overlooking the Pacific Ocean. [2]It has only one main street and [3]one ice cream shop. [4]St. Helm does not have a large bookstore.

5. Is Passage #1 an argument?

      A. Yes   B. No

6. What type of passage does Passage #1 represent?

      A. An argument

      B. An explanation

      C. An exposition

      D. An illustration

      E. A report

Read the following passage and answer the following questions.

Passage #2

[1]The New York Twin Towers with each of its 244 columns crumbled to the ground on September 11, 2001, because [2]the insulation that protected the steel from high heat was compromised by the fact that the sprinkler system gave way, and, in addition, since [3]the planes crashing into the building shifted the columns, putting elevated states of stress on them.

7. Is Passage #2 an argument?

    A. Yes   B. No

8. What type of passage does passage #2 represent?

    A. An argument

    B. An explanation

    C. An exposition

    D. An illustration

9. Does passage #2 contain any indicator words making it an argument?

    A. Yes   B. No

10. Are a series of opinions the same as arguments?

    A. Yes   B. No

Chapter 6 Pretest

1. In formal writing, what is the definition of rhetoric?

    A. The science of telling the truth

    B. When you read an essay out loud

    C. A type of fallacy

    D. The art of argumentation

    E. It is another word for "research"

2. Which rhetorical mode can be defined as "a discussion of the steps one needs to follow in order to achieve or complete some task"?

    A. Comparison/contrast

    B. Example/illustration

    C. Problem/solution

    D. Process analysis

    E. Narration

3. Which rhetorical mode can be defined as "telling a brief story in order to help make your point in a paper"?
   A. Narration
   B. Definition
   C. Example/illustration
   D. Description
   E. Problem/solution

4. Which rhetorical mode can be defined as "discussing the similarities and/or differences between two things in order to prove a larger point or argument"?
   A. Example/illustration
   B. Cause/effect
   C. Process analysis
   D. Argument/persuasion
   E. Comparison/contrast

5. If you wrote a personal essay which discusses what things from your past have caused you ultimately to decide you needed to go to college, what Rhetorical Mode will the overall essay be employing?
   A. Definition
   B. Argument/persuasion
   C. Process analysis
   D. Comparison/contrast
   E. Cause/effect

6. In a research paper, the research including research in a body paragraph would be considered which rhetorical mode?
   A. Description
   B. Cause/effect
   C. Example/illustration
   D. Process analysis
   E. Narration

7. Consider these paper topics: an exploration of how Amazon.com became the biggest retailer in America or what led to the popularity of electric and hybrid cars. Which rhetorical mode would best cover these topics?
   A. Cause/effect
   B. Problem/solution
   C. Comparison/contrast

D. Narration

E. Argument/persuasion

Read the following paragraph. Then, answer the questions below in reference to its content.

Paragraph #2

[1] In the *Star Wars* films, there are "force users" who can do supernatural abilities thanks to their use of a mystical power called the force. [2] One type of force user are the Jedi; they use their abilities to bring peace and justice to the galaxy. [3] Another type is the Sith. [4] The evil Sith Lords use their powers to dominate others and spread tyranny. [5] They both use a weapon called a light saber. [6] It is a glowing laser sword that can cut through anything with its bright, luminescent blade. [7] The saber ignites with a loud thrum and has become famous around the world for the ominous hum it emits and the drastic sparks that shoot when the two energy blades clash loudly during conflict. [8] The most famous of all the force users was the Jedi named Luke Skywalker. [9] He started as a young farm boy on a remote planet, and after he met his mentor, he went on a series of adventures that slowly made him a Jedi Knight and eventually a Jedi Master. [10] He helped defeat the evil emperor during his quest, and he ultimately redeemed his father.

8. Refer to Paragraph #2: Sentences [1] through [4] are an example of what type of rhetorical mode?

    A. Description

    B. Argument/persuasion

    C. Division/classification

    D. Narration

    E. Problem/solution

9. Refer to Paragraph #2: Sentences [5] through [7] are an example of what type of rhetorical mode?

    A. Description

    B. Argument/persuasion

    C. Division/classification

    D. Narration

    E. Problem/solution

10. Refer to Paragraph #2: Sentences [8] through [10] are an example of what type of rhetorical mode?

    A. Description

    B. Argument/persuasion

     C. Division/classification

     D. Narration

     E. Problem/solution

Chapter 7 Pretest

For each of the following, choose the term that most closely fits the definition provided.

1.   Existing or operating within; inherent.

     A. Immanent

     B. Imminent

     C. Eminent

     D. Inane

2.   To make complete

     A. Coefficient

     B. Coherent

     C. Complement

     D. Compliment

3.   To escape from something; to fail to be attained.

     A. Allude

     B. Elude

     C. Ensure

     D. Abdicate

4.   A result or consequence of an action or other cause.

     A. Affect

     B. Effect

     C. Defect

     D. Affectation

5.   To improve something by making small changes.

     A. Repair

     B. Restitute

     C. Refine

     D. Resolve

6.   To suggest or call attention to something indirectly or in a disguised way.

     A. Elucidate

     B. Elude

     C. Allude

     D. Ensure

7. To intervene between individuals in a dispute in order to bring about an agreement or reconciliation.
    A. Meditate
    B. Mitigate
    C. Moderate
    D. Mediate

8. An element placed at the beginning of a word to adjust or qualify its meaning.
    A. Affix
    B. Infix
    C. Prefix
    D. Suffix

9. An element added at the end of a word to form a derivative.
    A. Affix
    B. Infix
    C. Prefix
    D. Suffix

10. A book that lists words in groups of synonyms and related concepts.
    A. Thesaurus
    B. Encyclopedia
    C. Dictionary
    D. Journal

Chapter 8 Pretest

1. An independent (main) clause
    A. Is grammatically essential to the sentence it is in (removing it would change meaning)
    B. Is not grammatically essential to the sentence it is in (removing it would not change the meaning)
    C. Has a subject and a verb and can stand alone as a sentence
    D. Has a subject and a verb but cannot stand alone as a sentence

2. A dependent (subordinate) clause
    A. Is grammatically essential to the sentence it is in (removing it would change meaning)
    B. Is not grammatically essential to the sentence it is in (removing it would not change the meaning)

      C. Has a subject and a verb and can stand alone as a sentence

      D. Has a subject and a verb but cannot stand alone as a sentence

3. A restrictive element

      A. Is grammatically essential to the sentence it is in (removing it would change meaning)

      B. Is not grammatically essential to the sentence it is in (removing it would not change the meaning)

      C. Has a subject and a verb and can stand alone as a sentence

      D. Has a subject and a verb but cannot stand alone as a sentence

4. A nonrestrictive element

      A. Is grammatically essential to the sentence it is in (removing it would change meaning)

      B. Is not grammatically essential to the sentence it is in (removing it would not change the meaning)

      C. Has a subject and a verb and can stand alone as a sentence

      D. Has a subject and a verb but cannot stand alone as a sentence

5. Which of the following has only coordinating conjunctions?

      A. Of, against, between, from, with

      B. For, and, nor, but, or, yet, so

      C. Since, while, because, when, though

      D. However, therefore, consequently, nevertheless

6. Which of the following has only subordinating conjunctions?

      A. Of, against, between, from, with

      B. For, and, nor, but, or, yet, so

      C. Since, while, because, when, though

      D. However, therefore, consequently, nevertheless

7. Which of the following has only conjunctive adverbs?

      A. Of, against, between, from, with

      B. For, and, nor, but, or, yet, so

      C. Since, while, because, when, though

      D. However, therefore, consequently, nevertheless

8. Which of the following has only prepositions?

      A. Of, against, between, from, with

      B. For, and, nor, but, or, yet, so

      C. Since, while, because, when, though

      D. However, therefore, consequently, nevertheless

9. Which of the following has only pronouns in subjective case?
   A. She, he, whom, them
   B. Her, him, whom, them
   C. She, he, who, they
   D. Their, her, he, that

10. Which of the following has only pronouns in objective case?
    A. She, he, whom, them
    B. Her, him, whom, them
    C. She, he, who, they
    D. Their, her, he, that

Chapter 9 Pretest

1. All assignments in MLA format documents should be double-spaced
   A. True   B. False

2. What is the correct format for the volume and issue number of a journal in a works cited entry?
   A. Vol. 74, Issue 3
   B. Vol. 74, No 3
   C. 74: 3
   D. vol. 74, no. 3

3. When you have a works cited entry for an anthology with one editor, what should the entry begin with?
   A. The editor's full name, last name first, followed by a comma and "editor"
   B. The editor's full name, last name first, followed by a comma and "ed."
   C. The editor's full name, last name first, followed by a period.
   D. The title of the anthology

4. When you have a works cited entry for a source with two authors, what should the entry begin with?
   A. Both authors in alphabetical order by their last names, with the first and last names of each author reversed
   B. Both authors in the order they are presented in the source, with the first and last names of each author reversed
   C. Both authors in the order they are presented in the source, with the first and last names of only the first author reversed
   D. Both authors in the order they are presented in the source, with the last names of both authors followed by their first initials

5. When you have a works cited entry for a source with three or more authors, what should the entry begin with?
    A. Both authors in the order they are presented in the source, with the last names of both authors followed by their first initials
    B. All the authors in the order they are presented in the source, with the first and last names of each author reversed
    C. Just the first author presented in the source
    D. The first author presented in the source, with the first and last names reversed, followed by a comma and "et al."

6. When you find a journal article in a database, the database gives you the information in MLA format, so all you have to do is copy everything for the works cited entry.
    A. True   B. False

7. When you have page numbers in the same range of a hundred or a thousand in an in-text citation and a works cited entry, drop the first numeral of the last page number.
    A. True   B. False

8. In works cited entries, all months should be abbreviated except for May, June, and July.
    A. True   B. False

9. In-text citations do not need authors' last names if you have introduced the author before a quotation
    A. True   B. False

10. You need in-text citations for all information taken from sources, including summaries and paraphrases.
    A. True   B. False

Chapter 10 Pretest

Read the following two passages and, then, answer the questions below.

Passage #3

Being mindful of the confirmation bias, in addition to keeping us intellectually honest and increasing the likelihood of fair outcomes, can also help us to be more persuasive. The key is to focus on the stories in the heads of the people we hope to influence. This is done through a process called intellectual empathy, meaning seeing the world through the others' eyes, hearing through the others' ears, understanding the stories in their heads. (from John G. McCabe's article "It Has to Be Believed to Be Seen")

Passage #4

John G. McCabe's article discusses how important it is for us to be "mindful of the confirmation bias" because, "in addition to keeping us intellectually honest and increasing the likelihood of fair outcomes, can also help us to be more persuasive." He says we need intellectual empathy, which entails "seeing the world through the others' eyes, hearing through the others' ears, understanding the stories in their heads" (22).

1. Passage #4 would not be considered an example of plagiarism of Passage #3.

   A. True   B. False

Read the following two passages and, then, answer the questions below.

Passage #5

As the behavioral psychologist B. F. Skinner proved in the laboratory, the human mind seeks relationships between events and often finds them even when they are not present. Slot-machines are based on Skinnerian principles of intermittent reinforcement. The dumb human, like the dumb rat, only needs an occasional payoff to keep pulling the handle. The mind will do the rest. (from Michael Shermer's book *Why People Believe Weird Things: Pseudoscience, Superstition, and Other Confusions of Our Time*)

Passage #6

Psychologist B.F. Skimmer proved in the laboratory that the human mind seeks relationships between events and can see them even when not present. Stupid people, like rats, need only occasional payoff to keep pulling the handle of a slot machine. Their minds do the rest (Shermer 53).

2. Passage #6 would not be considered an example of plagiarism of Passage #5.

   A. True   B. False

Read the following two passages and, then, answer the questions below.

Passage #7

If the novel is the genre which affirms the common life, it is also the form in which values are at their most diverse and conflicting. The novel from Defoe to Woolf is a product of modernity, and modernity is the period in which we cannot agree on fundamentals. Our novels and beliefs are fragmented and discordant, and the novel reflects this condition. (from Terry Eagleton's book *The English Novel: An Introduction*.)

Passage #8

According to Terry Eagleton, a leading literary theorist, "If the novel is the genre which affirms the common life, it is also the form in which values are at their most diverse and conflicting (5). In his book on the English novel, he states that "The novel from Defoe to Woolf is a product of modernity, and modernity is the period in which we cannot agree even on fundamentals. Our novels and beliefs are fragmented and discordant, and the novel reflects this condition" (5).

3.   Passage #8 would not be considered an example of plagiarism of Passage #7.
      A. True   B. False

Read the following two passages and, then, answer the questions below.

Passage #9

Every single empire in its official discourse has said that it is not like all the others, that its circumstances are special, that it has a mission to enlighten, civilize, bring order and democracy, and that it uses force only as a last resort. And, sadder still, there always is a chorus of willing intellectuals to say calming words about benign or altruistic empires, as if one shouldn't trust the evidence of one's eyes watching the destruction and the misery and death brought by the latest mission civilization. (from Edward W. Said's book *Orientalism*)

Passage #10

All empires have said that they are unique among all other empires and that their goals are just and that they avoid force only if it can't be avoided. Many so-called intellectuals, unfortunately, are happy to support such assertions even when patently false.

4.   Passage #10 would not be considered an example of plagiarism of Passage #9.
      A. True   B. False

Read the following two passages and, then, answer the questions below.

Passage #11

Alcohol addiction casts a pall of alienation and misery over a great many of Raymond Carver's stories, and it contributes more powerfully to his vision of life than perhaps any other single human problem. The life of the alcoholic in Carver's work is one of pain and failure and broken promises. Carver himself lived such a life for many years until, with the help of Alcoholics Anonymous and several treatment centers, he finally quit drinking. (from H. Colon Messer's article "Fleeing the Wasteland of Alcoholism: Alienation, Recovery, and Hope in Raymond Carver's 'Cathedral'")

Passage #12

Raymond Carver's personal experiences with alcoholism colored much of his work, and protagonists in these stories were not only themselves wretched, they were undependable to others. Alcoholism influenced Carver's views more than other difficulties people can experience (Messer 43).

5.   Passage #12 would not be considered an example of plagiarism of Passage #11.
     A. True   B. False

Read the following two passages and, then, answer the questions below.

Passage #13

Orwell, arriving home, had become the writer we know today from *Animal Farm* and *1984*. Burma had made him an anti-imperialist, but it was his time in Spain that developed his political vision and with it the determination to criticize right and left with equal vigor. Before Spain, he had been a fairly conventional leftist, arguing that fascism and capitalism were essentially the same. Until this point, Orwell still clung to some of the views of the 1930s left. (from Thomas E. Ricks' book *Churchill and Orwell: The Fight for Freedom*)

Passage #14

Orwell's experience with and betrayal by a faction of leftist Republicans had a great impact. This experience made Orwell "the writer we know today from *Animal Farm* and *1984*" (Ricks 77). He had long criticized the right, but Spain "developed his political vision and with it the determination to criticize right and left with equal vigor" (Ricks 77).

6. Passage #14 would not be considered an example of plagiarism of Passage #13.
    A. True   B. False

Read the following two passages and, then, answer the questions below.
Passage #15

> We need to make sure that every vote is recorded on a piece of paper, too. Without paper, there may be no evidence we can go back and look at that would reveal vote tampering. We also need to make attacks as difficult as possible by making sure systems used to program ballot design are locked down and never accessible from the internet. (from Martin Giles' article "Your Vote Is in Jeopardy")

Passage #16

> We need to ensure that every vote is recorded on paper. "Without paper, there may be no evidence we can go back and look at that would reveal vote tampering." We must also make attacks as difficult as possible by ensuring systems used to program ballot design get locked down and are never accessible from the internet (Giles 44).

7. Passage #16 would not be considered an example of plagiarism of Passage #15.
    A. True   B. False

Read the following two passages and, then, answer the questions below.
Passage #17

> Parents refusing to immunize their children frequently emphasize it is their choice and right to do so. But this choice can have serious consequences — not only for the particular child, but for other children and society in general. Those who recognize the individual and public health benefits of immunization are rightly concerned about the anti-vaccine movement's growth and negative impact on vaccination rates. (from Allison M. Whelan's article "Lowering the Age of Consent: Pushing Back against the Anti-Vaccine Movement")

Passage #18

> People who understand vaccinations' safety and efficacy are understandably worried by the expanding anti-vaccine movement. While personal liberty is often cited by parents who don't vaccinate their children, the fact is that

exercising this liberty can harm their own and other people's children, as well as having a negative impact on our country overall (Whelan 467).

8. Passage #18 would not be considered an example of plagiarism of Passage #17.
    A. True   B. False

Read the following two passages and, then, answer the questions below.

<u>Passage #18</u>

According to statistics from the Olweus Bullying Prevention Program, one in seven students in K-12 is either a bully or a victim of a bully, and 15% of all school absenteeism is directly related to fears of being bullied at school. (from Beverley Goldberg's article "How Libraries Help Kids Stand Up to Bullying")

<u>Passage #19</u>

One in seven students in K-12 is either a bully or a victim of a bully, and 15% of all school absenteeism is directly related to fears of being bullied at school.

9. Passage #18 would not be considered an example of plagiarism of Passage #19.
    A. True   B. False

Read the following two passages and, then, answer the questions below.

<u>Passage #20</u>

The social media platforms nearly all of us use teem with "bots," artificial intelligence modules that impersonate human beings and tirelessly fill our heads with propaganda. Facebook admits its pages may harbor as many as 270 mil- lion fake accounts. That's more than all the people in Brazil. Or Indonesia." (from Clay Farris Naff's article "Call in the Robocops: With Democracy At Risk, Can We Quell Internet Bots and Trolls?")

<u>Passage #21</u>

"The social media platforms nearly all of us use teem with "bots," artificial intelligence modules that impersonate human beings and tirelessly fill our heads with propaganda. Facebook admits its pages may harbor as many as 270 mil- lion fake accounts. That's more than all the people in Brazil. Or Indonesia."

10. Passage #21 would not be considered an example of plagiarism of Passage #20.
    A. True   B. False

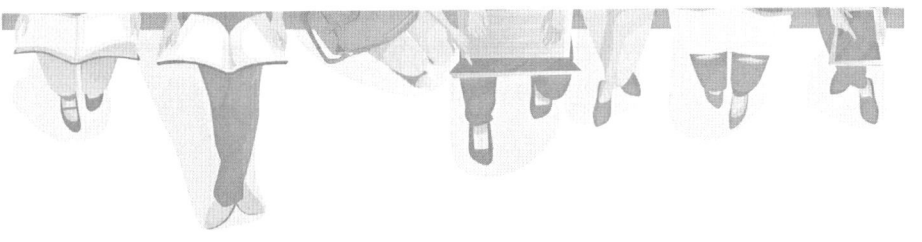

APPENDIX III

Posttests for Chapter 1-10

Chapter 1. Chapter Posttest

1. How many sentences does a rhetorical précis have?
    A. Four
    B. Five
    C. Six
    D. As many as you need

2. In the database EBSCOhost, the icon labeled "periodical" is used to indicate every kind of periodical.
    A. True   B. False

3. Which of the following is most likely to be re-tweeted?
    A. False information
    B. Genuine information

4. Which of the following is specifically designed to both critically read and also evaluate how accurate and reliable a source is?
    A. The rhetorical précis
    B. SQ3R
    C. The CRAAP Test
    D. Double-entry note taking

5. Which of the following domains probably indicates greater trustworthiness when you do research?
    A. .com
    B. .org

C. .edu

D. .com

6. Which of the following is likely to be the best type of source for a research paper?

   A. A tabloid

   B. A journal

   C. A magazine

   D. Both A and B

7. Which of the following is required to have a sentence that provides an explanation of how the author develops and supports the major assertion (thesis) of a work?

   A. The rhetorical précis

   B. SQ3R

   C. The CRAAP Test

   D. Double-entry note taking

8. Which of the following is good to use to search for scholarly information online outside of your college library?

   A. Directory of Open Access Journals

   B. Google Scholar

   C. Wikipedia

   D. Both A and B

9. In order to best ensure that the news one reads and hears is accurate, it is a good idea to use multiple news sources but to avoid social media as news sources.

   A. True

   B. False

10. A peer-reviewed periodical is one where the articles are reviewed after publication by readers who submit their opinions to the periodical's editors after they read and judge the articles.

    A. True

    B. False

Chapter 2. Chapter Posttest

Note #1: The formal writing process is made up of the following steps (but not necessarily in this order): researching (if required), revising, prewriting, drafting, proofreading, editing, outlining, thesis generation, and publication of the final draft. answer the questions below about these steps of the process.

1. Which of these tasks should come first for a college writer?
    - A. Thesis generation
    - B. Outlining
    - C. Editing
    - D. Proofreading
    - E. Prewriting
2. Which of these two should you complete first: drafting or outlining?
    - A. Drafting
    - B. Outlining
3. Which of these two should come first: research or prewriting?
    - A. Prewriting
    - B. Research
4. Which of these steps of the writing process is best defined by the following: "the act of reading the entire paper over and making changes to the content and flow of the essay"?
    - A. Proofreading
    - B. Editing
    - C. Drafting
    - D. Revising
    - E. Prewriting
5. Which of these steps of the writing process is best defined by the following: "the act of reading over your completed paper to look for errors"?
    - A. Drafting
    - B. Revising
    - C. Thesis generation
    - D. Prewriting
    - E. Editing
6. Which of these steps of the writing process is best defined by the following: "a formal way to map out your paper, so it is easier and more logically written"?
    - A. Thesis generation
    - B. Editing
    - C. Drafting
    - D. Outlining
    - E. Prewriting

Read this excerpt from a sample outline and answer the question below.

    <u>Sample Outline.</u>

    I. *Health epidemic*

    1. *Impact on youth*

        A. *Define youth*

        B. *Stats on rise in problems*

    2. *Premature high blood pressure*

    3. *Obesity*

    4. *Diabetes*

7.   True or False. The labels on this outline are correct (the letters and numbers such as I, 1, A)

        A. True   B. False

Read this excerpt from a sample outline and answer the question below.

    <u>Sample Outline.</u>

    I. *Health epidemic*

    A. *Impact on youth*

        1. *Define youth*

        2. *Stats on rise in problems*

    B. *Premature high blood pressure*

    C. *Obesity*

    D. *Diabetes*

8.   True or False. The labels on this outline are correct (the letters and numbers such as III, A, 1).

        A. True   B. False

Read this excerpt from a sample outline and answer the question below.

    <u>Sample Outline.</u>

    A. *Health epidemic*

    I. *Impact on youth*

        a. *Define youth*

        b. *Stats on rise in problems*

     II. *Premature high blood pressure*

    III. *Obesity*

    IV. *Diabetes*

9. True or False. The labels on this outline are correct (the letters and numbers such as A, 1, a).

    A. True   B. False

10. Which of the following is not listed in the chapter as a person you should get to help you proofread your paper?

    A. Your professor
    B. Yourself
    C. Tutor
    D. Librarian
    E. Classmate

Chapter 3. Chapter Posttest

1. A thesis statement for a college essay should be phrased as one sentence.

    A. True   B. False

2. The best place for a thesis statement in a college essay is at the end of the introductory paragraph.

    A. True   B. False

3. Declarative sentences end with

    A. Question marks
    B. Exclamation points
    C. Periods.
    D. Any of the above

4. A thesis statement should not be phrased as a question.

    A. True   B. False

5. A good thesis statement can be any number of sentences.

    A. True   B. False

6. A thesis statement for an expository essay

    A. Should not express an opinion or take a position on a topic
    B. Should take a stand on an issue and be debatable
    C. Should be answering a "how" or "why" question
    D. All of the above

7. A thesis statement for an analytical essay

    A. Should not express an opinion or take a position on a topic
    B. Should take a stand on an issue and be debatable
    C. Should be answering a "how" or "why" question
    D. All of the above

8. A thesis statement for an argumentative essay
    A. Should not express an opinion or take a position on a topic
    B. Should take a stand on an issue and be debatable
9. A good thesis statement for an essay may change as you write your paper
    A. True   B. False
10. Questions can be used to set up thesis statements.
    A. True   B. False

Chapter 4. Chapter Posttest

1. The chapter suggests you open your introduction with a phrase such as "In today's society" or "In the modern world" in order to set the stage for your paper.
    A. True   B. False
2. Which of these opening hooks does the chapter warn you about using, just in case your professor thinks it might be too casual?
    A. Rhetorical question
    B. Personal anecdote
    C. Background information
    D. Quote
    E. Interesting fact or statistic
3. True or false: A Thesis Sentence and topic sentence are the same exact thing.
    A. True   B. False
4. Which of the following elements is not a part of the body paragraph's primary content?
    A. Humor
    B. Rhetorical modes
    C. Argument/counter arguments
    D. Personal anecdotes
    E. Research
5. In this chapter, you are told that starting your thesis sentence with a phrase like "In this essay, I plan to…" is a good idea. It helps your reader understand your stance.
    A. True   B. False

6. According to the chapter, you should avoid using the phrase "In conclusion" at any point in your conclusion.
    A. True   B. False

7. According to the chapter, which of the following elements of the paper's introduction is considered optional?
    A. Thesis sentence
    B. Gradual buildup
    C. Topic sentence
    D. Opening hook
    E. None of the above

8. How long should a typical body paragraph be in a college essay?
    A. Exactly three sentences long
    B. At least two sentences long
    C. At least four sentences long
    D. There is no defined length
    E. None of the above

9. Which of these is not part of the paper's body paragraphs?
    A. Thesis reminder
    B. Opening hook
    C. Transition
    D. Topic sentence
    E. Critical discussion

10. Should a paper's introduction move from specific points to more general ones, or should it start with generic points and move to more specifics?
    A. Specific points to general points
    B. General points to specific points

Chapter 5. Chapter Posttest

1. A conditional statement, "if X, then Y," by itself is considered an argument.
    A. True   B. False

2. An argument and an explanation are the same thing.
    A. True   B. False

3. What is the definition of an argument?
    A. An argument is a statement that is debatable

B. An argument is a set of statements whereby at least one statement [called a conclusion] supports or proves another statement [called a premise]

C. An argument is a set of debatable statements that can be proven true

D. An argument is a set of statements whereby at least one statement [called a premise] attempts to support or prove another statement [called a conclusion]

E. An argument is a set of statements whereby at least one statement [called a premise] supports or proves another statement [called a conclusion]

4.   Which of the following represent conclusion indicator words:

A. Therefore, thus, as such, if,

B. Thus, because, wherefore, we may conclude

C. It follows that, inasmuch as, thus, then

D. Hence, as a result, we may infer, entails that

5.   What is an *explanans*?

A. A set of statements that provide what was previously unknown factual statement(s)

B. A set of statements that prove the evidence true

C. A set of statements that explain previously known facts

6.   Does an argument have to be true to have good reasoning?

A. True   B. False

7.   Is the following passage, an argument?

Spider Man is a famous fictional superhero, because Stan Lee and Steve Ditko believed that a spider, though a bit frightening, could spin an unbreakable web that could be used to ensnare bad guys. Spider Man, they believed, would capture the attention of any mind when he first appeared in the 1962 edition of Amazing Fantasy #15, published by Marvel Comics.

A. True   B. False

8.   Can a topic sentence also be a conclusion?

A. Yes   B. No

9.   Can an argument have more than one main conclusion?

A. True   B. False

10. What is the maximum number of statements that can make up an argument?

A. One

B. Two

    C. Ten

    D. As many as it needs to take

Chapter 6. Chapter Posttest

1. What is rhetoric?
    A. When you read an essay out loud
    B. The art of argumentation
    C. It is another word for "research"
    D. The science of telling the truth
    E. A type of fallacy
2. Division and classification are the same exact thing.
    A. True   B. False
3. Which rhetorical mode might be used to give directions on how to cook a recipe, repair a car, or even complete a level on a video game?
    A. Division/classification
    B. Problem/solution
    C. Process analysis
    D. Example/illustration
    E. Cause/effect
4. While using the definition rhetorical mode, you will only want to use formal definitions found in dictionaries and reference books. You don't want to use your own definitions of terms since it will be too casual.
    A. True   B. False
5. Which rhetorical mode can be defined as "using formal outside evidence such as a quote from an expert"?
    A. Problem/solution
    B. Example/illustration
    C. Process analysis
    D. Comparison/contrast
    E. Definition
6. If you wrote a paper that first discussed the fact that the drinking water in your community was polluted and then went on to argue that a luxury tax could pay for more water purification plants, what type of rhetorical mode would the overall essay be employing?
    A. Problem/solution
    B. Definition

C. Example/illustration
D. Division/classification
E. Comparison/contrast

Read the following paragraph. Then, answer the questions below in reference to its content.

Paragraph #1

[1] *The Avengers* movie have become the largest grossing films in history, and many people want to know what has caused their multi-billion dollar popularity. [2] Why are the Avengers and superheroes so popular right now? [3] Some say it is because the world is a mess, and we need hope. [4] War always looms in the Middle East. [5] America now finds itself embroiled in ongoing racial and political divides. [6] The gap between the rich and poor widens, and we are in the middle of a climate crisis. [7] Because of realities like this, we need to find stories to set our minds at ease. [8] So stories of heroes with super human abilities are the cause of much hope and wonder as opposed to the daily dread many people feel. [9] If we can look to the Avengers, even though fictional, we can find a world that is better than ours. [10] One example of the heroes on *The Avengers* team is Steve Rogers, aka, Captain America. [11] In a piece by Caitlin Busch, *SyFy Wire's* associate feature editor and expert on popular culture, she says, "Steve Rogers will always be the skinny kid who was willing to sacrifice himself to save his fellow soldiers. The other *Avengers* rely on this certainty" (Busch, par 6). [12] This quotation proves that Captain American is the most heroic of The Avengers. [13] He is not the same as other members of the team; indeed, Iron Man is seen as selfish and self-serving, a stark contrast to the giving and noble generosity embodied in Captain America.

7. Sentences 1 through 9 are an example of what type of rhetorical mode?
    A. Cause/effect
    B. Narrative
    C. Example/illustration
    D. Argument/persuasion
    E. Comparison/contrast
8. Sentences 10 through 11 are an example of what type of rhetorical mode?
    A. Cause/effect
    B. Narrative
    C. Example/illustration

      D. Argument/persuasion

      E. Comparison/contrast

9.   Sentences 12 through 13 provide an example of what type of Rhetorical Mode?

      A. Cause/effect

      B. Narrative

      C. Example/illustration

      D. Argument/persuasion

      E. Comparison/contrast

10. Collectively, though this paragraph uses different types of rhetorical modes, what rhetorical mode is the entire paragraph collectively an example of?

      A. Cause/effect

      B. Narrative

      C. Example/illustration

      D. Argument/persuasion

      E. Comparison/contrast

Chapter 7. Chapter Posttest

For each of the following, choose the term that most closely fits the definition provided.

1.   The official system of rules governing affairs of state or diplomatic occasions; the accepted or established code of procedure for an organization, group, or situation.

      A. Criterion

      B. Protocol

      C. Constitution

      D. Template

2.   Favorable to progress or reform; favorable to individual freedoms and rights.

      A. Civil

      B. Hierarchal

      C. Liberal

      D. Conservative

3.   Indicated but not plainly expressed; essentially or very closely connected with; always to be found in; potentially contained.

      A. Discreet

      B. Explicit

    C. Implicit

    D. Coherent

4. A proposition assumed as an argument's premise; a supposition made on the basis of limited evidence as a starting point for further investigation.

    A. Data

    B. Guess

    C. Hypothesis

    D. Significance

5. Open to two or more interpretations; equivocal; unclear because a choice between alternatives has not been offered.

    A. Ambidextrous

    B. Ambivalent

    C. Indecisive

    D. Quandary

6. Originating, based on, concerned with, or verifiable by observation or experience rather than theory or speculation.

    A. Empirical

    B. Pragmatic

    C. Practical

    D. Experimental

7. A standard or principle by which a decision or judgment is made.

    A. Archetype

    B. Exemplar

    C. Prototype

    D. Criterion

8. Factual information, such as statistics and results of scientific research, used for calculation and reasoning; in computing, information in digital form.

    A. Lore

    B. Data

    C. Dossier

    D. Results

9. Consist of; be made up of; constitute.

    A. Comprise

    B. Compass

    C. Contain

    D. Comprehend

10. Individually distinct; constituting a separate entry.
    A. Discreet
    B. Discrete
    C. Empirical
    D. Demonstrable

Chapter 8. Chapter Posttest

1. Which of the following sentences has no punctuation or grammar errors?
    A. David Robert Jones, known professionally as David Bowie, was a leading figure in the music industry and is considered one of the most influential musicians of the 20th century.
    B. David Robert Jones, known professionally as David Bowie was a leading figure in the music industry, and is considered one of the most influential musicians of the 20th century.
    C. David Robert Jones, known professionally as David Bowie was a leading figure in the music industry and is considered one of the most influential musicians of the 20th century.
    D. David Robert Jones, known professionally as David Bowie, was a leading figure in the music industry, and is considered one of the most influential musicians of the 20th century.

2. Which of the following sentences has no punctuation or grammar errors?
    A. Bowie's early albums include *The Man Who Sold the World*, which was released in 1970; *The Rise and Fall of Ziggy Stardust and the Spiders from Mars*, which was released in 1972; and *Aladdin Sane*, which was released in 1973.
    B. Bowie's early albums include: *The Man Who Sold the World*, which was released in 1970; *The Rise and Fall of Ziggy Stardust and the Spiders from Mars*, which was released in 1972; and *Aladdin Sane*, which was released in 1973.
    C. Bowie's early albums include *e Man Who Sold the World*; which was released in 1970, *The Rise and Fall of Ziggy Stardust and the Spiders from Mars*; which was released in 1972, and *Aladdin Sane*; which was released in 1973.
    D. Bowie's early albums include: *The Man Who Sold the World*; which was released in 1970, *The Rise and Fall of Ziggy Stardust and the Spiders*

from Mars; which was released in 1972, and *Aladdin Sane*; which was released in 1973.

3. Which of the following sentences has no punctuation or grammar errors?

    A. Bowie's early albums include the following *The Man Who Sold the World*, *The Rise and Fall of Ziggy Stardust and the Spiders from Mars*, and *Aladdin Sane*.

    B. Bowie's early albums include the following: *The Man Who Sold the World*; *The Rise and Fall of Ziggy Stardust and the Spiders from Mars*; and *Aladdin Sane*.

    C. Bowie's early albums include the following: *The Man Who Sold the World*, *The Rise and Fall of Ziggy Stardust and the Spiders from Mars*, and *Aladdin Sane*.

    D. Bowie's, early albums include, the following: *The Man Who Sold the World*, *The Rise and Fall of Ziggy Stardust and the Spiders from Mars*, and *Aladdin Sane*.

4. Which of the following sentences has no punctuation or grammar errors?

    A. Because Bowie was such a talented writer and performer he had a large cult following for decades.

    B. Because Bowie, was such a talented writer and performer, he had a large cult following for decades.

    C. Because Bowie was such a talented writer and performer, he had a large cult following for decades.

    D. Because Bowie was such a talented writer and performer; he had a large cult following for decades.

5. Which of the following sentences has no punctuation or grammar errors?

    A. Since automobiles were first marketed to consumers, there have been many safety scandals, including ones associated with the following companies: Ford, Takata, and Volkswagen.

    B. Since automobiles were first marketed to consumers, there have been many safety scandals, including ones associated with the following companies; Ford, Takata, and Volkswagen.

    C. Since automobiles were first marketed to consumers, there have been many safety scandals including ones associated with the following companies: Ford, Takata, and Volkswagen.

    D. Since automobiles were first marketed to consumers, there have been many safety scandals, including, ones associated with the following companies; Ford, Takata, and Volkswagen.

6. Which of the following sentences has no punctuation or grammar errors?

    A. *The Ballad of Buster Scruggs* is a 2018 American western anthology film written, directed, and produced by the Coen brothers; Tom Waits has a small role as a gold prospector.

    B. *The Ballad of Buster Scruggs*, is a 2018 American western anthology film written; directed; and produced by the Coen brothers. Tom Waits has a small role as a gold prospector.

    C. *The Ballad of Buster Scruggs*, is a 2018 American western anthology film written, directed, and produced by the Coen brothers; Tom Waits has a small role as a gold prospector.

    D. *The Ballad of Buster Scruggs*, is a 2018 American western anthology film, written, directed and produced by the Coen brothers; Tom Waits has a small role as a gold prospector.

7. Which of the following sentences has no punctuation or grammar errors?

    A. Tom Waits' and Patrick Fugit's 2007 black comedy is called *Wristcutters: A Love Story.*

    B. Tom Waits' and Patrick Fugit's 2007 black comedy, is called *Wristcutters: A Love Story.*

    C. Tom Waits and Patrick Fugit's 2007 black comedy, is called *Wristcutters: A Love Story.*

    D. Tom Waits and Patrick Fugit's 2007 black comedy is called *Wristcutters: A Love Story.*

8. Which of the following sentences has no punctuation or grammar errors?

    A. It's based on a story by Etgar Keret called "Kneller's Happy Campers," and its premise is set in an afterlife way-station.

    B. It's based on a story by Etgar Keret called "Kneller's Happy Campers," and it's premise is set in an afterlife way-station.

    C. Its based on a story by Etgar Keret called "Kneller's Happy Campers," and its premise is set in an afterlife way-station.

    D. Its based on a story by Etgar Keret called "Kneller's Happy Campers," and it's premise is set in an afterlife way-station.

9. Which of the following sentences has no punctuation or grammar errors?
   A. The U.S. womens' soccer teams victory over the Netherlands in the finals of the World Cup made world headlines.
   B. The U.S. women's soccer teams' victory over the Netherlands in the finals of the World Cup made world headlines.
   C. The U.S. women's soccer team's victory over the Netherlands in the finals of the World Cup made world headlines.
   D. The U.S. women's soccer team's victory over the Netherlands in the final's of the World Cup made world headlines.

10. Which of the following sentences has no punctuation or grammar errors?
    A. Lee's and Ann's voices are very good; between you and I, I think they are the best in the choir.
    B. Lee and Ann's voices are very good; between you and I, I think they are the best in the choir.
    C. Lee's and Ann's voices are very good; between you and me, I think they are the best in the choir.
    D. Lee's and Ann's voice's are very good; between you and me, I think they are the best in the choir.

Chapter 9. Chapter Posttest

1. The upper left identification information on the first page of a paper should be
   A. Single spaced
   B. Single spaced and followed by two spaces
   C. Double-spaced
   D. Double spaced and followed by two extra spaces

2. In the upper left identification information on the first page of a paper, professors with more than one section of the same class may want students to follow the class name with what?
   A. A colon followed by the starting time and then the class days abbreviated to the day's first letters
   B. A colon followed by the class days abbreviated to the day's first letters followed by the starting time
   C. A colon followed by the class's days spelled out and the starting time
   D. A colon followed by the class's starting time and the class's days spelled out

3. In the upper left identification information on the first page of a paper, the date the assignment is in should be in what format?
   A. The month abbreviated, followed by the day, a comma, and the year
   B. The month fully spelled out, followed by the day, a comma, and the year
   C. The day, the month abbreviated, and the year (no commas)
   D. The day, the month fully spelled out, and the year (no commas)
4. The titles of your own assignments should be
   A. Enclosed in quotation marks
   B. Italicized
   C. In bold font
   D. None of the above
5. Which of the following is the correct format for an MLA in-text citation when the author is not named before the information is presented?
   A. (Smith page 7).
   B. (Smith, p. 7).
   C. (Smith, 7).
   D. (Smith 7).
6. You should capitalize all words in titles except the following (unless they are the first or last words of a title or subtitle): articles ("a," "an", and "the"), prepositions ("of," "with," "above," "in," "over," "before," "at," etc.), coordinating conjunctions ("for," "and," "nor," "but," "or," "yet," "so"), and the "to" in infinitives.
   A. True   B. False
7. The cross-referenced works cited entries for two or more works from the same anthology typically include what information?
   A. The author's last name, the title of the work, the anthology editor's last name, and pp. and the page numbers
   B. The author's full name (last name first), the title of the work, the anthology editor's last name, and pp. and the first and last page numbers
   C. The editor's last name, the title of the work, the author's full name, and pp. and the first and last page numbers
   D. The anthology, the title of the work, the author's full name (last name first), and pp. and the page numbers

8. An entry for only one work taken from an anthology typically includes what information?

    A. The author's full name (last name first), the title of the work, the title of the anthology, "edited by" followed by the editor's full name (last name first), the publisher, year, and the first and last page numbers

    B. The author's full name (last name first), the title of the work, the title of the anthology, "edited by" followed by the editor's full name (last name last), the publisher, year, and the first and last page numbers

    C. The author's full name (last name first), the title of the work, the title of the anthology, "ed." followed by the editor's full name (last name first), the publisher, year, and the first and last page numbers

    D. The author's full name (last name first), the title of the work, the title of the anthology, "ed." followed by the editor's full name (last name last), the publisher, year, and the first and last page numbers

9. When you have two or more works by the same author, list the works alphabetically by the first important word of title (ignoring "a," "an" and "the" but leaving those in place) and use three hyphens instead of the author's name for every entry by that author after the first.

    A. True   B. False

10. When a work has two authors,

    A. Keep the authors in the same order that they are presented in the work, with the first author's name presented with the last name first, followed by a comma, "and," and the second author's name also presented with the last name first

    B. Arrange the authors in alphabetical order, with the first author's name presented with the last name first, followed by a comma, "and," and the second author's name also presented with the last name first

    C. Arrange the authors in alphabetical order, with the first author's name presented with the last name first, followed by a comma, "and," and the second author's name presented with the last name last

    D. Keep the authors in the same order that they are presented in the work, with the first author's name presented with the last name first, followed by a comma, "and," and the second author's name presented with the last name last

Chapter 10. Chapter Posttest

1. You need quotations marks for phrases that you copy from sources, not just entire sentences.
   A. True   B. False
2. Summarized and paraphrased information taken from sources must be cited.
   A. True   B. False
3. Mosaic plagiarism refers to situations when students
   A. Recycle a paper from an earlier semester
   B. Tutors or proofreaders make substantial changes using their own language and ideas
   C. Collaborate with friends on one master assignment together and then cut, paste, and change it somewhat in order to each submit it separately
   D. Plagiarize by combining ideas, reasoning, facts, or copied phrases and sentences from other people within a paper that they otherwise wrote
4. Self-plagiarism refers to situations when students
   A. Recycle a paper from an earlier semester
   B. Tutors or proofreaders make substantial changes using their own language and ideas
   C. Collaborate with friends on one master assignment together and then cut, paste, and change it somewhat in order to each submit it separately
   D. Plagiarize by combining ideas, reasoning, facts, or copied phrases and sentences from other people within a paper that they otherwise wrote
5. Buddy plagiarism refers to situations when students
   A. Recycle a paper from an earlier semester
   B. Tutors or proofreaders make substantial changes using their own language and ideas
   C. Collaborate with friends on one master assignment together and then cut, paste, and change it somewhat in order to each submit it separately
   D. Both B and C
6. You cannot plagiarize from yourself.
   A. True   B. False

7. "Common knowledge" refers to
   A. Information known by the average person
   B. Information known by the average scholar in a particular discipline
   C. Information that is repeated in many different sources
   D. All of the above

8. The percentage of direct quotations that you have in a paper usually doesn't matter.
   A. True   B. False

9. Your professors recognize students' writing styles, including choices of vocabulary and syntax.
   A. True   B. False

10. When direct quotations are over four lines, you don't need quotation marks; you need to indent the quotations one inch from the left margin.
    A. True   B. False

Cuerpos y Escalas del subgrupo A2 (cuerpos especiales) de la Generalitat Valenciana

Julio 2025